PERSPECTIVES OF EMPIRE

Photograph by Tim Marlborough

GERALD SANDFORD GRAHAM

Perspectives of Empire

Essays presented to
GERALD S. GRAHAM

edited by
JOHN E. FLINT
and
GLYNDWR WILLIAMS

BARNES & NOBLE

BOOKS

10 East 53d St., New York 10022
(a division of Harper & Row Publishers, Inc.)

LONGMAN GROUP LIMITED
London
Associated companies, branches and representatives
throughout the world

First published 1973

Published in the U.S.A. 1973 by:
HARPER & ROW PUBLISHERS, INC.
BARNES & NOBLE IMPORT DIVISION

ISBN 06-492129-8

Printed in Great Britain

CONTENTS

NOTES ON CONTRIBUTORS

E. A. AYANDELE, BA, PhD (London); Acting Principal of the University of Ibadan at Jos, northern Nigeria, and Professor of History in the University of Ibadan; author, *The Missionary Impact on Modern Nigeria 1842–1914: A Political and Social Analysis* (London, 1966); *Holy Johnson 1836–1917: Pioneer of African Nationalism* (London, 1970); *Visionary of the African Church: Dr Mojola Agbebi 1860–1917* (Nairobi, 1971).

PETER BURROUGHS, BA, PhD (London); Professor of History, Dalhousie University; author, *Britain and Australia 1831–1855: A Study in Imperial Relations and Crown Lands Administration* (Oxford, 1967); *The Colonial Reformers and Canada 1830–1849* (Toronto, 1969); *British Attitudes towards Canada 1822–1849* (Scarborough, Ont., 1971); *The Canadian Crisis and British Colonial Policy 1828–1841* (London, 1972).

K. ONWUKA DIKE, BA (Durham), MA (Aberdeen), PhD (London), Hon LLD (Aberdeen, Columbia, Leeds, London, Northwestern, Princeton), Hon. DLitt, (Birmingham, Boston, Ahmadu Bellu), Hon DSc (Moscow); Fellow, American Academy of Arts and Sciences; Professor of History, Harvard University, formerly Vice-Chancellor of the University of Ibadan; author, *Report on the Preservation and Administration of Historical Records in Nigeria* (Lagos, 1954); *Trade and Politics in the Niger Delta 1830–1885* (Oxford, 1956); *100 Years of British Rule in Nigeria 1851–1951* (Lagos, 1958).

JOHN E. FLINT, BA (Cambridge), PhD (London); Professor of History, Dalhousie University; author, *Sir George Goldie and the Making of Nigeria* (London, 1960); *Nigeria and Ghana* (New Jersey, 1966); editor, Mary Kingsley's *West African Studies* (London, 1964) and *Travels in West Africa* (London, 1965); contributor to R. Oliver and G. Mathew, eds., *History of East Africa*, Vol. 1 (Oxford, 1963) and L. H. Gann and Peter Duignan, eds., *Colonialism in Africa 1870–1960*, Vol. 1, *The History and Politics of Colonialism 1870–1914* (Cambridge, 1969).

JOHN S. GALBRAITH, BS (Miami), AM, PhD (Iowa), LLD (Mt Union College); Professor of British Empire History, University of California, Los Angeles, formerly Chancellor of the University of California, San Diego; author, *The Establishment of Canadian Diplomatic Status at Washington* (Berkeley and Los Angeles, 1951); *The Hudson's Bay Company as an Imperial Factor, 1821–1869* (Berkeley and Los Angeles, 1957); *Reluctant Empire: British Policy on the South African Frontier 1834–1854* (Berkeley and Los Angeles, 1963); *Mackinnon and East Africa 1878–1895* (Cambridge, 1972).

Notes on Contributors

GEORGE P. GRANT, BA (Queen's, Ont.), DPhil (Oxford), FRSC; Professor of Religious Studies, McMaster University; author, *Philosophy in the Mass Age* (Toronto, 1959); *Lament for a Nation* (Toronto, 1965); *Technology and Empire* (Toronto, 1969).

A. F. McC. MADDEN, MA, BLitt, DPhil (Oxford), Fellow of Nuffield College and Reader in Commonwealth History in the University of Oxford, formerly Director of the Institute of Commonwealth Studies, University of Oxford; editor of *Imperial Constitutional Documents 1765–1952* (Oxford, 1953); (with V.T. Harlow) *British Colonial Developments 1774–1834* (Oxford, 1953): (with Kenneth E. Robinson), *Essays in Imperial Government* (Oxford, 1963); contributor to V.T. Harlow, *The Founding of the Second British Empire 1763–1793* (London, 1964), *The Cambridge History of the British Empire*, III (Cambridge, 1959); H.R. Trevor-Roper, ed., *Essays in British History. Presented to Sir Keith Feiling* (London, 1964).

P. D. MARSHALL, BA (Oxford), MA, PhD (Yale); Professor of American History and Institutions, University of Manchester; author of articles on British imperial policy and the American Revolution in *English Historical Review, History, Journal of American Studies, Past and Present*.

GEORGE METCALF, BA, MA (Toronto), PhD (London); Associate Professor of History, University of Western Ontario; author, *Royal Government and Political Conflict in Jamaica 1729–1783* (London, 1965); (with F. C. Jones) *New Worlds to Conquer* (London, 1969); editor, *Long's History of Jamaica* (London, 1970).

DONALD SCHURMAN, BA (Acadia), MA, PhD (Cambridge); Professor of History, formerly Director of Commonwealth and Comparative Studies Institute, Queen's University, Ontario; author, *The Education of a Navy* (Chicago and London, 1965).

GLYNDWR WILLIAMS, BA, PhD (London); Reader in History at Queen Mary College, University of London, General Editor of the Hudson's Bay Record Society; author, *The British Search for the Northwest Passage in the Eighteenth Century* (London, 1962); *The Expansion of Europe in the Eighteenth Century : Overseas Rivalry, Discovery and Exploitation* (London, 1966); editor, *Documents relating to Anson's Voyage round the World 1740–1744* (London, 1967); *Andrew Graham's Observations on Hudson's Bay 1767–91* (London, 1969); *Peter Skene Ogden's Snake Country Journals 1827–28 and 1828–29* (London, 1971).

ACKNOWLEDGEMENTS

The help given at the following archives and libraries to the authors of contributions in this volume is here gratefully acknowledged.

Rhodes House, Oxford
University of Durham
Rhodesian Archives, Salisbury
Public Record Office, London
University of the Witwatersrand
London Missionary Society
Royal Commonwealth Society, London
Christ Church, Oxford
British Museum
Guildhall Library, London
India Office Library
Royal Archives, Windsor
University of Birmingham
Church Missionary Society, London
Methodist Missionary Archives, London
University of Ibadan

PREFACE

It is not the editors' intention to analyse the distinguished career of Gerald Sandford Graham. To have done so would have been, for either of us, a labour of love, but we could not have written such an appreciation jointly. Each person whose life and career have been touched by Graham's fine scholarship and extraordinary personality would paint a different picture of the many facets of his impact. Graham's tenure of the Rhodes Chair of Imperial History in the University of London coincided with the emergence to independence of the Commonwealth nations of Asia, Africa and the Caribbean, and we feel that it is singularly appropriate that his first African doctoral student, K. Onwuka Dike, who rose to be Vice-Chancellor of Africa's finest University and is now Professor of History at Harvard, should have fulfilled that task. Here we shall limit ourselves to a brief factual outline of Graham's career.

Born at Sudbury, Ontario, on 27 April 1903, Graham graduated from Queen's University, Ontario, in 1924 with a BA in History and Political Science. The next year he was awarded an MA from Queen's, together with the Gowan Prize in Political Science, and a University Travelling Fellowship to Harvard University where he obtained the degree of AM. The award of the Sir George Parkin Scholarship enabled Graham to spend the years 1927 to 1929 at Trinity College, Cambridge, where he was awarded a PhD for his dissertation on British policy towards Canada in the late eighteenth century. A Rockefeller Fellowship took Graham in 1929 to the Universities of Berlin and Freiburg-im-Breisgau to study German colonial policy, and in 1930 he returned to North America to begin his teaching career as instructor and tutor in the department of history at Harvard. In 1936 Graham became assistant professor at Queen's University, and was later promoted to associate and then full professor of history at his old university. In 1941 a Guggenheim Fellowship took Graham back to the United States to investigate the relationship between sea power and North American colonisation; but in 1942 his academic career was interrupted when he was commissioned into the Royal Canadian Naval Volunteer Reserve as an instructor lieutenant-commander. At the end of the war Graham was transferred to the Historical Section of the Canadian Army Overseas, and then in 1946 he took up a lectureship (a readership from 1947) in history at Birkbeck College, University of London.

In 1949 Gerald Graham was appointed to the Rhodes Chair of Imperial History at King's College, University of London, where his main under-graduate teaching commitments were in the special subject in Commonwealth History, 1880–1932, and in the optional subject in British Colonial History. His lectures and classes in these courses, covering as they did the whole span of British imperial history from the Tudors to the twentieth century, attracted students from many London colleges. Graham's own postgraduate seminar in imperial history met weekly at the Institute of Historical Research throughout his tenure of the Rhodes Chair, and he also helped to organise the regular series of seminars in modern Commonwealth history held at the Institute of Commonwealth Studies. As a senior teacher in the university Graham served on a myriad of committees and boards, and although never an enthusiastic committee-man he was assiduous in his attendance at these meetings.

Away from the university Graham was closely associated with the work of the Royal Commonwealth Society, to which he was elected in 1928 and of which he is now a Life Fellow and Vice-President. He was a member of the Library Committee from 1948 to 1955, and of the Imperial Studies Committee from 1952 to 1957, when he became Chairman of the new Academic Committee. This was responsible for awarding the Walter Frewen Lord Prize for the best essay by a postgraduate student in the field of imperial history, and also for reviving the Imperial Studies Series. This series of monographs, begun in the 1920s to encourage scholars 'mature in mind but young in years' (and in which Graham's first book appeared, in 1930), had lain dormant for some years. Under Graham's editorship volumes XXII to XXIX appeared between 1961 and 1970. Another series of which Graham was general editor was the West African History Series, published by the Oxford University Press. At the time Graham established the series it was assumed that the market for books on West African history was small, and the venture was backed by financial assistance from West African Newspapers Ltd. The series was designed to facilitate the publication of collections of documentary material illustrating the whole span of the history of the new West African nations, and to allow young scholars to publish full-length studies, or short biographical analyses of Africans. Virtually all the publications of the series have now become standard works in West African historiography, and by demonstrating that there existed a considerable reading public for scholarly works in West African history, the series made itself redundant in a few years as most major publishers began publishing similar studies and series of their own, without the need for financial subsidies.

During his tenure of the Rhodes Chair Graham toured and lectured extensively overseas: in Canada, West and East Africa, Australia, New Zealand, South Africa, Fiji, Ceylon, India, Borneo, Hong Kong, the United States and Germany. In 1964 he was honoured by an invitation to deliver the Wiles Lectures at Queen's University, Belfast, and these were published the next year under the title *The Politics of Naval Supremacy*. In 1970 Graham retired from the Rhodes Chair, and was made Professor Emeritus of the University of London. He spent the first two years of his 'retirement' as visiting Professor of Military and Strategic

Studies at the University of Western Ontario, and at his home in Sussex remains actively involved in research and writing.

Even so bald a summary will indicate the difficulties which faced the present editors when they undertook to compile this volume of essays. To select ten contributors to write essays in honour of Gerald Graham is to practise an intolerable form of academic *apartheid*, for there are few historians of empire in the English-speaking world who have not been influenced, personally and directly, by him. One of the editors has four colleagues in his own department who were Graham's former students. In Canada his pupils teach in university history departments which when listed sound like overnight stops on the trans-Canada Highway: at Memorial University in Newfoundland, at Dalhousie, Acadia, New Brunswick, McGill, Queen's, Toronto, Western Ontario, Manitoba, Saskatchewan, Edmonton, Calgary and British Columbia. His students teach in every English-speaking university in West Africa, in Ceylon, Hong Kong, the West Indies, South Africa, at several Indian universities, in Malaya, the universities of Australia and New Zealand, and they are scattered across the United States and throughout Britain. The first step in preparing this volume was to ask Mrs Marjorie Sutton, who for several years was Graham's personal secretary at King's College, to scour the files to produce a list of his former students now occupying university teaching posts. The result was a list of more than two hundred names. To these we could have added many other scholars, who, like several of our contributors here, have never been his students but whose association with him in scholarly and academic matters has led them to a profound respect and admiration. We were thus in the invidious position of having to compile a representative sample which by the nature of things could never be truly representative. We did not use Mrs Sutton's list, we scarcely dared ask for contributions, or we should have been inundated and embarrassed by the riches offered. Instead we selected from the essays which came to us, many unsolicited, in response to mere rumours of this project, and tried to make the best balance we could between youth and seniority, colleagues and former pupils, differing nationalities and topics, in order to form these *Perspectives of Empire*.

In doing so we are only too aware of the many distinguished names absent from this volume who would have been glad to appear. We are also aware, as Professor Dike's essay emphasises, that to limit this volume to topics in British imperial history is to make an arbitrary selection of only one important aspect of Graham's scholarship. It would have been perfectly feasible to have assembled two quite different groups of essays by other authors, the one a collection of essays in naval history by an international group of the foremost authorities in that field; the other a book of essays in Canadian history written by Graham's compatriots. This volume is thus what Gerald Graham might like to consider an accident of history, fortuitously emerging as one of several possibilities. Many potential themes, and many potential authors, have been excluded from its pages by the rigours of publishing economics, time, space, and the bludgeonings of chance.

For help in various ways with this most congenial of tasks we wish to thank Mrs Mary Graham and John Graham, Mrs Marjorie Sutton, Professor S.T. Bindoff, Dr P. J. Marshall and Mr D.H. Simpson.

J.E.F.

G.W.

1

K. ONWUKA DIKE

Gerald S. Graham: Teacher and Historian

From my student days I have always regarded Gerald Graham as a close personal friend. It is now twenty-five years since I had the great privilege of sitting at his feet and I can only speak for my own generation of students, but I undertook to write this introductory chapter not only because I recognise the profound influence which he had on my own intellectual development and career but because I know many of his past students, several distinguished now in public life, with whom he has been in touch for over forty years and who still speak of him with great affection. Furthermore, the deluge of tributes which poured in from far and near on the occasion of his retirement bears witness to the devoted and generous involvement of GSG in his students' interests over the years. Apart from strictly academic supervision and introductions to appropriate authorities, he exercised an almost pastoral oversight on the affairs of students committed to his charge: the tedious chores of mediation on their behalf with the dispensers of patronage in the form of scholarships, appointments, publishing facilities, were meticulously performed. Letters were answered by return post; endless manuscripts were read with care and annotated with perception and wit. Quite clearly the qualities which endeared him to my generation persisted throughout his tenure of the Rhodes Chair in London.[1] A friend writing about GSG must guard against being too frivolous. His wit, humour and sense of the ridiculous could at times be overwhelming, but those whose reaction to him is merely flippant, simply do not understand the man and have failed to discern that beneath the genial exterior is a scholar whose contribution to learning is solid and distinguished.

I first met Gerald Graham in 1947 just before he succeeded the late Professor Vincent Harlow to the Rhodes Chair of Colonial History at King's College in the University of London. He came to London a mature, well-established historian, whose contributions were mainly in the fields of Canadian and naval history,[2] and who had taught history at Harvard

---

[1] I owe some of the material used in writing this introductory chapter to several of GSG's students of more recent years. But it was the communications from his wife, Mrs Mary Graham, and Mrs (Dr) Heather Gilbert that were most useful.

[2] See 'The Historical Writings of Gerald Sandford Graham', *infra*, pp. 198–200.

University and Queen's University, Ontario. This is not the place nor the time to dwell on Graham's distinguished contributions in his chosen fields of study. I will refer very briefly to his areas of specialisation and to his basic qualities as teacher and historian. GSG, as most of his students will recall, was anything but a doctrinaire; in seminar and out of it, his animated and penetrating comments on books and scholars were not burdened with lengthy discourses on weighty philosophies of history. Indeed, he tended to view with suspicion any attempt to reduce complex issues and situations to tidy systems, and his conclusions were invariably determined by his analysis and meticulous use of the available evidence. Partly for this reason his major books have taken long to write and have been rewritten many times as new material which shaped his conclusions appeared. This basic element characterises his writings, no matter whether he is involved with the history of Canada or with the British Navy in the Indian Ocean.

His deep interest in the history and politics of his native land continued long after he left Canada to settle in London. The publication of his *A Concise History of Canada* in 1968 showed GSG's scholarship at its best in this area of his interest: the book embodies his very individual views of Canadian history and there is perforce less narrative and more interpretation and distillation of a subject of which he is a master. While the sun never set on GSG's legitimate fields of activity as Rhodes Professor, those close to him know that the problems of his native Canada were always in his mind. His lecture[3] to the Royal Commonwealth Society in Canada's Centennial Year dealt with that country's relations with the United States, with the question of Quebec ('the once-cloistered land of Maria Chapdelaine'), and with Canada's 'negative nationalism':

> The ideal of a common nationhood has not lost meaning for most Canadians. National association on a transcontinental scale is, in their view, too precious a heritage to be whittled away in the interest of regional rights and privileges. Although the idea of a distinct national identity may be a myth, they pray for a leadership possessing sufficient vision and inspiration to make their country's government effective at home and acceptable abroad. Mutual understanding between race and region is still far away, but an *entente cordiale* should not be beyond the reach of men of imagination capable of rising to the level of events.

I do not wish to imply that GSG's interests were entirely national and imperial. An extract from the same lecture reveals his wide sympathies as well as his vigorous style: 'The 'thirties were flaccid, ineffective and sick years of good intentions, when the evil peril of Nazism could be reduced to commonroom proportions, and when bustling, bright

[3]'Canada, 1867–1967', 27 April 1967; printed in abridged form in *Commonwealth Journal*, x (1967), 111–17.

and provocative scholars could seek bubble reputations by intellectual exercises that ignored the world the locusts were already devouring.' But strong links bound him to his motherland; and Canadian contemporaries such as Harold Innis, Donald Creighton, A.L. Burt, George V. Ferguson, and several others were men he continued to hold in respect as friends and scholars. It was Canada that fashioned and possessed him. He cannot forgive Canadian political leaders who fell below what was expected of them and in a brilliant review article, 'Canadian destinies', which appeared on the front page of *The Times Literary Supplement*[4] he carried out a masterly survey of the ups and downs of Canadian history from the time of the French settlement to the diminished status of that country in international affairs at the present time, praising or castigating politicians in measure as they took into account or not the realities of our time. The role of international peacekeeper which Canada assumed after the last war he considered unrealistic, and Lester Pearson, its advocate, came in for critical comment:

> Moral strictures on the part of Canada's future prime minister could not alter the fact that the use of force, even through the United Nations, was not a basic Canadian interest. 'Canada,' wrote L.B. Pearson in 1965, 'has developed a special interest in international peace-keeping in many of the world's trouble spots and has played a leading part — with men, equipment, money and ideas — in the effort to make peace-keeping activities effective'. . . . It is a mistake for any government to assume the mantle of international peace-keeper, unless that government is prepared in the last resort to back up intervention with armed men necessary to make the effort effective. Like Britain, Canada must come to terms with her diminished role in the world. . . . The life of Canada is now too closely interwoven with that of the United States to permit too zealous a scramble for even the worthiest ends. . . . The vital decisions for Canada . . . will continue to be made in the United States.

GSG's comments on men and events are always refreshing, candid and detached. Not only is he very outspoken about Canadian Liberal politics, but he despises academic politicians who employed devious methods to advance their own interests or those of their protégés. To be sure, he would fight to the last to uphold the cause of a student or teacher worthy of support, but he would not back men of little or no merit or mislead those in authority about a scholar's real abilities. A highly principled man of transparent integrity, there was little of this kind of politics in him: one gains the impression that on account of this he tended to judge politicians a little harshly and to underestimate the tangled mesh with which they have to grapple.

His second love was the seas and the men and ships that sail on them.

[4] *The Times Literary Supplement*, 7 December 1967.

During the Second World War he saw active and dangerous service as an officer in the Royal Canadian Navy in the North Atlantic, but these were experiences to which few of his students ever heard him refer.[5] They undoubtedly gave him a sense of the hard realities of seafaring life in wartime which intensified the quality of his writings on naval history. His studies in this subject culminated in the publication of what may be termed his magnum opus — *Great Britain in the Indian Ocean*. This together with his earlier *Empire of the North Atlantic* must be regarded as his main contribution in the field of oceanic history. The former, which appeared in 1967, is dedicated 'To those members of my Seminar in British Imperial History — 1949–1967'. To his students this dedication did not come as a great surprise. GSG was by instinct a lover of his fellow men and it is characteristic of the man — who always expected his students to produce the best of which they were capable — to decide that only his best is good enough for dedication to his seminar. This book, which took fourteen years to write, has been much praised, and a reviewer on the front page of *The Times Literary Supplement* described it as an 'uncommonly distinguished book, as magnificent in sweep and as artfully put together as it is felicitous in style and grounded in fresh research'.[6] It confirmed GSG's position as one of the leading naval historians of his day.

Yet, in spite of his distinguished contribution to historical scholarship, many of his former students will agree that above all else, people fascinate him: he has uncommon genius for friendship. GSG was not only an effective and dedicated teacher whose relationship to his pupils was that of a friend and companion rather than that of teacher and taught, but he went out of his way to keep track of many of them and to offer unstinted support in their quest for advice and advancement. There are men whom he taught over forty years ago at Harvard or Queen's who to this day cling tenaciously to the connection. His own interest had always been in teaching, and — except for a momentary toying with journalism[7] — he never wanted to do anything else. In London his work was mainly with graduate students; judging by the number of references to him in their published works, they found him extremely helpful, a careful and understanding teacher and, for a naturally impatient man, extraordinarily patient where the interests of his students were concerned.

---

[5]All he wrote concerning his war service was 'Convoy Diary', *University of Toronto Quarterly*, XIII (1943), 102–16, and 'The room in Dover', *Queen's Quarterly*, LIII (1946), 12–14.
[6]*The Times Literary Supplement*, 10 Oct. 1968.
[7]Graham's abilities in this direction can be glimpsed in the many articles he wrote for such periodicals as the *Queen's Quarterly*, the *Queen's Review* and the *Canadian Banker*. These ranged from a lighthearted 'Some impressions of Cambridge' in the *Queen's Review* for 1928 to later series of articles of a more serious nature such as, to take a few instances, 'War guilt and war aims', *Queen's Quarterly* (1939), 'The future of Poland', *Queen's Quarterly* (1940), and 'The German economic drive in the Balkans', *Canadian Banker* (1940).

During my first year of graduate work in London, I was supervised first by the late Professor Vincent Harlow, a kind and courteous scholar, albeit rather aloof and official in his relations with students. 'Colonial' students like myself tended to view him, rightly or wrongly, as too close to the Colonial Office (with all that implied in the 1940s). Although there was absolute freedom of discussion in his admirably conducted seminars, there were students who suspected that their criticism of British rule (a dangerous exercise in those days) might be held against them. In retrospect, I am sure that none of us was ever victimised for the views he held, yet at the time the feeling lingered on, to be dispelled by the impact of the very different temperament shown by GSG when he succeeded Harlow as Rhodes Professor. In his own blunt way — as he sometimes admitted, a jocular rudeness was his way of showing real affection for a person — he made it clear from the beginning that what really mattered to him was the quality of the individual; his race and nationality were of little account. His obvious abhorrence of any form of arrogance or condescension partly explains the high esteem in which he was held by students, particularly those who were close enough to know him well. Even more important, GSG is modest in the best sense of the word. His intimate friends know that he has no great self-regard, and no vanity whatsoever. This, I think, has a bearing on his very shrewd judgment of people, students or colleagues. He never lets personal feelings enter into his judgment of persons: he has, of course many prejudices: he prickles with them. Anyone who cares about people the way he does must be this way. But his determination to be scrupulously fair in his appraisal of people is too evident to be missed. That is why in judging he is cool and fair.

When GSG first came to King's everyone looked out for the new professor, who soon showed himself to be open and approachable. Several evenings after seminar, he would invite us out to dinner at Olivelli's in Store Street, and real friendship developed between teacher and pupils. I came to take him for granted and was therefore not a little surprised when one evening after reading the first draft chapter of my thesis, he expressed himself shocked by my sloppy thought and shoddy writing. In place of well argued, analytical writing, he stated, I had presented him with a series of anecdotes loosely strung together, and he simply ordered me to scrap the entire chapter and begin all over again. This reprimand made no difference to our personal relations and when a few months ago I reminded him of the incident, he had forgotten it. But this tough and hidden aspect of the man's character made a profound impression on my mind and helped shape my academic career. GSG never suffered fools gladly and I suspect that the care and attention which, as I have already indicated, he lavished on his students, were reserved mainly for those who could work and who had demonstrated that they had the capacity to

5

learn. Years later when I paid occasional visits to his room at the Chesham in Surrey Street, I saw him with different eyes — a vigorous, kindly figure dispensing advice or chastening from behind his desk as the occasion demanded.

The same impression of physical and intellectual vigour characterised his presence at the end of the table at the Monday evening seminar at the Institute of Historical Research. Quick reaction; complete absence of affectation or pomposity; on the contrary, a touching humility, as if in recognition of the fact that the newest graduate student could turn up a hitherto unknown piece of information. Generations of students will recall particular *mots*: for example, his lightning response to the visiting professor who asked in somewhat pungent terms, 'Have I the freedom...?' 'Within the law, Sir.' Another generation will recall the evening when, in mid-session, the student assistant's alarm-clock went off suddenly inside her briefcase. Seated between two Roman Catholics, the Presbyterian professor's split-second reaction was, 'What's this? Another Popish plot?'

His seminars always attracted a vast field of potential scholarship, and the seminar topics — like the British Empire — were inevitably very varied indeed, seldom touching at the edges; but somehow GSG succeeded in providing a measure of cohesion by throwing out the occasional clear guidelines, historical or literary. He waged war on sloppy thought and writing (especially on anachronisms); encouraged 'streamlining' — interpretation with events well in perspective. His last words to his former students, gathered to do him honour on retirement, were a warning against the temptations of prostitution — in this case journalistic history. On an earlier more formal occasion he had spoken eloquently on this same theme, supporting the plea of his old friend the late Harold Innis 'to guard the University against the menace of commercialism, popular journalism and obsession with power and status'. As GSG put it:

A true scholar's curiosity is likely to be eccentric, because his work separates him from most of his fellows. If he is inspired to toil day and night in his little vineyard he may well become a little peculiar. None the less, it is this dedicated concentration that gives him his dignity, the University its vitality, civilization many of its material benefits.[8]

There remains the question of GSG's position with regard to the British Empire. After all, he held one of the two most important chairs on the subject in Britain. The present title, 'Rhodes Professor of Imperial History' is, in a sense, an anachronism today: only the acute observer can tell to what extent GSG gloried in the imperial past. He makes no

[8]'In defence of the ivory tower', an address given on the occasion of the twenty-fifth anniversary of Founders' Day at the University of New Brunswick, March 1967.

secret of the fact that he was a product of the age of empire and with characteristic candour described his early impressions of the Empire in his opening of the First Reid Lecture, delivered at Acadia University, Nova Scotia, in 1969:

> Fifty years ago, my generation believed in the beneficence of an Empire for which so many Canadians had gladly offered their lives. Most of us were brought up in a tradition which held that the 'Old Country' was home, or at least a second home, and we found in the Royal Navy and the Indian Army, in Henty and Kipling, in Roberts and Kitchener, the inspiration that reinforced our faith.
>
> We waved Union Jacks when we sang of Empire fifty years ago, but we were romantics rather than jingoes. Few of us felt called upon to beat 'the war-drum of the white man'. We sang *Rule Britannia*, but we were not racialists. (The word did not exist in those days; and we spoke politely of 'backward' not under-developed countries.) Admittedly there was something arrogant and vulgar about certain aspects of the Imperial idea, and the notion of white superiority was probably taken for granted. On the other hand, we were not unprepared to combine our adolescent patriotism with sturdy faith in a God of Battles who would act as impartial umpire; God would judge the fruits of Empire in the years to come.[9]

As with Canada, GSG has a very deep attachment to the 'Old Country'. His family background has contributed not a little to this. His father was English/Scottish, a Presbyterian minister who emigrated to Canada as a young man: his mother was of Anglo-Irish descent, a woman of great drive and intelligence who also settled in Canada when young. There were missionaries on both sides of the family, and GSG's young life in small Ontario towns was certainly coloured by this missionary connection with its letters and mementoes from 'outposts of Empire'. In spite of these early influences, I do not believe that there was ever much 'imperialism' in his attitude. His humanity, his freedom from rigid views, his willingness to experiment with the new, indeed his flexibility, enabled him to grow and develop with the times. Unlike his predecessors such as the late Reginald Coupland and A.P. Newton, he developed a much wider view of colonial history. Indeed the new attitude to the history of the non-white Commonwealth and to the cultures of Black Africa — areas in which revolutionary changes have taken place during the past quarter of a century — owes more than is often realised to GSG's encouragment of young scholars from these areas and his healthy attitude to the study of the history of non-European peoples. Although his work has been in the Canadian and naval fields, his first years in London as Rhodes Professor coincided with a succession of greatly loved African and West Indian

---

[9]'Colonies by repulsion', the First Reid Lecture delivered at Acadia University, Nova Scotia, in 1969.

students — of whom I had the good fortune to be the first — men and women to whom GSG literally gave more than the normal share of attention. Years afterwards whenever he visited his former students in their respective countries it was easy to detect from his openly expressed joy at meeting them again that his attachment to his African students, like everything else he valued in life, was deep and sincere.

The years of his tenure of the Rhodes Chair in London were critical years for the British Empire. As is well known, following the end of the Second World War, India, Pakistan, Burma, Ceylon, and the rest gained their independence: between 1950 and 1960 nearly all the tropical African dependencies recovered their sovereignty. During these years and as far as African and Asian members were concerned, the British Empire was transformed into the Commonwealth. It is fortunate for the University of London and for the new Commonwealth that the occupant of the Rhodes Chair during these memorable years understood and accepted the forces that were transforming the old empire into the Commonwealth: his personal integrity and his wide sympathies attracted Western and non-Western postgraduate students to his seminar. His work went beyond the community of students and the seminar room. He travelled extensively throughout the new Commonwealth, lecturing, broadcasting, meeting scholars and politicians and generally interpreting one area of the Commonwealth to the other. Even in London he ran courses for overseas civil servants, and this in addition to his regular courses for students. When we take into account his prodigious output, it is clear that his wife and children must have seen all too little of him. Yet his many accomplishments could only have been achieved within the calm setting provided by Mary Graham, for GSG is sensitive to his immediate environment; and as a friend of the family aptly observed: 'To read a thesis while seated in a deck chair under an apple tree ("This is great!" he says, waving his pipe) is probably the nearest he will ever come to retirement.'

2

A.F. McC. MADDEN

1066, 1776 and All That: the Relevance of English Medieval Experience of 'Empire' to Later Imperial Constitutional Issues[1]

Like Wesley, historians of empire have 'the whole world for their parish', for few areas of the world's surface have at no time been within an empire, whether as metropolis or as dependency. Historians of European expansion alone will find materials in nearly all continents; and historians of the Commonwealth need yield to none in the compass, complexity or diversity of their subject matter. We need not then be narrow or apologetic. In the contemporary fashion for comparative studies we have a rich abundance of material to make our patterns, to build our models, to liberate ideas or to demolish generalisations. While strengthening our base in a special area — North America, South Asia, Australasia or Africa — or century or decade, we should venture into other territories and periods. We should not be content to be 'Africanists' or 'Asianists', or worse still specialists in that non-subject, the so-called 'Third World', for the whole range of imperial existence from John Smith's Virginia to Ian Smith's Rhodesia is our oyster.

But the time span is much longer than that, though for the most part we neglect or forget it. Before ever Elizabethan adventurer set foot in the New World there were five centuries (or more) of precedent stored away in the minds and archives of English officials. Issues had been joined, questions asked, expedients found, a system formed; and such experience was not irrelevant to the subsequent history of British empire, and indeed was crucial in the great debate which preceded the schism of 1776. Perhaps the folk memory was not always accurate, and advocates were careless of respect for their sources in their spirited partisanship. In the later propaganda battle between British and American pamphleteers in the mid-eighteenth century myth would suffuse fact in ambiguity; and precedents would be abused with an ignorant temerity which would shock the jealously

[1]This article is based on a lecture I was encouraged to write in the fall of 1970 for Queen's University, Ontario, by Professor D.M. Schurman (of the Institute of Commonwealth Studies) and Professor G.A. Rawlyk (of the History Department). My researches into the medieval empire were stimulated by R.L. Schuyler's *Parliament and the British Empire* (New York, 1929) and J. Goebel's introduction to J.H. Smith, *Appeals to the Privy Council from the American Plantations* (New York, 1950).

exclusive professionalism of later medievalists. But historians of a post-medieval period should not be surprised. Did not seventeenth-century lawyers, like Coke, use medieval history as a precept for his own times?[2] Did not the protagonists in the conflict between king and parliament justify their causes by researching selectively among the medieval archives: the king's men in the periods of royal despotism, the parliament men in those of royal weakness? So too did American pamphleteers in the eighteenth century employ history as a guide for present discontents or a handmaiden of the revolutionary principle.[3]

The history of governance overseas thus began near at home in the British Isles and in Europe: an English medieval empire was the seedbed of forms used later. Though it is an anachronism to use the word, in 1066 England became by conquest a 'colony' of Normandy; yet by inverting roles (which might perhaps have been repeated if the thirteen colonies had not become independent) the 'colony', England, with its greater resources and the king's presence, became the metropolis of a considerable empire in western Europe. Henry II a century later ruled territories overseas much larger than England and with a system of government more coordinated and probably more efficient than in any other European realm. To inheritance of dominions outside the realm of England (and these included the pre-Conquest Norman 'empire' of the Channel Islands) were added, by marriage, inheritance, conquest and plantation, an empire on the continent consisting of Anjou, Aquitaine and Gascony, and another in the British Isles themselves of Ireland, Wales and the Isle of Man. Though all the continental possessions were lost to the English crown (Calais last of all) by the mid-sixteenth century, traditions and usages deriving therefrom passed into British colonial practice in the modern period. What were these? First, it was established that the monarchy was unitary and that 'dominions' were possessions of the crown of England, not mini-kingdoms in their own right as in the Spanish empire. Secondly, these dependencies would, like Quebec in 1774, retain their own laws and customs, except in so far as common law, ordinance or statute might be imposed on them. Thirdly, both the king in council and the king in parliament could legislate for 'dominions', though in fact it was usually the king in council. Acts of the English parliament, in which they were

[2]See, for example, J.G.A. Pocock's admirable *The Ancient Constitution and the Feudal Law* (Cambridge, 1957); also J.E.C. Hill, *The English Revolution, 1640* (London, 1955).

[3]See, for example, R.G. Adams, *Political Ideas of the American Revolution* (Durham, N.C., 1922) and H. Trevor Colbourn, *The Lamp of Experience; Whig History and the Intellectual Origins of the American Revolution* (Chapel Hill, N.C., 1965). See also Martin Howard and James Otis in B. Bailyn, ed., *Pamphlets of the American Revolution* (Cambridge, Mass., 1965) and James Wilson in S.E. Morison, ed., *Sources and Documents illustrating the American Revolution* (Oxford, 1923).

not represented, could bind the subjects in 'dominions' and indeed tax them. But though few did, some Acts purported to do so, and some did. Fourthly, the king in council could hear appeals from his 'dominions' and indeed often did so.

Such were some of the means whereby a degree of imperial unity and authority was asserted within the medieval empires. On the other hand it had been also established that on the frontier, almost beyond effective control, 'dominions' in march or palatinate possessed a considerable amount of sturdy, local self-government with legislatures of their own. It was government at a distance and on the cheap. The crown, not wishing to get directly involved, was content with some supervision only. Nominally at least local legislation might be subject to royal initiative, and more probably to royal veto. In practice local autonomy would of course depend on the relative strength, or resolution, of king, marcher lord or palatinate; and on the distance between metropolis and 'dominion'. Therefore, long before the grant of powers of government to merchant companies (like those of Virginia or the East Indies) in identical phrases to those for guilds, or to proprietors (like Baltimore of Maryland or Carlisle for the Caribbees) of fiefs similar to those for Man or Durham, England had a 'colonial' system in embryo. Moreover she had had experience of the crucial and universal dilemma of empire: how to secure a reasonable and inexpensive balance between local diversity and central unity, between independence and interdependence, between freedom and a continuing association. This was the balance Jefferson, Madison, Franklin and others sought for in vain in their writings in the 1770s:[4] equal partnership in union under a common crown – a concept owing something perhaps to the relations of the sister kingdoms of England and Scotland between 1603 and 1707 and ultimately achieved in the 'dominion status' of the 1930s.

It was the inequality of realm and dominions which was the central theme of the pamphleteers of the American Revolution: the imbalance between colonial self-government and imperial authority; more precisely with reference to the legitimacy or otherwise of metropolitan decision- and law-making overseas by crown or parliament. The crown could grant power, could check its use (as by *quo warranto*)[5], could revoke powers, could assert jurisdiction and could exercise supervision over justice in all 'dominions' by claiming appeals. To merchants overseas in Flanders (1359) or Calais (1363)[6], or to distant barons or prelates such as the Bishop

---

[4]See W.P.M. Kennedy, *Essays in Constitutional Law* (London, 1934), pp. 19–20.
[5]Statute of Gloucester (6 Ed. I. cap. 1) 1278, and subsequently that of 1290 (18 Ed. I). The charter of the Virginia Company was held void in May 1624 by *quo warranto* process.
[6]W Cunningham, *The Growth of English Industry and Commerce* (Cambridge, 1890), I, 544–5; *Foedera* (1830 edn.), III, ii, 690; H. Knighton, *Chronica* (London, 1652), IV, 2626.

of Durham (1153–75)[7] the king — who could maybe do little else — granted substantial powers of self-government. At Calais merchants accepted as 'heirs denizen of England' were recognised as possessed of all 'the rights of Englishmen'[8] (a phrase so prominent in the 1770s), as if they had been born in England. They could elect their own governor and assembly and could try their own cases according to their own laws and usages. The king's supreme remedial jurisdiction affirmed in the realm by the Statute of Marlborough (1267)[9] was asserted similarly over the frontier marches by the Statute of Westminster I (1275): if crime 'be done in the marches of Wales or in any other place where the King's writs be not current, the King who is Sovereign Lord over all, shall do right there, unto such as will complain'.[10] In time such appeal would be extended over 'dominions', for example (as we shall see most significantly for the future) over the Channel Islands.

As for the powers of 'parliament' we must remember cautiously its nebulous origins. But though the representative commoners might stand mutely around dressing the stage like extras in a Cecil B. de Mille epic, it is clear that what the crown had power to do in council it had apparently more power to do effectively in 'parliament', their silent presence indicating assent. Some of this 'parliamentary' legislation affected the 'dominions'. As early as 1275 an ordinance, made in an unwontedly large 'parliament', imposed the collection of new customs on exports from England, Wales and Ireland, though neither Wales nor Ireland was annexed to the realm of England.[11] It is true that there were a dozen Irish (or rather Norman Irish) magnates present, a reminder that Edward I regarded his English parliament as an imperial one and encouraged petitions from all his dominions. One of the first calls on such revenues from Irish customs was indeed for an 'imperial' war elsewhere — in Wales:[12] the issue of military contributions sought later, with little success, from the American colonies in 1765, Ireland in 1785, or Canada in 1887 and 1897. Nevertheless, Acts of 1413 and 1536 provided for the paying of taxes in Calais for defence, while one of 1535 required the burgesses there to pay tithes.[13] Many

---

[7] J. Raine, ed., *Historiae Dunelmensis Scriptoris Tres* (London, Surtees Society, 1839), App. xxxi–xxxv, cxxv; T.D. Hardy, ed., *Register of Richard de Kellawe 1311–1316* (1873 etc.), i, 9–17; ii, 116–17; iii, 61–7; iv, 225–8. See also G.T. Lapsley, *The County Palatine of Durham* (Cambridge, Mass., 1900), and Jean Scammell, 'The origins and limitations of the Liberty of Durham', *English Historical Review*, lxxxi (1966), 449–73.

[8] See also 25 Ed. III St. 2. and 42 Ed. III, cap. 10.

[9] 52 Hen. III cap. 19.

[10] 3 Ed. I cap. 17.

[11] F. Palgrave, ed., *The Parliamentary Writs...* (1827 edn), i, 1. Rot. fin. 3 Ed. I m. 24d. Writs issued on 25 May 1275 show that the King's agents were authorised to collect the customs forthwith without waiting for the formal assent of the Irish Parliament: H.S. Sweetman, ed., *Calendar of Documents relating to Ireland* (London, 1875 etc.), *(1251–84)*, p. 243.

[12] *Ibid.* *(1284–92)*, pp. 35ff., 300.

[13] 1 Hen. V cap. 9; 27 Hen. VIII cap. 63; 27 Hen. VIII cap. 20.

English statutes purport to legislate for 'the realm and the dominions': for example most of the Reformation statutes against papal jurisdiction (1533, 1534, 1536).[14] So did the Royal Style (Defender of the Faith) Act of 1544 and the Elizabethan Acts of Supremacy and Uniformity of 1559,[15] the latter with some significance in the religious issues of Quebec after 1763. The Export Customs Acts of 1535 and 1566 and the Tonnage and Poundage Act of 1604[16] expressly apply to 'this realm and any your Majesty's dominions': so do the statutes requiring yearly thanksgiving for 5 November or punishing profanation of Sundays.[17] Surely this is the lie direct to MacIlwain's claim that it was not until the Puritan revolution that parliaments in, for example, the Act declaring England to be a Commonwealth[18] or the 'first' Navigation Acts of 1650 and 1651,[19] claimed to legislate overseas.[20] If these were indeed the 'first' Navigation Acts, what then were the Statutes of 1381 and 1390 directing the use of ships of the realm,[21] or the Act of 1540 which laid down freight rates for realm and dominions and had a resoundingly mercantilist preamble setting out the need for England's defence — 'compassed and invironed' as it is 'by and with grete seas' — of a large merchant fleet, for the mariners it trained and the craftsmen it employed and the families in sea ports it supported?[22]

Let us look a little more closely at some of this English medieval empire. Since the continental 'dominions' were all lost by 1558 and indeed raise somewhat special and complex problems of overlordship and homage,[23] we can concern ourselves with the remnants. When Ralegh prayed to God 'who had raised up this empire of the Britaynes with all her attendant daughter islands about her to an envious height', it was the remnants of this medieval empire which he had in mind.[24]

---

[14]24 Hen. VIII cap. 12; 26 Hen. VIII cap. 1; 28 Hen. VIII cap. 10.

[15]35 Hen. VIII cap. 3; 1 Eliz. I cap. 1, cap. 2. See also 5 Eliz. I cap. 1; 25 Eliz. I cap. 1; 35 Eliz. I cap. 2.

[16]27 Hen. VII cap. 14; 8 Eliz. I cap. 3; 1 Jac. I cap. 33.

[17]3 Jac. I cap. 1; 1 Car. I cap. 1.

[18]S.R. Gardiner, *The Constitutional Documents of the Puritan Revolution, 1625–1660* (3rd edn, Oxford, 1906), p. 388.

[19]C.H. Firth and R.S. Rait, eds., *Acts and Ordinances of the Interregnum 1642–1660* (London, 1911), II, 425–9; Gardiner, *Constitutional Documents*, pp. 467ff.

[20]C.H. MacIlwain, *The High Court of Parliament and its Supremacy* (New Haven, 1910), *The American Revolution: A Constitutional Interpretation* (New York, 1923).

[21]5 Rich. II St. 1 cap. 3; 14 Rich. II cap. 7.

[22]32 Hen. VIII cap. 14.

[23]See E.C. Lodge, *Gascony under English Rule* (London, 1926) and M.G.A. Vale, *English Gascony 1399–1453* (London, 1970). Even in Bracton's time the law accepted that a man might be a subject both of the French, and of the English king: F. Pollock and F. Maitland, *History of English Law* (London, 1898), I, 443ff.

[24]By contrast, the word 'empire' had been used as an assertion of English independence. If the Holy Roman Empire was so styled then the realm of England could certainly claim equal dignity. See 24 Hen. VIII cap. 12: 'Where by divers sundry old authentic histories and chronicles it is manifestly declared and expressed that this realm of England is an empire and so hath been accepted in the world...'

The Channel Islands were dominions of the king as duke of Normandy, separated from their homeland by the French conquest of Normandy in 1204 and confirmed as possessions of the English king in 1360.[25] But long before that King John, by a generous grant of autonomy, had bid for, and bought, their allegiance: by charter he recognised their right to their own systems of ancient Norman (and often very uncertain) island custom, and to their own *Cour Royale* of bailiff and *jurats*, a self-perpetuating oligarchy of seigneurs, as interpreters of them.[26] The 'rights of Englishmen', and indeed more — quittance from tolls in England and from military service — were also granted.[27] Furthermore, charters of Edward VI, Elizabeth, and Charles II granted the islanders a remarkable privilege of neutrality in war: 'in time of war the merchants of all nations and others, as well aliens as inhabitants, as well enemies as friends, may freely, legally and with impunity come go and frequent the said islands' on their lawful business without molestation.[28] Though firmly abolished by proclamation of William III in 1689, one wonders whether some Acadian of Nova Scotia, having known of this, lived in hopes of securing similar liberties in the forty years after 1713.[29]

The seigneurs in the Channel Islands then enjoyed substantial home rule, though always in their skirmishes with the king's governor they claimed to acknowledge that the king himself as duke had the *sole* right to initiate taxation. 'It is a maxime of State that noe authority whatsoever under yours can leavye or impose any kind of taxe or impost ... without your expresse Command, and that the leavying of any such taxe is a Prerogative Royall essentially adhering to your Crowne which to violate is felony.'[30] The king indeed did from time to time show his solicitation for their security — 'farthest remote from the rest of our saide domynions' in James I's words, 'thereby most exposed to daunger of invasion'[31] — by requiring taxes for defence. But if the islanders protested their respect for the prerogative royal they also argued that 'the Lord King of England has nothing in these islands save the status of Duke' and therefore parlia-

---

[25]*Foedera*, III, pt 1, p. 487. See J.H. Le Patourel, *The Medieval Administration of the Channel Islands 1199–1399* (London, 1937).

[26]P. Falle, *Account of the Island of Jersey* (Jersey, 1837 edn.), pp. 222–3; *Col. Pat. Rolls (1225–32)*, p. 330; *(1332–47)*, p. 18. Jersey Prison Board, II, 111; III, 885.

[27]Jersey Prison Board, II, 156, 158; III, 881; and Warburton's *Treatise on ... Guernsey* (1822), pp. 148–9.

[28]Jersey Prison Board, I, 35ff.; II, 203–6, 216ff.

[29]Phillips to Board, 26 November 1730. C.O. 217/6. Proclamation 1 August 1749. C.O. 217/40. T.B. Akins, *Selections from the Public Documents of the Province of Nova Scotia* (1869), pp. 28–9, 31, 168–9, 171, 174–5, 251–3. B. Murdoch, *A History of Nova Scotia or Acadie* (Halifax, NS, 1865–7), II, 283, 299–301. The expulsion of the Acadians had a medieval precedent in that of the burghers from Calais.

[30]Jersey Prison Board, II, 428. Governor Morgan had levied customs on exports and enforced the Navigation Act (12 Car. II cap. 18).

[31]*Documens relatifs à l'Ile de Guernsey* (Guernsey, 1814), no. 1, pp. 6ff.

mentary statutes did not, they said, automatically extend to islands never annexed to the realm. Three conditions had, they declared, to be fulfilled: the islands must be expressly named in an Act, the king must have ordered the Act to be registered in the local *Cour Royale*, and the *Cour Royale* must have done so.[32] Since the islanders were not represented in parliament, they asserted in 1679, such exemplification was necessary to secure the general local 'cognisance of new measures'.[33] But English attorneys general in 1681 and 1698[34] argued that a general reference to 'plantations' or 'dominions' was sufficient for an Act to extend to the Channel Islands: registration by the *Cour Royale* was only a convenient, not a legally necessary, procedure. The Navigation Act[35] referred to did not, indeed, name the Channel Islands generally or specifically in § 17 but in other sections (e.g. 3, 4, 6 and 14) did enumerate both Jersey and Guernsey; and though never registered, it was observed, at least as effectively as in Massachusetts.

Some enterprising home rulers argued that, since the Statute of 1542, restraining the use of crossbows and handguns, expressly excluded the Channel Islanders,[36] parliament had recognised that it could not legislate without the consent of their island legislatures, the States; but surely such express mention in the Act would argue that parliament had to make positive exemption if the statute were *not* to apply, and in the context it is clear why the islanders were exempted, for others excluded were subjects living within five miles of the coast, or on the Scottish borders, or in the town of Calais — in other words, frontiersmen who would be the first line of 'home guard' defence against hostile invasion. Though there is little legal doubt about the right of parliament to legislate for the islands even by 'necessary intendment' and not with express words, in practice parliament left legislation to the king in council and to the island States.

The most momentous contribution of the Channel Islands to later imperial history, however, concerned appeals to the privy council. In 1641 the Long Parliament abolished prerogative jurisdiction, including

---

[32]Jersey Prison Board, II, 428.
[33]Order in Council, 21 May 1679. PC 2/68, pp. 43–4, 320–2.
[34]Jersey Prison Board, I, 76; a similar decision was given in *AG v Le Marchant*, 1772; and in 1832 it was held that, though the Habeas Corpus Act (31 Car. II cap. 2) was never registered, it nevertheless was in force there on the authority of the Privy Council alone. PP 1861 XXIV (2761) p. 273. In 1906 the Law Officers strongly endorsed a memorandum of Sir Almeric Fitzroy's which sought to correct Lloyd George's uninstructed answer to a parliamentary question about the extension of the Merchant Shipping Act to the Channel Islands (Hans. 4th CLIX 775). Fitzroy had asserted the 'undefeasible right of Parliament to enforce such laws as it chooses' in the islands: *Memoirs* (London, 1925), I, 296–7. This was also the conclusion of the Commissioners of 1861 (PP 1861 XXIV (2761) p. vi), but they added that except on general imperial matters the extension of parliamentary legislation is 'unusual'.
[35]12 Car. II cap. 18.
[36]33 Hen. VIII cap. 6, § 23.

the Star Chamber and the courts of the North, of Wales, of Lancaster and of Chester;[37] but it happened that section 5 in effect limited such abolition to the realm itself by its reference specifically to 'this kingdom' and by its acknowledgement of 'the ordinary course of law'. Appeals had indeed come to the Privy Council from the Channel Islands by the ordinary course of law, at least (it was claimed) since the fourteenth century.[38] When Charles II sought to assert royal supervision over the American plantations in the 1670s, the continuing existence of appeals overseas from Jersey and Guernsey proved both precedent and pretext for a regular system of appeals from the colonies to the privy council.[39]

If the Channel Islands conquered England, Ireland, Wales and Man were dominions conquered by England and only one of these — Wales — was formally annexed to the realm before the seventeenth century. Ireland was 'conquered' under papal sanction, the bull *Laudabiliter* of Adrian IV, the English pope, in 1156;[40] but it was little more than a paper conquest. An expatriate Anglo-Norman garrison, with a small enclave in 'The Pale', a group of settler magnates ('the middle nation') becoming more Irish each year, and 'the wild Irishry' themselves — 'the King's Irish enemies', as the tribesmen were called: such was the dominion of Ireland, a large island for the most part quite unaffected or influenced by its nominal conquerors who, even within the area round Dublin where they clung to some of the trappings of *imperium*, found themselves, more often than not, being conquered in turn by their environment. The extension of English law and custom was nominal, little more than a matter of favour for individuals or a vague criterion for judgment.[41] English kings would send ordinances and statutes to be observed in Ireland as Henry III did with Magna Carta in 1217 and Edward I with the Statutes of Westminster and Gloucester in 1285;[42] but even within 'the Pale' they could not always be enforced. The Statute of Kilkenny in 1366 showed concern to prevent loyal settlers in the 'obedient shires' from becoming 'celticised' in language, dress, law and custom like the 'degenerate' Norman-Irish of the remoter

[37]16 Car. I cap. 10.
[38]Certainly such appeals were recognised in the orders in council of 3 November 1494, 22 June 1565, 13 May 1572 and 9 October 1580: Jersey Prison Board, I, 40; II, 176, 234; III, 915; and PC 2/10.
[39]Appeals had continued to be heard by the Council in England under the Protectorate.
[40]The invasion did not take place until 1172, when Pope Alexander III wrote in approval to Henry II for extending 'the plenitude of his peace' to a barbarous and pagan race.
[41]At the request of 'all the men of Ireland' (i.e. the Anglo-Norman magnates) King John in 1210 decreed that English law should be observed in Irish Courts. See also H.F. Berry ed., *Statutes and Ordinances, and Acts of the Parliament of Ireland* (1907 edn.), I, 20–1; *Foedera*, I, 266, 540; Sweetman, *Calendar* (1285–92), 33, 38.
[42]Berry, *Statutes*, I, 47. See also a writ from Edward II in 1320: D. Pickering, ed., *Statutes at Large*, I, 357.

areas,[43] but it was in vain. A long period of Norman-Irish home Celtic and aristocratic, succeeded, and a large part of Ireland was abandoned to native law and tribal custom. Leaders of the 'middle nation', such as the Butlers, Burkes and Geraldines, ruled large autonomous territories partly as feudal seigneurs and partly as Gaelic kings, and played prominent roles, even as king's deputies, in a Gaelic renaissance.

The Statute of Drogheda a century later reads like a declaration of Irish legislative independence: 'Whereas the land of Ireland is and at all times has been corporate of itself by ancient laws and customs used in the same, freed of the burden of any special laws of the realm of England', save only such as were confirmed in the Irish parliament itself.[44] For Irish customary law (*brehon*) the courts officially had little respect and as early as 1229 by the so-called 'Statute of Ireland' it was to be set aside in certain matters in preference for English common law. Though the rule of succession by *tanistry* and *gavelkind* persisted,[45] the individualisation of tenure gradually eroded the tribal system as chiefs built up their power at the expense of their clansmen. As for the application of English statutes to Ireland, even the courts in England had some doubts until the late fifteenth century. In *Pilkington's Case* (1441) the judges were divided: one indeed argued that since 'they have no order by our writ to come to our Parliament' the Irish were not bound by English statutes: a tithe (he said) granted by the English parliament would not bind the men of Durham.[46] In this view there could be no legislation without representation. But in 1486, in the case of the *Merchants of Waterford* it was agreed unanimously in King's Bench that English statutes could legally be applied to Ireland.[47]

There was an Irish parliament too of course: afforced meetings of the king's Irish council which in the later fourteenth and fifteenth centuries dwindled in authority and numbers till it was representative of little more than parts of Leinster and Meath and a few towns. Though indeed it might be prudent to obtain its approval, the king's deputy could both legislate and tax without its assistance, and similarly the English parliament continued at the request of Irish petitioners to pass special Acts for

---

[43] Berry, *Statutes*, I, 435–7.
[44] 38 Hen. VI cap. 1; H.F. Berry, ed., *Statute Rolls of the Parliament of Ireland, reign of Henry VI* (1907 edn.), 645–7.
[45] The last notable judgment according to *brehon* law was probably not until 1584, though a statute of 1495 (10 Hen. VII cap. 11) had proscribed it. See also the judges' resolution of 1605 in Sir John Davies, *Les Reports des Cases en les Courts des Roy en Ireland* (London, 1674), pp. 49–50.
[46] Year Book 20 Hen. VI, fos. 8–9.
[47] Year Book 1 Hen. VII, fo. 3. In the Exchequer in 1485, however, when not all the judges had been present, some had held that since the Irish did not have knights of parliament (*quia hic non habent milites parliamenti*) English statutes relating to land and property did not extend to Ireland: Year Book 2 Richard III, fo. 12.

Ireland.[48] In 1495 the Irish parliament passed Poynings' Law, a measure which recognising the king's sole initiative in all law-making gave the crown a sort of veto on legislation proposed and not yet passed.[49] The Act was not, as it was later considered, the legislative enslavement of Ireland: it was in the circumstances of the late fifteenth century an attempt to secure the standing and procedure of the Irish parliament as a safeguard against the over-mighty deputies who had exploited Irish autonomy for their own interest.[50] It should be remembered how subordinate the contemporary English parliament was to the king's mandates. It was only when a century later the English parliament had won its legislative initiative, and the Irish parliament remained frozen static in subservient posture to the king's will by Poynings' Law that the Act was seen to be a grievance. It was indeed a remarkable control, and one which in the 1670s Charles II tried in vain to fasten on Jamaica.[51] But the decisive attack on Norman-Irish home rule was not launched till Henry VIII's excommunication prompted fears of an Irish rising to rid a heretic king of his papal fief. The English reformation statutes were applied to Ireland; the crowns of England and Ireland were united by statute in 1542,[52] and gradually, in law at least, Ireland became subordinated to the realm of England — even more completely of course with the Declaratory Act of 1719,[53] the exact replica for that of 1766 for America.

In Ireland the infiltration of English law had been individual: in the conquered principality of Wales it was territorial. Magna Carta in 1215 had recognised Welsh law as the law in Wales, but in 1277, after Llewelyn had given his allegiance to Edward I, Welsh law was restricted to Snowdonia by the Treaty of Aberconway and English law was gradually introduced into the ceded counties to the south.[54] Despite Llewelyn's plea that every province in the king's *imperium* had its own laws — 'Gascon in Gascony, Scots in Scotland, Irish in Ireland (an error of course) and English in England'[55] — seven years later in the Statute of Rhuddlan[56] the king, while recognising Welsh *civil* law, insisted on English *criminal* law (the same compromise as in the Quebec Act). Edward I, with qualms

---

[48]See H.G. Richardson and G.O. Sayles, eds., *Parliaments and Councils of Medieval Ireland* (Dublin, 1947), *The Irish Parliament in the Middle Ages* (Philadelphia, 1964).

[49]10 Hen. VII cap. 4.

[50]See D.B. Quinn, 'The early interpretation of Poynings' Law, 1494–1534', and R. Dudley Edwards and T.W. Moody, 'The history of Poynings' Law: Part I, 1494–1615', *Irish Historical Studies*, II (1941), 241–54, 415–24.

[51]There was a similar intention to impose this legislative control on Virginia; see instructions to Culpeper, December 1679. C.O. 5/1355, p. 334.

[52]33 Hen. VIII cap. 1.

[53]6 Geo. I cap. 5.

[54]*Foedera*, I, 545.

[55]J. Conway Davies, ed., *The Welsh Assize Roll 1277–1284* (University of Wales, 1940), p. 266.

[56]I. Statutes of the Realm 55.

reminiscent of George III's conscience about Catholic emancipation, argued that his coronation oath prevented him from accepting bad, unjust and unreasonable custom. Indeed, but for the battle of Bannockburn Scots law, an amalgam of Celtic, Norman feudal and Roman civil law, would have suffered a similar fate, for it is clear that in the aftermath of his arbitration in the matter of the Scottish succession, Edward I's conception of his overlordship included the role of his English parliament (though with a few Scottish representatives added) as the supreme court and legislature of his *imperium*.[57] But Scotland's independence survived this threat, and though the English parliament continued occasionally to claim to legislate for Scotland[58] and English sovereigns to claim homage till 1560, Edward III in 1328 had virtually acknowledged Scotland's freedom. Furthermore the persistent independence of Scotland and the coexistence of the twin kingdoms even after the union of crowns in 1603 provided the future British empire with an example of 'union in diversity',[59] the distinguishing feature which alone made that empire able to persist into Commonwealth. But Wales was in 1536 firmly annexed and absorbed into the realm by a statute which, by making provision for inquiry into residual Welsh law,[60] made clear that any distinct Welsh custom was doomed. Unity was seen here in terms of uniformity, anglicisation. This was not the case with Scotland, or Quebec, or the new conquests of the second British Empire. Uniformity was not confused with imperial unity after the 1770s. That was the lesson of American independence.

But from the earliest period of empire substantial powers of self-government had been granted to responsible magnates on the frontiers as indeed they were to merchant adventurers overseas in Flanders or Calais.[61] The Isle of Man, first Norse, then Scots, was conquered by the English and in 1406 granted to the Stanleys as a proprietary fief.[62] The island had its own Manx laws, its own judiciary (Tynwald) and legislature (the House of Keys).[63] Though the Keys declared in 1608 that their consent to the lord proprietor's taxation was necessary,[64] this claim was premature: indeed it was not till the mid-twentieth century (1958) that they secured full control of taxation and appropriation. In practice the proprietor had

[57]For example, in 1296 and 1305.

[58]For example, 11 Ed. III caps. 2, 3.

[59]American advocates of the revival of such a relationship for America and Britain would have been less keen had they realised that Scotland had been economically subordinated to the stronger kingdom of England.

[60]27 Hen. VIII cap. 26, and the supplementary 34 & 35 Hen. VIII cap. 26.

[61]Cunningham, *English Industry and Commerce*, I, 544–5; *Foedera*, III, ii, 690; C.P. Lucas, *The Beginnings of English Overseas Enterprise* (Oxford, 1917), pp. 184–7; G. Cawston and A.H. Keene, *The Early Chartered Companies* (London, 1896), pp. 249–54.

[62]J.R. Oliver, ed., *Monumenta de insula Manniae* (Douglas, Manx Society, 1860–62), II, 232–6.

[63]Not until 1866 were members of the Keys elected directly.

[64]A.W. Moore, *A History of the Isle of Man* (London, 1900), II, 766, 769.

the sole right to initiate law making.[65] There was no question that the crown could revoke what it had granted, as indeed Elizabeth did for a period after 1594;[66] and from case law Coke argued in the *Fourth Institutes* that English parliamentary statutes would apply if Man were expressly named.[67] In 1663 it was shown that the Restoration Act of Indemnity, though it specifically mentioned Ireland, Wales and Channel Islands but not Man, applied there because of mention of 'other his Majesty's dominions'.[68] Therefore a Commonwealth anti-proprietor leader, William Christian, should have been released and not judicially murdered by the local court,[69] just as Thomas Scott was at Red River by Riel and Lepine in 1870. It is interesting that when in 1765 the crown decided to buy out the proprietor because of the evasions of customs duties and Navigation Laws in Man,[70] this had to be done by statute[71] to overcome certain restrictions on the crown's power of alienation in a previous Act of 1610.[72] This was nine years before Lord Mansfield gave that momentous decision in *Campbell v Hall* on the exhaustion of the crown's powers as conqueror, an opinion which had already led to the use of parliamentary omnicompetence in the Quebec Act a few months earlier. It is significant that Mansfield, whose judgment did so much to protect French civil law in Quebec, had leased lands in the Isle where *deemsters* had preserved their own local law and custom. After the Isle had been reinvested in the crown, local custom continued to be recognised by the courts even on appeal in the Privy Council;[73] and though 'no doubt' can be entertained of 'the legal competency of Parliament to make laws to bind the Isle of Man',[74] British statutes rarely applied.[75]

As for the bishop palatine of Durham on the Scottish borders he was permitted substantial powers to help maintain the King of England's peace. He had his own council and assembly; he raised his own taxes and was exempt from the king's; and virtually he exercised powers of making foreign policy by frequent negotiations with the Scottish king.[76] No doubt bishops might exaggerate their powers and strong kings could reduce

---

[65]J. Gell, ed., *An Abstract of the laws, customs, and ordinances of the Isle of Man* (Douglas, Manx Society, 1867).
[66]Following the case of the Stanley inheritance, 2 And. LX 116.
[67]E. Coke, *Fourth part of the Institutes* (1797 edn.), cap. 69, 283.
[68]12 Car. II cap. 11.
[69]W. Harrison, *Illiam Dhône and the Manx Rebellion of 1651* (Douglas, Manx Society, 1877), p. 55.
[70]This 'coercion Act' was nine years before the Boston Port Act.
[71]5 Geo. III cap. 26.
[72]8 Jac. I cap. 4.
[73]e.g. *A.G. v Mylchreist* 1879: 4 AC. 294.
[74]Law officers' report, 10 November 1802. PP 1805 v, pt ii (79).
[75]For the most part those which did concerned customs duties, e.g. 20 Geo. III cap. 42, 28 Geo. III cap. 63, 45 Geo. III cap. 99, 50 Geo. III cap. 42, and 6 Geo. IV cap. 105.
[76]Lapsley, *County Palatine of Durham.*

them.[77] But Durham is important to the Commonwealth historian, for it links the medieval empire with the American. In proprietary grants — for example, as to Lord Baltimore for Avalon and Maryland — there was regularly the phrase granting 'powers as plenary and ample as ever claimed by the Bishop in the county palatine of Durham'. In the proprietary colonies the powers belonging to the crown elsewhere — the veto, disallowance, appeals — were exercised by the proprietor; and all the normal restrictions on colonial self-government in royal or company plantations were present, not least 'repugnancy' to English law. Laws should 'stand with reason and be not repugnant, nor contrary, but as near as conveniently may be agreeable to the laws, statutes and customs of this our Kingdom of England'.[78] Incidentally this limitation, persisting ambiguously till the Colonial Laws Validity Act of 1865, was a routine copying out of the restriction made in charters to gilds in England relating to their competence in making by-laws. Complaints from municipal officials against the wide powers granted to guilds led to a statute in 1437 restraining unlawful orders made by the latter and one in 1504 requiring guild laws to be examined and approved by the chancellor, the treasurer and the king's chief justices.[79] The charters from Edward IV incorporating the barber-surgeons of London in 1462 and that from Elizabeth I to the Worcester clothiers in 1596 both required by-laws not to be contrary to the laws and statutes of England.[80] Furthermore courts could declare such laws null and void if they were so repugnant.[81] The rule of repugnancy of course did not mean complete identity with English law in the colonies. Differences were tolerated, even expected. To hold otherwise would be to nullify the law-making powers granted. Indeed the power delegated sometimes, as to William Penn later, explicitly included the power 'to alter' the law.

To sum up, then why was this medieval experience of empire relevant? First of all, because the Elizabethan and Jacobean administrators thought it was so. The only conceivable law of empire was that of personal land holding from the crown on the analogy of feudal tenure, and that of the delegated use of the crown's powers within regulated limits to adventuring

[77]Scammell, 'Origin and limitations of the Liberty of Durham', pp. 472–3.
[78]The letters patent for Avalon, 7 April 1623, C.O. 195/1. Similarly for the Caribbees, 2 July 1627, C.O. 29/1; for the Muscovy Company, 6 February 1555, R. Hakluyt, *The Principal Navigations...* (Glasgow, 1903–5 edn.), II, 304ff.; for the Guinea Company, 3 May 1588, *ibid.*, VI, 443ff.; for the East India Company, 31 December 1600, J. Shaw (ed.), *Charters relating to the East India Company from 1600 to 1761* (London, 1887), pp. 1–15; or for Massachusetts, 4 March 1629, W. Macdonald (ed.), *Select Charters and other documents illustrative of American history 1606–1775* (New York, 1899), pp. 37–42
[79]15 Hen. VI cap. 6 and 19 Hen. VII cap. 7.
[80]S. Young, *The Annals of the Barber-Surgeons of London* (1890), pp. 56–7; V. Green, *The History and Antiquities of ... Worcester* (London, 1796), II, lxxi–lxxv.
[81]*The Case of the Tailors of Ipswich*, 1614: 11 Coke 53b.

proprietors or merchant corporations. The link between councils in England, Ireland or Gascony was the king. So too the government of new projections of England in America were not conceived save as an integrated part of the regular government of the realm. There was no new executive machinery devised, no new separate department, no new blue print for the New World. Clerks entered the details of colonial administration in the same ledgers and decisions were taken by the same officials as dealt with the internal affairs of the realm. Concerned (as administrators ever are) with a routine, they pressed into service what precedents of imperial governance were available. The experience of the relics of the medieval empire were still a conscious part of the English constitutional heritage: they constituted the only ready model, which the 'realm' had available, of extended extra-territorial control. What the crown could not control directly it might supervise indirectly. Substantial powers could be devolved on those who might be strong enough to use them in the main for the good of the realm. What was of local importance only might be left to local decision. Sturdy self-government in Bordeaux, Dublin, Calais or St Helier might be permitted to wrestle in local matters on the frontier with the king's trusted representative, whether he were Seneschal of Gascony, Deputy in Ireland, Captain of Calais or Warden of Jersey. Those Tudor civil servants who had witnessed the closing of the English frontiers in the north or in the Celtic west,[82] the rejection of external overlordship at the Reformation,[83] and the loss of an open door to a continental destiny at Calais, tackled the new problems of expansion overseas with the traditional devices they had at hand: a little amateur and makeshift no doubt, but the law of the fief or guild was made to fit colonial circumstances, just as Rome had extended the municipal law of a city to the outlying provinces of a wide empire. So the administrators adopted and adapted what they had from tradition into a patchwork for the future.

Secondly, because, as we have seen, the colonial charters themselves go back to medieval precedents — the palatinate of Durham, for example. The patent to Sir Humphrey Gilbert in 1578 sought to make him a vassal of the queen with all the royalties and jurisdiction of a royal fief[84] just as the Black Prince had in Chester or Gascony, or the Stanleys had in Man. Again, the charters to the embryonic joint stock companies in the East Indies, Virginia or Shakespeare's 'much vexed Bermoothes',[85] echo those to the merchants of the Staple. These were the normal methods for regulating guilds, now developed for small self-governing merchant com-

---

[82]e.g. Cornwall and Wales. See A.L. Rowse, *The Expansion of Elizabethan England* (London, 1955).

[83]See, for example, the 'Act in restraint of appeals' (24 Hen. VIII cap. 12).

[84]11 June 1578: Hakluyt, *Principal Navigations*, III, 17–23.

[85]Shaw, *Charters*, pp. 1–15; MacDonald, *Select Charters*, pp. 1–11; J.H. Lefroy, *Memorials of the discovery and early settlement of the Bermudas. . .* (1877), I, 90.

munities in Muscovy or the Levant[86] — nurseries for imperial government.

Thirdly, because the lawyers considered these medieval precedents authoritative. In 1606 in *Calvin's Case*[87] it was the leading jurists of the age — Bacon, Dodridge, Hyde, Sandys, Popham, Ellesmere and Coke — 'divers sages of the law', who brought these very precedents from the old empire to the cradle of the new. They used Gascony, Ireland, Scotland, Man, Anjou, Jersey, Wales and Guienne to discuss the rights of the crown in colonies by descent and by conquest; the rights of king and of subjects; the extension of English law and statutes.

Fourthly, because the pamphleteers used these examples, if often incorrectly. Darcy, Molyneux and other Irish patriots challenging the sovereignty of parliament from the 1640s onwards, constantly referred to them;[88] so did the pamphleteers of the American Revolution a century later. Francis Maseres, one not unknown to Canadian historians of the mid-eighteenth century, wrote in 1777 a curious dialogue between an Englishman and a Frenchman in favour of conciliating America. In this pamphlet, *The Canadian Freeholder*, he argued that Lord Mansfield's judgment in *Campbell v Hall* was too permissive to conquered peoples and that it attributed too much discretionary power to the crown as conqueror. Mansfield had employed the medieval precedents of Ireland, Wales, Man, Gascony, Guienne and Calais in coming to his *ratio decidendi*.[89] Maseres favoured a statutory assertion of parliamentary power to insist on English law and to reduce the prerogative: he rehearsed illustrations from the medieval empire to throw doubt on Mansfield's judgment, but he claimed that these precedents from 'ancient and obscure times' provided a very doubtful case for the crown's absolute power as conqueror.

The issue of parliament's sovereignty overseas was of course the substance of the debate between Professor MacIlwain and Professor Schuyler half a century ago.[90] But if Schuyler's evidence is legally unanswerable,[91] is that the end of the matter? It is not difficult to show that medieval parliaments claimed to legislate and to tax dominions; but are what purport to be precedents really so? What may be accepted by lawyers in advocating a case need not necessarily convince historians. Did the makers of Magna

[86]Hakluyt, *Principal Navigations*, II, 304–16.
[87]Also called 'Colvil's case': 2 Howell St. T. 559–695.
[88]Patrick Darcy, *An argument. . .* (Waterford, 1641, repr. Dublin, 1764); William Molyneux, *The Case of Ireland's being bound by Acts of Parliament in England* (Dublin, 1698).
[89]A. Shortt and A.G. Doughty, eds., *Documents relating to the Constitutional History of Canada, 1759–1791* (2nd edn, Ottawa, 1918).
[90]MacIlwain, *High Court of Parliament*; Schuyler, *Parliament and the British Empire*.
[91]See H. Wheeler, 'Calvin's case (1608) and the McIlwain–Schuyler debate', *American Historical review*, LXI (1955–56), 587–97.

Carta, for example, mean by '*liber homo*' what Coke did four centuries later? Here we are involved in one of the perpetual dilemmas of English constitutional history. And what do we mean by parliament? In the shifting sands of historical interpretation fashions change. Was it a court (as MacIlwain declared) or a legislature (as Wilkinson argued), or both (as Edwards demonstrated)?[92] In the thirteenth and fourteenth centuries a flexibility of convenience prompted the king whether to make a law in council or in parliament. Even in the presence of parliament it may be claimed that the authority derived from the king. Many things were done in parliament which were not done by parliament. Even when we can prove that parliament in the fourteenth century made laws for subjects unrepresented in its counsels, have we an answer? If the 'parliament' of Edward I or Henry VIII had legislative authority over the dominions, does that imply that that of George III had too? A great constitutional change – a shift of balance between king and parliament – took place between such parliaments. Historians cannot overlook the gulf between a period of royal dictatorship and one of embryonic cabinet government, or between one of fundamental law and one of parliamentary omnicompetence. Of necessity too the growing power of the realm and the increasing authority of the English parliament tended to subordinate the 'dominions'.[93] Can arguments from one side of this great divide be solved by reference to precedents from the other?

Oddly enough this leads to a fifth and final reason for studying the medieval empire. A typical colony moves from a period of absolute royal, 'crown colony' government to representative, to responsive, to responsible government and on to dominion status. The thirteenth and fourteenth centuries were the 'crown colony' stage of the English constitution. It contributes to the understanding of the evolution of the British constitution to see the metropolitan model itself going through the same 'colonial' process.

There are, of course, ways, other than those relating to the application of metropolitan law, wherein the medieval empire can give comparative depth to the Commonwealth history. The laws of the Anglo-Saxons about frontier cattle-thieving are not unfamiliar to students of early nineteenth-century South African history. There are many parallels between the moving frontier in Ireland and that in America, Australasia or Africa: the impact on tribal structure, the search for a middle 'buffer', for collaborators, and for means of control. In the mid-sixteenth century Queen

[92]MacIlwain, *High Court of Parliament*; B. Wilkinson, *Studies in the Constitutional History of the Thirteenth and Fourteenth Centuries* (Manchester, 1937); J.G. Edwards, '"Justice" in Early English Parliaments', *Bulletin of the Institute of Historical Research*, xxvii (1954), 35–53.

[93]Contrast the equality of the phrase 'this realm *and* the dominions' in sixteenth-century statutes with 'this realm and the dominions *thereunto belonging*', the form used from the mid-seventeenth century.

Elizabeth, William Cecil and Henry Sidney conducted an interesting discussion on the relative merits of controlling Ireland,[94] by the chiefs, by Norman-Irish magnates, or by expatriate English officials and plantations of settlers. To students of Gordon in Fiji or Lugard in Africa this is the familiar debate on 'direct' or 'indirect' rule. At first Edward I had employed in Gascony the feudal counterpart of indirect rule, but then he had opted more directly for an official, careerist bureaucracy. (Incidentally he organised a sort of 'Devonshire course' for the sons of seneschals and brought them on short visits to his Court to observe him at work.) Moreover those concerned with plantations in the New World — Grenville, Sidney, Gilbert and Thomas Smith — were also involved with those in Ireland. The English frontier was moving westwards. The Tudors had been forging a greater national unity by absorbing the outlying Celtic fringe in Cornwall, Wales and the Northern marches into the realm. That done, England entered the imperial game — a little late perhaps and with the rich prizes gone.

A knowledge of the history of the pre-seventeenth century 'empire of the Britaynes' is, then, illuminating and can also sometimes be corrective. Historians of Canada have often pointed to two new liberal principles in the Quebec Act: that local law had been recognised, and that a non-Anglican religion was accepted as established in the colony. But if French civil law was accepted, so too had been Jersey, Manx and Welsh custom: *brehon* law was an exception. And if the formula of *'cuius regio, eius religio'* had prevailed since the Reformation, a duality of systems of religion had been accepted successfully in the Union of England and Scotland in 1707 and attempted unsuccessfully in Nova Scotia for a period after 1713. But there is a much earlier precedent. For sixty years after 1565 Presbyterianism was recognised by Elizabeth I and James I as the established religion in the Channel Islands: the islanders were being permitted to be Protestant in their own way and Norman Huguenot Protestantism was Calvinistic.[95] It is true that promises were made in the terms of capitulation for Quebec, but if the Treaty of Limerick had been broken, that of Quebec was not.

Precedents can be useful to us. But they could give little comfort to the American publicists in the mid-eighteenth century. Since there had been taxation without representation, since charters granted could as legally be revoked, since 'rights of true born Englishmen' themselves were imprecise and derivative, an act of grace, so in a necessary process of self-determination historical precedents must be invented, romanticised, and misinterpreted to create a national folklore, just as Plantagenet kings

---

[94]*Cal. State Papers*, 63/26, 18,
[95]'Articles to be considered by the Privy Council', *Calendar of the Manuscripts of the Earl of Salisbury*, Part XIII (Addenda), (London, Historical Manuscripts Commission, 1915), 93.

claimed links with Brutus of Troy,[96] or Tudors with Arthurian legend, or Gold Coasters discovered 'Ghana'. It was safer to base claims on Tom Paine and the rights of men than those of Englishmen, and to rely on a display of force against a remote authority rather than on tedious unrewarding processes of legal argument, in which indeed the new aspirations would founder. And among the 'rights of men' could be included all that a national folklore required. The game could be played by ear, without respect for any moth-eaten precedents. And that after all was a revolutionary, *not* a constitutional, principle.

[96]e.g. Edward I to Boniface VIII, 7 May 1301, justifying his claim to homage from Scotland. *Foedera*, I, ii, 932ff. Similarly the Maltese in the nineteenth century, asserting a demand for the right to representative government, invented a fictitious 'popular council' granted in the eleventh century by Count Roger of Normandy: see C. Mitrovich, *The Claims of the Maltese* (London, 1835).

3

GLYNDWR WILLIAMS

'The Inexhaustible Fountain of Gold'[1] : *English Projects and Ventures in the South Seas, 1670–1750*

Late starters in the maritime expansion of western Europe, Englishmen long looked with covetous eyes at the rich domains of Spain in central and south America. The hope that the precious metals which existed in such profusion in Peru and Mexico might also be found farther north lured many English across the Atlantic to the eastern coastline of north America; but they found no Potosí in New England, no Zacatecas in Virginia. As the northern colonists forgot their early dreams of silver and gold, and instead built up a more mundane economy along the Atlantic seaboard, protagonists of overseas expansion in England continued to regard with speculative interest Spain's colonial empire. The magnificent churches and public buildings of the cities of Spanish America were visible evidence of the wealth of the region. From the plantations of the Caribbean islands to the grassy pampas of the southern regions stretched great tracts of fertile land. Exports of sugar, tobacco, cotton, hides and dye-woods swelled the value of the cargoes of precious metal shipped across the Atlantic; but it was the latter which caught the attention of Europe. As far as the popular imagination was concerned, 'the wealth of the Indies' lay in the holds of the treasure fleets which crossed the ocean each year. From the mid-seventeenth century onwards an infinite variety of schemes was put forward to tap the silver lifeline of the Spanish empire, ironically enough at a time when Spain's bullion imports and her trans-Atlantic trade in general were in serious decline.[2]

With many of England's foreign trades running an adverse bullion balance, it was the more frustrating that the country's merchants could not gain direct access to the Spanish American market, whose demands for woollens, manufactured goods and dried fish Spain was quite unable to meet. English merchants could send their American-bound goods only

[1]The phrase was in common use at this time to describe the wealth of Spanish America. It appears, for example in [Daniel Defoe], *An Historical Account of the Voyages of Sir Walter Raleigh* (London, 1720), p. 43; and in a slightly different form ('the only inexhaustible Fountain of those Treasures') in a government-inspired pamphlet of the period, *A Letter to a Member of Parliament on the resolution of the House to settle a trade to the South Seas* (London, 1711), p. 8.
[2]See J.H. Parry, *The Spanish Seaborne Empire* (London, 1966), pp. 246–50.

as far as Spain, and although this trade brought in some bullion, the costs, delays and uncertainties associated with the Casa de la Contratación at Seville acted as a constant irritant and a strong incentive to attempt a direct trade with Spanish America.[3] Most efforts towards this were centred on the Caribbean, where traders, privateers and smugglers sought to breach the wall of restriction and prohibition which Spain had erected around its lucrative American trade. The Caribbean became a focal point in the struggle for trade and dominion between the maritime nations of Europe, for it was at once an area of bustling commercial activity, and a strategic bottleneck which the galleons from Portobello and the *flota* from Vera Cruz had to negotiate before they broke clear into open sea. The story of English ambitions and achievements in the West Indies is a familiar one but the attempts to approach Spain's American empire by way of its remote but vulnerable Pacific seaboard have received less attention. Until the mid-eighteenth century it was this motive, rather than any disinterested zeal for exploration, which sent English ships into the South Seas.

After the Pacific exploits of Drake, Cavendish and Richard Hawkins in the late sixteenth century, the western coasts of Spanish America were left undisturbed by English seamen until Charles II's reign, when an expedition of very different stamp left the Thames for the South Seas. It was commanded by a naval officer, John Narborough, who sailed in September 1669 in the *Sweepstakes*, accompanied by a hired merchant vessel. He carried with him trade goods worth £300, and orders from the Duke of York (at this time Lord High Admiral) which revealed that 'the Design of this Voyage on which you are employed, being to make a Discovery both of the Seas and Coasts of that part of the World, and if possible to lay the foundations of a Trade there'.[4] On board was a Spanish pilot, but once Narborough passed the River Plate and headed south towards the famed Strait of Magellan his guide's pretensions evaporated: 'He told me I might do what I would', complained Narborough, 'for he did not understand the coast, nor where 'twas inhabited.'[5] To add to Narborough's troubles, his consort disappeared, and turned back for home. Narborough sailed on, taking possession of one or two harbours on the way south, and hopefully inspected the shoreline for signs of gold or silver. He negotiated and charted with considerable skill the tortuous windings of the Strait of Magellan, and in September 1670 reached his destination, the small Spanish garrison town of Valdivia in Chile. Here

---

[3]See Jean O. McLachlan, *Trade and Peace with Old Spain 1667–1750* (Cambridge, 1940), ch. 1.
[4]*An Account of several late Voyages & Discoveries to the South and North, Towards the Streights of Magellan, the South Seas ... By Sir John Narborough, Captain Jasmen Tasman, Captain John Wood ...* (London, 1694), p. 10.
[5]*Ibid.*, p. 19.

relations with the Spaniards seemed friendly enough for the first day or so. Narborough's officers learned that the Spaniards knew little of the country to the south, and that they were at war with the local Indians, who were reputed to possess immense amounts of gold. They observed for themselves that their Spanish hosts used nothing but utensils of silver, even down to cooking pots and pans. Narborough also noted that since Valdivia lay at the far end of a long and complex trade route from Spain via the Isthmus and the ports of South America, European manufactures were both scarce and expensive.

On the third day after his arrival Narborough sent eighteen of his sharpest men ashore to inspect 'the manner of the Harbour, and the Fortifications the Spaniards have, and the disposition of the People; and that it was my whole desire to have Conference with the Natives of the Country that are at Wars with the Spaniards, if by any means possible it may be obtained; for it is my whole desire to lay the Foundation of a Trade there for the English Nation for the future'.[6] The foolhardiness of this mission was exposed when the Spaniards promptly seized four of Narborough's men, including a lieutenant. After failing to negotiate their release Narborough could do nothing but return home. He would have been surprised, perhaps gratified, if he had realised the turmoil which his brief visit had caused. As reports of the expedition made their way north to Lima they were inflated by a process of Falstaffian exaggeration until his solitary vessel was transformed into a fleet of twelve men-of-war which had seized all the shipping in Valdivia harbour and was thought to be on its way to attack Panama — a prospect which caused the Viceroy of Peru to halt the regular silver shipments to Panama.[7] In reality, Narborough was quietly retracing his course through the Strait of Magellan (he was the first seaman to navigate the Strait both ways), and reached England in June 1671.

His ill-conceived venture had failed miserably. It was a casual attempt to combine a trading enterprise with a reconnaissance mission, and its motives were so transparent that Narborough was fortunate to withdraw his head from the Spanish noose with the loss of only four men. At home his voyage caused little stir, and indeed was probably a source of embarrassment to the government since during his absence England and Spain had negotiated the Treaty of Madrid (1670), whose only concession to the shipping of either nation was that it allowed help to be given in American waters to vessels in genuine distress.[8] Narborough's detailed map of the Strait of Magellan was published in 1673 and remained the standard

[6]*Ibid.*, pp. 96–7.
[7]These Spanish reports, dated January 1671, are now in BM, Add. MS 21,539, fos. 1–13.
[8]F.G. Davenport ed., *European Treaties bearing on the History of the United States and its Dependencies*, II (Washington, 1929), p. 195.

authority for decades to come, but his journal was not published until more than twenty years later. In it Narborough reported that the amount of gold in Chile, the proximity of the great silver mine at Potosí, and the feebleness of Spanish control over the region, meant that 'the most advantageous Trade in the World might be established in those parts'.[9] But he also had to confess that his own experience had revealed that this was practical only if the Spanish government was willing to admit foreign traders — an unlikely proposition — or if the English were prepared to use force to open a trade. In these sentences Narborough expressed the dilemma which was to afflict attempts to trade with Spanish America for the next hundred years and more.

After Narborough's unsuccessful venture, little more was heard about the South Seas in official circles, but interest in England was attracted by the wanderings and adventures on the Pacific coast of those disreputable marauders, the buccaneers. Although their usual sphere of operations was the Caribbean, Morgan's assault on Panama in 1671 was followed by forays across the Isthmus, or round Cape Horn, and on to the thinly defended coasts of Chile, Peru and Mexico. Neither exploration nor trade featured high on their list of priorities — 'Gold was the bait that tempted a Pack of Merry Boys of us', one of them wrote,[10] but the activities of the buccaneers proved of unending interest to the reading public at home. Lawless, argumentative, mutinous, they pillaged and burnt their way along the Pacific coasts from Acapulco to Valparaiso. Some held commissions of one sort or another to give a touch of legality to their work; most sailed under the authority set out in a truculent note from Captain Sawkins to the President of Panama when he warned him that he and his crew would 'bring our Commissions on the muzzles of our Guns, at which time he should read them as plain as the flame of Gunpowder could make them'.[11] Amid the havoc created by the buccaneers, the occasional expeditions sent from England in the hope of opening a legitimate trade with the ports of Peru or Chile had faint chance of success. Captain Charles Swan in the *Cygnet* carried £5000-worth of trade goods on board, but after being repulsed from Valdivia in 1684 decided he had no alternative but to sell his wares cheap to the nearest buccaneers and join their number.[12] John Strong, commanding the *Welfare* on a voyage in 1689–90, received the same brusque welcome at Valdivia as Narborough and Swan; and instead of the 1600 per cent profit which the promoters anticipated they

---

[9]*An Account of several late Voyages & Discoveries*, p. 110.
[10]Philip Ayres, *The Voyages and Adventures of Captain Bartholomew Sharp* ... (London, 1684), preface.
[11]A.O. Exquemelin [J. Esquemeling], *Bucaniers of America*. . . (London, 1684), p. 38.
[12]See William Dampier, *A New Voyage round the World* (with an introduction by Sir Albert Gray, 1937), pp. 100, 136–7.

were faced with a £12,000 loss.[13] Whatever indication individual Spanish merchants and even local officials might give of their willingness to trade, the governmental policy of total prohibition of the foreigner remained intact.

Given the conditions under which the buccaneers operated, it is remarkable how many of them managed to keep journals. Among their ranks were men with the instincts, if not the training, of scholars and scientists: Basil Ringrose, who had enough classical learning to negotiate with the Spaniards in Latin, and whose book 'Containing the dangerous Voyage, and bold Assaults of Captain Bartholemew Sharp, and others, performed in the South Sea' formed the supplement to the English edition in 1684 of Esquemeling's *Bucaniers of America*; the surgeon Lionel Wafer, whose notes on the Indians of southeast Panama have remained of interest to anthropologists in the present century;[14] and William Dampier, a man of immeasurable zest and curiosity who waded through the rivers of Darien with his journal secured in a length of bamboo cane, and whose books were to become classics of travel and adventure. If Dampier was frank enough in his admission of the buccaneers' objectives — 'our business was to pillage' — he also stressed the amount of information they amassed, though some of the more erudite of the queries he listed probably reflected his own interest in Spanish American society rather than that of the general run of his buccaneer companions:

For they make it their Business to examine all Prisoners that fall into their Hands, concerning the Country, Town, or City that they belong to; whether born there, or how long they have known it? how many Families, whether most Spaniards? or whether the major part are not Copper-colour'd, as Mulattoes, Mustesoes, or Indians? whether rich, and what their Riches do consist in? and what their chiefest Manufactures? if fortified, how many great guns, and what Number of small Arms, whether it is possible to come undescrib'd on them? How many Look-outs or Centinels; for such the Spaniards always keep? and how the Look-outs are placed — whether possible to avoid the Look-outs, or take them? If any River or Creek comes near it, or the best Landing; with innumerable other such Questions, which their Curiosities led them to demand.[15]

Other information brought back to England came from captured Spanish documents and maps. On his expedition of 1680–81 Bartholomew Sharp acquired a rare haul of Spanish coasting instructions and charts; and when turned over in London to William Hack these were copied,

---

[13]See Richard Simson's journal of the voyage in BM, Sloane MS 87, pp. 4, 113; copies of Strong's less interesting journal are in Harleian MS 5101 and Sloane MS 3295.

[14]See L.E. Elliott Joyce, ed., *A New Voyage and Description of the Isthmus of America by Lionel Wafer* (Oxford, The Hakluyt Society, 1934).

[15]Dampier, *New Voyage* (1937 edn), p. 28.

translated and presented as a 'Wagoner of the Great South Sea' to Charles II in 1682.[16] Its maps and views were set out in beguiling colours, but were ludicrously imprecise, lacking latitudes, scales and other information considered normal even by the standards of late seventeenth-century navigation. So although it is interesting to see Juan Fernandez recommended at this early date as a port of call for privateers or traders — 'This Isle is nearest continent. . . afforded us great relief it is destitute of Inhabitance but here was found aboundance of fish and goates likewise good water and wood'[17] — only freakish good luck would enable a seaman to find the island from Sharp's information.

Many of the buccaneers' journals were acquired by Sir Hans Sloane, secretary to the Royal Society, who had visited the Caribbean as a young man in 1687–88, and they still repose among his papers in the British Museum.[18] Those which were published whetted public and mercantile interest in the South Seas. After more than twenty years delay Narborough's journal was printed in 1694. Dampier's first and best book, *A New Voyage round the World*, was published by James Knapton in 1697, and was in its fourth edition by 1699. In the same year Knapton published Wafer's *New Voyage and Description of the Isthmus of America*, and William Hack's *Collection of Original Voyages*, which included the journal of Narborough's mate John Wood, and descriptions of Sharp's Darien adventures of 1680–81 and Cowley's voyage round the world in 1683–86. This spate of books on the South Seas marked the beginning of the vogue for 'voyages and travels' which was to reach such enthusiastic proportions in the eighteenth century.[19] It also came at a critical moment, for as the long-impending crisis of the Spanish Succession broke over Europe the future of Spain's American empire became of acute concern to statesmen and merchants alike. To meet the growing interest in England in the potentialities of the South Seas trade only the buccaneers' accounts could provide firsthand information. Despite Dampier's insistence on the accurate information gained by him and his companions, most of the journals were careless and repetitive compilations, but in them their readers found what they wanted to hear. The Spaniards in the South Seas were poor seamen and indolent traders, their ships and settlements were vulnerable, they were eager to engage in illicit trade, they lived in fear of Indian insurrection. General opinion on Spanish officialdom was summed up by Dampier when he wrote: 'The Spaniards have more than they can well

[16]Now in BM, K. Mar VIII, 15. For an assessment of Hack's work see E. Lynam, *The Mapmaker's Art* (London, 1953), pp. 101–16.
[17]BM, K. Mar VIII, 15, p. 264.
[18]See especially BM, Sloane MSS 44–49, 54, 87, 239, 819, 1050, 2752, 3236, 3295, 3820, 3833.
[19]See G.R. Crone and R.A. Skelton, 'English collections of voyages and travels, 1625–1846', in E. Lynam, ed., *Richard Hakluyt and his Successors* (London, The Hakluyt Society, 1946), pp. 63–140.

manage. I know yet, they would lie like the Dog in the Manger; although not able to eat themselves, yet they would endeavour to hinder others.'[20]

Interest in the South Seas was further excited by William Paterson's attempt to colonise Darien, and supporters in England for a similar project were not deterred by the disaster which overtook the unfortunate Scots. The second edition of Wafer's book in 1704 found him still advocating a settlement on the Isthmus, a project he had already expounded at length in a memorandum of 1698 or 1699 to the Duke of Leeds (formerly the Earl of Danby) and Charles Montagu, later Lord Halifax.[21] More original were his proposals for trade and settlement in the South Seas proper. He provided the two statesmen with thumbnail sketches of the most important ports on the Pacific coast, and went on to suggest that if Spain persisted in keeping these harbours closed to foreign traders, then the English should establish settlements by force of arms, preferably in Chile. If the English occupied either Valdivia, or Coquimbo farther north, they would hold a position with clear strategic and commercial advantages. Both ports were conveniently placed for English vessels rounding the Horn; the local Indians were bitterly hostile to the Spaniards; and, to cap it all, 'there Country abounds with all Sorts of Riches as Gold Silver &c.'[22]

Wafer was not the only advocate of this scheme. As international tension increased that prolific pamphleteer and controversialist, Daniel Defoe, produced in 1701 his *Reasons against a War* with France, which argued in favour of a lucrative maritime war rather than a profitless continental struggle, and stressed the wealth and vulnerability of Spain's American colonies. It was at about this time that Defoe sent William III, to whom he acted as unofficial adviser in the last years of his reign, a plan resembling Wafer's, but which proposed in addition to a settlement in Chile a supporting one on the Atlantic coast between the River Plate and the Strait of Magellan. As a young merchant Defoe had gained firsthand experience of trading conditions in Spain,[23] and he was well aware of the profits which an open trade with Spanish America would bring, free from the various duties and impositions levied on existing trade. Defoe always maintained that the king approved his scheme, and that only his death in March 1702 prevented it being put into operation,[24] but the documentary

[20]Dampier, *New Voyage* (1937 edn), pp. 189–90.
[21]BM, Add. MS 28,079, fos 39–50; printed in Joyce, *A New Voyage . . . by Lionel Wafer*, pp. 133–51.
[22]*Ibid.*, p 145.
[23]See J.R. Moore, *Daniel Defoe: Citizen of the Modern World* (Chicago, 1958), pp. 85–8.
[24]See Defoe to Robert Harley, 23 July 1711, printed in G.H. Healey, ed., *The Letters of Daniel Defoe* (Oxford, 1955), pp. 345–6; D. Defoe, *The Essay on the South-Sea Trade . . .* (London, 1712 [1711]), p. 46.

evidence for William's general intentions during this critical period provides no support for this contention.[25]

When war came in May 1702 it proved to be more continental than maritime; and others besides Defoe regretted that military operations in the Low Countries and Spain replaced their vision of operations against Spain's overseas empire.[26] During the long war it was the French who took advantage of Spain's damaging internal weaknesses to exploit her overseas wealth, and nowhere was this more evident than in the South Seas. Although Louis XIV and Philip V of Spain were allies, there was no formal relaxation of Spain's prohibition of foreign traders within her American empire, but in practice enterprising French traders found it a simple and profitable matter to sail for Chile and Peru. The weakness of the Spanish navy was such that it was unable even to protect home waters; to patrol the South American littoral lay well beyond its capabilities. In 1707 only three Spanish naval vessels were available to guard the entire Pacific coastline from Chile to California.[27] From St Malo, Toulon and other French ports increasing numbers of ships left for the South Seas, often with the connivance of the French authorities. Between 1695 and 1705 twenty-two French ships had sailed for the Pacific (though by no means all had reached there); in the three years 1705, 1706 and 1707 no fewer than thirty-seven vessels left France for the South Seas.[28] By opening a regular trade route round the Horn or through the Strait of Magellan the French proved that the voyage was not as fearsome as earlier mariners had reported. At Callao, Concepción and Valparaiso they exchanged manufactured goods for silver or oriental luxuries shipped into Acapulco in the annual galleon from Manila. At first they found an eager market, for during the war the whole elaborate structure of convoys, trade fairs and the rest had collapsed in ruin. Some expeditions continued their voyage to China and the East Indies,[28] a later development which was helped by the

[25]See A.F. Pribram, *Osterreichische Staatsvertänge : England*, I (1907), 218; Paul Grimblot, *Letters of William III and Louis XIV 1697–1700* (London, 1848), I, 301, 326, 344, 360, 362, 395, 414, 426, 462; II, 10. I am grateful to Mr. G.C. Gibbs of Birkbeck College, London, for help on this and other points.

[26]See Geoffrey Holmes, 'Post-Revolution Britain and the historian' in *Britain after the Glorious Revolution 1689–1714* (London, 1969), pp. 20–1; the most notable contemporary statement of this view was of course Swift's pamphlet of November 1711, *The Conduct of the Allies*.

[27]See Woodes Rogers, *A Cruising Voyage Round the World* (London, 1712), p. xiii; Henry Kamen, *The War of Succession in Spain 1700–15* (London, 1969), p. 141. The standard work on this subject remains E.W. Dahlgren, *Les Relations commerciales et maritimes entre la France et les ctoes de l'Ocean Pacifique au commencement du XVIIIe siecle* (Paris, 1909), vol. I; there is a useful summary in John Dunmore *French Explorers in the Pacific*, vol I *The Eighteenth Century* (Oxford 1965), pp., 10–31.

[28]See Louis Dermigny, *La Chine et L'Occident : Le Commerce à Canton au XVIIIe siècle 1719–1833* (Paris, 1964), pp. 152–4

dismaying discovery that the Spanish American market was a more limited one, and easier to glut, than had been thought. Despite repeated protests from the Spanish government, no firm action was taken by the French government against these illegal traders until near the end of the war, and their activities were not completely halted until the 1720s.[29]

After some delay reports of French enterprise and profits in the South Seas filtered back to England, where they were greeted with incredulity and indignation. When Dampier returned from an unsuccessful privateering voyage in 1707 his men told of French trading vessels along the Pacific coasts, one of which Dampier had twice tried to capture.[30] Another privateering venture was put on foot, under the command this time of the capable Woodes Rogers, with Dampier sailing in the less arduous capacity of 'pilot to the South Seas'. Rogers had read French accounts of the profits being made in the Pacific, though his own guesses at the sums involved were wildly exaggerated.[31] Further evidence came from captured letters from Spanish merchants at Lima, dated 1708, 'which clearly prove', a memorandum among the papers of Vice-Admiral Sir John Norris noted, 'that the French by carrying a Trade into the So. Sea and selling their goods at easier Rates to the Spaniards at Peru at their own doors than the South Galleonists can afford them at, have quite alter'd the Channel of that Trade'.[32] Another indication of the scale of the French trade came from the complaints of the Governor of Jamaica in 1710 and 1711 that his colony's illicit commerce with the Spaniards had almost vanished because of the competition from cheap French goods finding their way inland from the Pacific ports.[33]

Chagrin at French dominance in the South Seas helps to account for the enthusiasm which greeted the announcement by the Harley government in 1711 of the proposed formation of an English 'South Sea Company', but within the government the most impelling reasons for this decision

---

[29]The French government's ambivalent attitude was shown by the voyage to Chile and Peru in 1712–14 of Frézier, a capable engineer and mathematician, who (if the English editor of his account is to be trusted) was ordered by Louis XIV 'to chart the coast while the French could still enter the Pacific, and before the expected ban on such voyages became operative. Thus, if war should break out between France and Spain, the French would have a sound knowledge of the coast for possible military operations against the poorly defended Spanish Pacific . . .' A.F. Frézier, *A Voyage to the South-Sea, and along the coasts of Chili and Peru in the years 1712, 1713, and 1714* (London, 1717), preface.

[30]Dampier did not publish an account of this expedition, being forestalled by his mate William Funnell, who produced a rather dull book, *A Voyage round the World, containing an Account of Capt. Dampier's Expedition into the South-Seas in the Ship St. George, in the Years 1703 and 1704* (London, 1707).

[31]See Rogers, *A Cruising Voyage*, pp. ix–x.

[32]BM, Add. MS 28,140, fo. 27d.

[33]Cecil Headlam, ed., *Calendar of State Papers, Colonial Series, America and West Indies 1710–1711* (London, 1924), pp. 109, 111, 428.

were to be found in the political and financial situation.[34] By August 1710 the Whig-dominated ministry of Godolphin had given way to a Tory administration in which Robert Harley, Chancellor of the Exchequer, and Henry St John, Secretary of State, were determined to end the war on the continent in a way which would strengthen their new political power. First, an imminent financial crisis had to be surmounted. A credit collapse in England and on the continent had made more acute the growing problem of the floating debt, which now stood at the alarming figure of more than £9 million. By the late autumn Harley was considering the erection of a joint stock company as a way of funding this massive debt, and was also in touch with William Paterson (the originator of the ill-fated Darien scheme of the previous reign) about 'the Indies'.[35] In March 1711 Harley was wounded in an assassination attempt, and it was during his two-month convalescence that he seems to have reached a firm decision to link the proposed new company with the development of trade to Spanish America. Hopes of securing concessions within the Spanish territories had risen when in April the French foreign minister, the Marquis de Torcy, had signed six secret articles outlining the general shape of a peace settlement which included 'seuretez réelles' for British trade in Spain, the Mediterranean and the Indies.[36] This would gratify in particular St John, the only one of Harley's ministerial colleagues who had made any serious attempt to direct England's waning war effort overseas. One of his plans early in 1711 for an American expedition was dropped because of Harley's opposition, and the Quebec expedition which the Secretary of State set in motion during the spring would no doubt have met a similar fate if Harley had not been removed from the scene by his injury.[37] On the South Seas project the two men were more likely to be in agreement. The xenophobic St John expressed his feelings on the direction of the war when he complained to the British ambassador at the Hague, Lord Raby, of those continental allies who

> have always looked first at home, and the common cause has been served by the best of them in the second place. From hence it is that our commerce has been neglected, while the French have engrossed the South-Sea trade to themselves, and the Dutch encroach daily upon us, both in the East-Indies, and on the coast of Africa.[38]

[34]The best short account of the origins of the South Sea Company is J.G. Sperling, *The South Sea Company: An Historical Essay and Bibliographical Finding List* (Boston, Mass., 1962), pp. 1–14.

[35]*Manuscripts of the Duke of Portland*, IV (London, Historical Manuscripts Commission, 1897), *Harley Letters and Papers*, II, 583–4.

[36]See Davenport, *Treaties*, III, 141. A good recent summary of the peace negotiations from the British side is A.D. MacLachlan, 'The Road to Peace 1710–13', in Geoffrey Holmes, ed., *Britain after the Glorious Revolution 1689–1714* (London, 1969), pp. 197–215.

[37]See G.S. Graham, ed., *The Walker Expedition to Quebec, 1711* (London, Navy Records Society, XCIV, 1953), pp. 9–21.

[38]G. Parke, ed., *Letters and Correspondence of . . . Viscount Bolingbroke* (London, 1798), I, 193.

On 2 May (os) Harley presented his scheme to the House of Commons, and the next day a pamphlet appeared with impeccable timing which described the riches of South America, set out in urgent terms the extent of French activity there and argued the case for British intervention. In conclusion the helpful author appended a long list of goods 'proper for a Trade to the South-Sea', ranging from Devonshire serges to Cheshire cheese.[39] In the Commons a Bill was introduced on 17 May, under which the government's unsecured creditors were to be incorporated as 'the Governor and Company of Merchants of Great Britain Trading to the South Seas and other parts of America and for running the Fishery'; and on 12 June 1711 it received the royal assent. The scheme was, one commentator wrote later with keen hindsight, 'a gross, palpable illusion; Nevertheless, the same being gilded over by the glittering Prospect of having a Share in the Trade of the South-Seas (by which the French got immense Riches) Mr Harley's Scheme was received with general Applause.'[40] At the time, it had all the appearance of a master-stroke by Harley, who before the end of May had become Earl of Oxford, and lord treasurer. He had disposed of the immediate problem of the floating debt; had set up a company with a directorate he could pack with those Tory merchants, financiers and politicians who were excluded from the Whig-dominated Bank of England and East India Company; and was sure of support from the Tory country gentry and the mercantile community for his move away from the endless continental campaigns towards the more alluring prospect of war or trade, or both, in Spanish America.

Under the terms of the Act the Company's privileges were gargantuan enough to satisfy even St John's appetite for overseas enterprise. The Company was granted:

> the sole trade and traffick into, unto, and from all the kingdoms, lands, countries, territories, islands, cities, towns, ports, havens, creeks, and places of America, on the east side thereof from the river of Aranoca, to the southermost part of the Terra del Fuego; and on the west side thereof, from the said southermost part of the said Terra del Fuego, through the South Seas, to the northermost part of America, and into, unto, and from all countries, islands, and places within the same limits, which are reported to belong to the Crown of Spain, or which shall hereafter be found out or discovered within the said limits, not exceeding three hundred leagues from the continent of America.[41]

How these paper concessions were to be transformed into commercial reality was left unsaid; and it was doubtful if enlightenment would come

---

[39] *A Letter to a Member of Parliament on the resolution of the House to settle a trade to the South Seas* (London, 1711), pp. 12–14.
[40] Abel Boyer, *The History of the Life and Reign of Queen Anne* (London, 1722), p. 495.
[41] 9 Anne, cap. XXI.

either from the Company's (honorific) first governor, Harley, or its thirty-three directors, none of whom had any experience of trade with Spanish America. A hostile versifier lampooned them thus in his *South Sea Whim*:

> We are a wretched motley crew,
> More various than the weather,
> Made up of debtors old and new,
> Tumbled and rocked together;
> Tars, soldiers, merchants, transport, tallies,
> Chained in a row like slaves in galleys.[42]

Such comment could be put down to the resentment of the government's Whig opponents, and certainly most of the public discussion in the summer and autumn of 1711 exuded a lighthearted optimism about the potentialities of the new company. Among Harley's papers are a number of memoranda sent to him on the South Seas question at this time, some at least in response to his request for information and advice.[43] In June Thomas Pindar advocated both an overland trade with Chile and Peru from the Atlantic coast, and a coastal trade enforced by a powerful expedition sent from England into the South Seas. Another memorialist told Harley that he could see no reason why a dozen well-armed ships should not glean as much profit along the Pacific coasts as the French had done, particularly if they could be supplied across the Isthmus. In July Sir George Byng, future victor of Cape Passaro and at this time a lord commissioner of the Admiralty, sent in a list of practical points designed to ensure the success of any expedition sent to secure a base in the South Seas. In September Thomas Bowrey, a London merchant with many years experience in the Eastern Seas, and an indefatigable projector, made precise proposals about the ports he thought should be taken in Spanish America.[44] If a seaborne trade by way of the Strait of Magellan or Cape Horn was seriously contemplated, then a harbour on the Atlantic seaboard was essential, and his preference was for Anegada Bay in latitude 39 S, described by Drake 130 years before. On the Pacific side of the continent Valdivia was Bowrey's choice. It lay only five hundred miles overland from Anegada Bay; the Spanish population of the area was scattered, and hemmed in by hostile Indians; the country was productive, with a temperate climate (and therefore offered good prospects for the sale of English woollens); and the hinterland was rich in gold.

A refreshing note of scepticism is to be found in an unsigned memoir of the same period among Harley's papers. It began with conventional

[42]Quoted in John Carswell, *The South Sea Bubble* (London, 1960), p. 58.
[43]These memoranda are in BM, Portland Loan 29/288; the volume has no page or folio numbers.
[44]Copies of Bowrey's proposals are in BM, Add. MS 28,140, fos 31–33d, and among the Bowrey Papers at Guildhall Library, London: MS 3041/2.

proposals for seizing bases here, there and everywhere, but then went on to take a critical look at the hopeful projects being aired in the months following the formation of the new company. The writer pointed to the earlier unsuccessful attempts to establish trading contacts with South America, and was full of foreboding about the fate of vessels which after an arduous voyage would reach the South Seas to find closed ports and a hostile population. Whether he considered the Atlantic or the Pacific seaboards, navigational hazards or trading difficulties, the writer could see little reason for optimism. The southern extremities of the continent formed 'an Iron Coast' with few harbours, and even if English vessels did manage to secure a base farther north along the Chilean or Peruvian coasts they would find the market completely satiated with French goods.[45]

In an attempt to remedy the lack of accurate information about the vast region which lay within the Company's charter rights, the geographer Herman Moll produced in 1711 two editions of a careful work, *A View of the Coasts, Countrys, & Islands within the Limits of the South-Sea Company*. In this Moll made intelligent use of the printed journals of Narborough, Cowley, Sharp, Dampier and others to produce an orderly survey which he hoped would be of value to navigators and merchants alike. Its limitations were those of its sources, and in Moll's work the deficiencies of the buccaneers' accounts were plain to see. It would have been a rash sailing-master who took his vessel into the Bay of Quiaquil in darkness with Moll's book as his only guide: 'If you fall in there in the Night, keep your head going, and mind your depth, till you either can get out, or with Conveniency come to an Anchor.'[46]

In the public prints of the day the fullest and most perceptive discussion appeared in the pages of Defoe's *Review*.[47] He did not welcome the scheme with the eagerness that might have been expected from his long-standing interest in the South Seas; indeed he did not mention it until the issue of 28 June 1711, eight weeks after Harley's introduction of the subject in the House of Commons. Defoe's position was an awkward one. He was trying to re-establish close relations with Harley, but he was also concerned about several features of the new company, and alarmed by the adulatory public reaction to it. As a result he had to pick his way between 'your wild Expectations on the one Hand, or your Phlegmatick Discouraging

[45]BM, Portland Loan 29/288.
[46][Herman Moll], *A View of the Coasts, Countrys, & Islands within the Limits of the South-Sea Company* (2nd edn, London, 1711), p. 113.
[47]The relevant issues in the summer of 1711 of Defoe's thrice-weekly *Review of the State of the British Nation* are: no. 41, 28 June; no. 42, 30 June; no. 43, 3 July; no. 44, 5 July; no. 45, 7 July; no. 47, 12 July; no. 49, 17 July; no. 50, 19 July; no. 53, 26 July; no. 54, 28 July; no. 58, 7 August; no. 68, 30 August.

Notions on the other'.[48] When he turned over four consecutive numbers of the *Review* in late June and early July to the subject he at first kept on safe ground by limiting himself to a factual account of the trade of Spanish America. This forms as good a summary of the state of informed knowledge of the area as can be found in any English publication of the period, except for those passages where Defoe's fear of French activities in the South Seas led him into the realms of fantasy. The French, he wrote, had taken possession of Lima, were fortifying bases all along the coast, and had been promised any unoccupied territories they wanted south of Potosí. At the time of writing fifty French ships were on the Pacific coast, and would each bring home up to £200,000 in silver, thereby allowing Louis XIV to continue the war indefinitely.[49] To Defoe the French presence in South America made nonsense of much of the talk in England about the potentialities of the area. The French were so firmly entrenched that as long as the war lasted no English trade on any scale was possible. He continued:

> What are we to understand by the Trade to the South-Seas? — I say frankly, If we mean that we shall take Possession of some Port or Place, Ports or Places, on the West side of America, which being to be allow'd as our, by the Treaty of Grand Alliance, we shall possess after the Peace is made, and that from this, or these Places, we shall carry on a free Trade with the Spaniards of America, throughout the rest of their Plantations, that is, with Peru, Mexico &c. as the French do now: If, I say, this is understood by the South-Sea Trade, then I must say, I doubt the Success of it, and that we can never carry on such a Trade, make 40 Acts of Parliament, Erect 40 Companies, and take possession of 40 Ports in the South-Seas.[50]

While the war continued French influence would stiffen Spanish resistance in America to English interlopers, and even when peace came Defoe could not envisage any reversal by Spain of her traditional policies of exclusion. 'New Spain is the Spouse of Old Spain, and they will no more prostrate her to be debauch'd in Trade by us, than they, the most Jealous People in the World, should allow us to come to Bed their Wives'.[51] He derided current speculation that convoys would soon be leaving England for South America, and within a matter of months would 'bring

---

[48]Of the former there was certainly no shortage. Among the lunatic fringe of pamphleteers pride of place must go to the writer who advocated the establishment of a settlement colony on the barren, galeswept coasts of Terra del Fuego – 'a fruitful and pleasant country'. *The Considerable Advantages of a South-Sea Trade to our English Nation* (London, *c.* 1711). Of pamplets critical of the South Sea project one of the most lucid was *A Letter from a Merchant in Amsterdam to a Friend in London about the South Sea Trade* (London, 1712).

[49]*Review of the State of the British Nation*, nos. 44 and 45, 5 and 7 July 1711.

[50]*Ibid.*, no. 47, 12 July 1711.

[51]*Ibid.*, no. 49, 17 July 1711.

Home Potosi, and the Gold of the Andes.' Rather, as he pointed out, any attempt by England to break into the trade of Chile, Peru and New Spain would meet stern countermeasures. All contact with the intruders would be prohibited, and retaliatory action would be taken not only against the English but against any Spaniards who had been tempted to trade with them. Under these conditions a profitable trade would be impossible.

Defoe did not state his own proposals until the *Review* of 17 July, and then they were guarded and vague. Instead of incursions into Spanish-held territories, he supported the establishment of a trade along the Pacific coast 'without Injuring, Encroaching on, or perhaps in the least Invading the Property or Commerce of the Spaniards', but the location of this region was nowhere mentioned. The reason for his secretiveness was revealed in a letter of the same date to Harley in which Defoe explained that 'I have put a Stop to what I was saying in Print Till I may kno' if my Thoughts are of any Consideration in your Ldpps Judgemt'.[52] In this, and two other letters to Harley in the next week, Defoe repeated his general sentiments as expressed in the *Review*, and gave more precise details of his own plan. This proved to be little more than a copy of the scheme he had put to William III a decade earlier — the settling of English colonies in Chile and on the Atlantic coast of southeast America, well away from the main centres of Spanish power. The Chilean colony would form the lynchpin of the new trade, with its temperate climate, friendly Indians, fertile land and gold mines. With the opportunities it offered for private trade it would play in the South Seas the role of Jamaica in the Caribbean — 'Tho' the Spaniards will Not Open Their Ports and Markets for us to Sell, we Shall allways have an Open Port and Market for Them to buy'.[53]

Harley's reaction to these proposals is not known, but it could not have been reassuring to Defoe, for in the late summer of 1711 he launched an open attack on the very essence of Harley's South Sea scheme. In later numbers of the *Review*, and in his *Essay on the South-Sea Trade*, published in September, he lamented lost opportunities: '. . . how this Golden Ball, now it is in our Hands, toss'd up and down among us, with Contempt, with Regret, with Reproach; Envy on one Hand, Stock-Jobbing on the other, and ill Management on both Hands; giving us no Heart to make a right Use of the Advantage now it is put into our Hands.'[54]

Defoe bitterly regretted that the whole South Sea project had become intertwined in the fierce domestic politics of the day, and that two quite separate issues had become fused: the problem of the floating debt, and the opening of Spanish America. The politicians' attempt 'to cure them both with One Plaister, or as we say more vulgarly, Kill both these Birds

[52]Defoe to Harley, 17 July 1711; printed in Healey, *Letters of Defoe*, p. 338.
[53]Defoe to Harley, 23 July 1711. *Ibid.*, pp. 347–8.
[54]*Review*, no. 68, 30 August 1711.

with 'One Stone' threatened disaster. At the same time, as Defoe explained to the public at large his plan for colonies in South America, he stressed the threat which hung over it as a result of the political and financial manipulations attending the birth of the South Sea Company. Although disillusioned with the government's approach Defoe retained his belief in the potentialities of the Pacific trade:

> This is so far from being little or inconsiderable, however it may be less than the Golden Mountains some People have form'd Notions of in their Imagination, that this Trade is not only probably to be Great, but capable of being the Greatest, most Valuable, most Profitable, and most Encreasing Branch of Trade in our whole British Commerce . . . a Trade, which had it been offered to the Merchandizing Part of Mankind, who understood Trade, who were employ'd in Commerce, and accustom'd to Adventures, and not unhappily join'd in and tied down to a Rabble of casual Subscribers, neither inclin'd to, capable of, or in the least having a Genius to trade, it would no doubt have met with another kind of Reception than now it has.[55]

Away from the litter of pamphlets and memoranda, the fate of the South Sea scheme depended on the crucial peace negotiations on which Harley had staked his political future. Diplomatic conversations during the summer of 1711 had soon revealed the difficulty of turning the vague pledges of April about 'seuretez réelles' for British commerce into specific concessions. In a confidential mission to France in July Matthew Prior informed the French foreign minister, the Marquis de Torcy, that as far as Spain's overseas empire was concerned Britain required four bases, two in the Caribbean and two on the Pacific coast of South America. Prior's arguments for this were ingenuous and unconvincing: the bases were necessary to protect the new British trade against pirates; the Spaniards themselves would benefit; and, finally, to quote Prior's notes, 'in a tract of land of above seven hundred leagues it was impossible that four places should annoy the Spaniards',[56] or (to turn to Torcy's summary) the King of Spain 'y auoit si grande estendüe de terre depuis la Californie jusqu'au detroit de Magellan que le Roy d'Espe pouuoit aisement et sans aucun risque donner aux Etrangers quelques etablissemens pour le bien de la paix'.[57] Torcy's response to this wheedling was forthright enough to make Prior blench: 'my heart ached extremely and I was ready to sink', he reported home. Added to British territorial

[55][Daniel Defoe], *An Essay on the South-Sea Trade* (London, 1712 [1711]), pp. 37–8.

[56]Prior's report home is contained in *Manuscripts of the Duke of Portland*, v (London, Historical Manuscripts Commission, 1899), *Harley Letters and Papers*, iii, 34–41.

[57]Torcy's memorandum to Louis XIV has been printed in L.G. Wickham Legge, 'Torcy's Account of Matthew Prior's negotiations at Fontainebleau in July 1711', *English Historical Review*, xxix (1914), 525–32.

claims in the Mediterranean and North America, these further demands in Spanish America were evidence of Britain's determination to gain world commercial dominance, Torcy insisted. 'It was a constant ruling of Spain', he reminded Prior, 'not to let in any other nation amongst them in America; so that he was assured, and told me plainly that this article was impossible to be granted.' The activities of French traders in Spanish America seem not to have been mentioned by either diplomat. Two days later Torcy expressed himself in even more direct language: 'Your maritime force is such as renders all the commerce of the two crowns, even the possession of Spain, precarious, but your demands in the Indies are such as the crown of Spain, by all the laws, maxims, and interests of the kingdom, can never consent to.'

Faced with this obdurate refusal to negotiate on the matter of Spanish American bases, the Harley government had by September dropped its demand; and in October it accepted instead a 15 per cent reduction in duties on English goods entering Spain, and the transfer of the slave *asiento* from France to England for a period of thirty years.[58] It was a far cry from this limited concession to the original ambitious hopes of dominating a vast market from Chile to Mexico which had accompanied the formation of the South Sea Company only a few moи.ths earlier. Ironically, at this moment interest in London in the South Seas was quickened by the return from the Pacific of Woodes Rogers, bringing with him up the Thames a spectacular prize, an Acapulco treasure 'galleon' (in fact a frigate-built vessel). The voyage had been a triumph for method and organisation. With Dampier released from the burdens of command, and able to act as pilot and adviser, Rogers had conducted a successful privateering enterprise which brought a financial return of £150,000. Rogers and one of the subordinate commanders, Edward Cooke, spent the winter writing rival accounts of the venture which were published in 1712. Both stressed the potentialities of Chile, Rogers in a long introduction which bore the imprint of Defoe's style and opinions. Like Defoe, Rogers gave a highly coloured account of French activities in the South Seas, claiming that a 'modest computation' from the reports of Spanish merchants they had questioned would put French profits in the early years of the trade at £25 million. He regretted that the English had not forestalled the French in the region at the beginning of the war, and continued: 'I am sorry to hear so noble a Design talk'd of with so much indifference by some, and exploded as impracticable by others.'[59] As to future activity in the area, Rogers was convinced that no regular trade was possible without a settlement. This should be on the Chilean coast, and here both he and Cooke simply repeated the arguments of Defoe, Bowrey and others; the

[58]See Davenport, *Treaties*, III, 147–51.
[59]Rogers, *A Cruising Voyage*, p. x.

climate was healthy, the Spaniards were few and intimidated by hostile Indians, there were mines of silver and gold in the interior.

During the winter of 1711–12 Rogers and Cooke were called into consultation by the South Sea Company. Cooke sent in a list of locations of the best harbours on the Pacific coast, and advised that a trading factory might be set up at either Valdivia or Juan Fernandez.[60] Rogers for his part met the sub-governor of the Company, James Bateman, and notes of their conversation have survived.[61] Rogers gave a good deal of practical advice about the dispatch of an expedition, and the possibility was put to him that he might be taken into the Company's service. In consulting Rogers and Cooke the Company seems to have been prompted by more than idle curiosity; and one of the most baffling aspects of the whole convoluted history of the Company is the evidence that throughout 1712 it was preparing to send an expedition of force to the Pacific coast of South America — though the diplomatic manoeuvring of Harley and St John the previous autumn would seem to have put an end to hopes of securing bases, or even trade, in the region.

The evidence is contained in the minutes of the Court of Directors, which show that at the end of January 1712 the Board wrote to Harley outlining an expedition which it hoped might be sent to South America.[62] It was of prodigious size: one 80-gun ship; four of 70; five of 60; five of 50; two of 40; three of less than 40; forty transports; bomb vessels; hospital ships; and four thousand soldiers. What exactly this sledgehammer of an expedition was intended to do was not made clear, though the directors hoped that the ships would be ready to sail by June. In March St John wrote pledging government support for 'their making a Settlement in the South Seas for their security and better carrying on the Trade to those Parts', but his letter was studiously vague about the size of the force and the date of its dispatch.[63] Further minutes show the directors busy hiring vessels and collecting cargo, but by May they were betraying signs of anxiety about the government's silence on the subject.[64] Letters to the queen and Harley about the lateness of the season, and the fact that the Company had laid out £120,000 in trading goods, evidently brought no response; and the only other mention of the venture comes in a reproachful note of February 1713 which informed Harley that the cargoes bought the previous year would soon decay unless they were sold.[65]

It is difficult to see rhyme or reason behind this exercise. Time and money had been spent in organising an expedition which was never likely

---

[60]BM, Add. MS 28,140, fos 29–30.
[61]*Ibid.*, fos 30–30d.
[62]BM, Add. MS 25,559, fos 8d. –9.
[63]BM, Add. MS 25,494, fo. 66.
[64]*Ibid.*, fos 69d., 75, 87, 93, 94; BM, Add MS 25,559, fos 8, 10–11.
[65]*Ibid.*, fo. 14.

to sail after the diplomatic agreements of the previous autumn. Why Harley and St John allowed the farce to continue, and why the directors devoted energy to playing it out, is a mystery. It may have been connected with the jockeying for position within the government of the two politicians; or possibly the paper expedition was intended as a reminder to France and Spain of the consequences of a breakdown in the negotiations for a definitive treaty which began at Utrecht in January 1712. Whatever the reason, the projected expedition was the first and last attempt by the South Sea Company to take advantage of its Pacific privileges outlined in the 1711 Act; and as mention of it disappears in the Company records it is replaced by more realistic discussion on the exploitation of the *asiento* concession.

After 1713 circumstances combined to discourage any revival of practical English interest in the South Seas. In Bourbon Spain, British merchants found it difficult to regain their prewar position,[66] and the problems of trading with remote American regions in the face of official Spanish opposition now appeared greater than ever. During the brief bouts of Anglo-Spanish hostilities in 1718 and 1727, Defoe and a few other writers resurrected plans for conquest or settlement in South America,[67] and in 1727 Admiral Sir Charles Wager (soon to become First Lord of the Admiralty) tried without success to persuade Walpole to send a naval force round Cape Horn and into the South Seas.[68] These efforts lacked conviction; even the irrepressible Defoe seems to have given up hopes of government support, and instead wrote of the importance to overseas enterprise of 'the little Adventures of single Men, and the small Undertakings of a few'.[69] Such an undertaking was the privateering cruise of George Shelvocke and John Clipperton in 1719–22, but this attempt to emulate Woodes Rogers's achievement was a failure. The expedition reached the South Seas, only to lose one of its vessels at Juan Fernandez, and it came back with more casualties than prize money.[70] Moreover, it returned to an England where for years to come mention of the South Seas raised a spectre — that of the South Sea Bubble of 1720. The financial manipulations and chicanery which led to the crisis had little to do with the overseas trade, actual or potential, of the South Sea Company, but when the catastrophe came it had a chastening effect on promoters and investors alike. Although under Walpole's patient guidance financial and mercantile confidence was slowly restored, to raise money for distant ventures became

---

[66]See McLachlan, *Trade and Peace with Old Spain*, pp. 53–9.
[67]See e.g. [Daniel Defoe], *Reasons for a War* . . . (London, 1729).
[68]See William Coxe, *Memoirs of the Life and Administration of Sir Robert Walpole* (London, 1798), ii, 514.
[69][Daniel Defoe], *A General History of Discoveries and Improvements* (London, 1726–7), p. iii.
[70]Accounts were written by George Shelvocke, *A Voyage round the World* . . . (London, 1726), and William Betagh.

more difficult than ever. Defoe, in one of his last works, noted the change in attitude:

> As for new Colonies and Conquests, how do we seem entirely to give over, even the Thoughts of them . . . as if we had done our utmost, were fully satisfied with what we have, that the enterprising Genius was buried with the old Discoverers, and there was neither Room in the World nor Inclination in our People to look any farther.[71]

No serious attempt was made to revive interest in projects to the South Seas until the imminence of war with Spain in 1739 once more brought a flood of schemes for the exploitation, occupation or even dismemberment of Spain's colonial empire. There was a general determination in England that the new war would see no repetition of the costly continental campaigns of Marlborough's day; instead it was to be a maritime struggle in which the navy would be lucratively employed striking at Spanish colonies and shipping. Among the several areas of operations considered the Pacific figured almost from the beginning,[72] and in the autumn of 1739 Sir Charles Wager, now First Lord of the Admiralty, and Sir John Norris, Admiral of the Fleet, began detailed discussions on a South Seas expedition. Both men had long shown interest in the region: Wager as we have seen put forward a project in 1727, and among Norris's papers are proposals for a South Seas venture dating from his days as a vice-admiral during the War of the Spanish Succession.[73] Another link with the past was provided by two former factors of the South Sea Company who played an important part in the planning of the expedition, Hubert Tassell and Henry Hutchinson. Tassell had served as a Company factor in Havana in the 1730s; Hutchinson had seen service as a Company factor at Panama and Portobelo between 1728 and 1732, and was among the few Englishmen to have visited Lima, probably in 1736 or 1737.[74]

In September 1739 Tassell and Hutchinson wrote to Walpole suggesting that an expedition carrying fifteen hundred soldiers should be sent around Cape Horn to attack the Pacific coasts of Spanish America, and later in the month they put their full plan before Wager and Norris.[75] To anyone who had read Defoe, Rogers and the rest it had a familiar ring: the expedition was to conquer Chile, plunder Lima and perhaps establish a government there well disposed towards the British, seize coastal towns,

---

[71][Daniel Defoe], *A Plan of the English Commerce* (2nd edn, London, 1730), pp. xiii–xiv.
[72]The South Seas were first mentioned at a meeting of the Cabinet Council on 3 June 1739, some months before the formal declaration of war in October; see BM, Add. MS 32,993, fo. 59.
[73]BM, Add. MS 28,140, fos 20–34.
[74]See BM, Add. MSS 25,510 and 25, 558 *passim.*
[75]See BM, Add. MSS 32,694, fos 41–5 and 28,132 ('A Journal of My Proceedings' by Sir John Norris, 1739–40), 17, 29 September, 1739.

and then attack Panama. Despite the insistence of the two traders that Spanish defences along the Pacific seaboard were weak, and rebellion among the Creole or Indian inhabitants probable, the reaction of Wager and Norris to these sweeping proposals was cautious. Both were doubtful about the wisdom of sending land forces to the Pacific, and thought that an attack on Panama would be better mounted across the Isthmus; but by mid-October they had endorsed the principle of a raiding expedition along the Pacific coasts of Spanish America.[76]

This agreed, two days later Wager and Norris met James Naish, a former supercargo of the East India Company who had made several voyages to China before being accused by his employers of fraud and smuggling.[77] He produced a detailed scheme for seizing Manila, the great Spanish entrepôt in the North Pacific and the destination of the Acapulco treasure galleon. Like Hutchinson and Tassell, Naish was concerned with the wider implications of a predatory expedition to the Pacific, and he argued that the retention of the Philippines would give British traders in the East a decisive advantage over their foreign rivals 'for extending of commerce to Cochin-China, Cambodia, Siam, Ichore, the coasts of China, and in any islands upon them; and to Japan, and even to the coasts of Mexico, Peru, and Chile; and to every island and place in the vast Pacific Ocean'.[78]

Wager and Norris caught some of Naish's enthusiasm, and despite a frosty comment by Newcastle that 'this was a small affair, and that greater matters had been under consideration',[79] the two veteran seamen put both the South Seas and Manila schemes before a meeting of leading ministers at the end of October.[80] Newcastle and Harrington continued to have reservations about the proposed voyages, and Norris himself was beginning to suspect that they might be used as a cover for private trading. After further hesitation Walpole came to a decision: the expedition round Cape Horn was to go ahead, but the forces needed for the Manila expedition could not be spared. The main weight of the British war effort was to fall on the Caribbean.[81]

At Wager's suggestion George Anson, an experienced naval captain forty-two years old, had been chosen for the Manila project, and on its abandonment he was given command of the Cape Horn expedition. His

---

[76] *Ibid.*, 16 October 1739.
[77] Naish's career with the East India Company can be followed through the Company records at the India Office Library, especially in the Court Minutes, vols 43 to 58.
[78] Notes written by Naish on his copy of *A Voyage round the World . . . by George Anson* (London, 1748), pp. 1–13, now in BM 10025, fo. 8; see also BM, Add. MS 28,132, 18, 20 Oct. 1739.
[79] *Ibid.*, 23 Oct. 1739.
[80] *Ibid.*, 29 Oct. 1739.
[81] *Ibid.*, 5, 7 Dec. 1739.

orders were drawn up personally by Wager,[82] and reveal that the expedition was still regarded as something more than a plundering raid. It is true that attacks on Spanish American shipping and ports were routine privateering objectives, but there were also clauses which dealt with the implications of possible rebellion in Peru and the establishment there of a government sympathetic towards British merchants. A draft manifesto drawn up before Anson sailed promised British protection, freedom of trade and religious liberty to all who rose against the authority of the Spanish crown. Other documents reveal that if the wealthy creole inhabitants did not rebel, then Anson was to win over the mulattoes and Negro slaves.[83] Although the possibility of rebellion within the Spanish colonies had been hopefully mentioned in earlier proposals, Anson's instructions contain the first evidence of any awareness in government circles that the most promising openings for British commerce would come if Spain's American colonies, with or without British help, moved towards independence.

The plans of the Spanish Succession war had at last come to fruition it seemed; British naval forces were to be used as instruments of commercial imperialism in the Pacific. In fact the hopes which prompted the sending of Anson to the Pacific were even less realistic than those of the earlier period. The projects of Tassell, Hutchinson and Naish paid little attention to reactions in Old and New Spain to foreign incursions into the colonial empire; nor did they take account of the diplomatic pressures which would be brought to bear (as they had been in 1711 and were to be again in 1762) on any attempts at territorial adjustments within the Spanish colonial empire. Anson's sailing orders reveal other difficulties. In one hand he held instructions to destroy Spanish American towns and shipping; in the other exhortations to gain the confidence of all Spanish Americans ready to rebel against viceregal rule. The inquiries of Antonio de Ulloa and Jorge Juan in Peru were providing disturbing evidence for the Spanish government of discontent in its American possessions;[84] but there was little likelihood that, outside the Indian tribes, any substantial section of the colonial populace would have welcomed marauding heretics with open arms.

Anson's squadron consisted of his flagship *Centurion* (60 guns), *Gloucester* and *Severn* (50), *Pearl* (40), *Wager* (28), *Tryal* (8), and two merchant vessels carrying supplies and trade goods. The land forces on board comprised a mixed detachment of Chelsea pensioners and raw marines. Administrative ineptitude and contrary winds prevented the expedition from sailing until September 1740, and it was soon overwhelmed by sickness and disaster. The *Severn* and *Pearl* were forced back by tem-

[82]See PRO, SP 42/81, fos 293–8, 42/88, fos 2–10.
[83]BM, Add. MS 19,030, fos 470–2.
[84]See Jorge Juan and Antonio de Ulloa, *Relacion Historica del Viage a la America Meridional* (Madrid, 1758).

pestuous seas off Cape Horn, their rigging shattered, and most of their crews dead or dying. The *Wager* was driven ashore on the desolate coast of southern Chile, and when Anson's remaining warships, the *Centurion, Gloucester* and the tiny *Tryal*, limped one by one into the old privateer rendezvous of Juan Fernandez they had lost two-thirds of their crews through scurvy. Anson's instructions to attack the great cities of Spanish America, encourage rebellion against Spanish rule, and open the region to British traders, had become a mockery. The most which he could accomplish was a series of hit-and-run raids on Spanish shipping, and a repetition of Shelvocke's inconsiderable feat of sacking the small Peruvian town of Paita. During his Pacific wanderings Anson was forced to scuttle first the *Tryal* and then the *Gloucester*, and when he arrived at Macao in November 1742 he had only 210 men and one ship left. As he wrote to Naish in his characteristic style of terse understatement, 'I am certainly unfortunate, and a fatality attends me'.[85]

One exploit alone could redeem this dismal story of hardship and catastrophe — the taking of the Acapulco galleon on its way into Manila. After a month's wait off the Philippines Anson encountered the galleon, the *Nuestra Señora de Covadonga*, and captured her after a ninety-minute action. On board, Anson's men found one of the richest treasures ever taken by an English ship: 1,373,843 pieces of eight, and 35,682 ounces of virgin silver. Together with smaller amounts of silver and coin taken from earlier prizes and at Paita, Anson brought home in the *Centurion* approximately £400,000, a sum whose modern equivalent would be ten or twenty times as much. It was this colossal treasure which stirred imagination in England, and the return of the *Centurion* in the summer of 1744 provided good copy for the London newspapers. After the Mediterranean fleet's failure off Toulon in February the navy stood in need of a popular triumph, and the capture of a treasure galleon was the next best thing to a fleet victory. Certainly it was of more public interest than the incomprehensible continental campaigns and alliances which dominated the government's attention. Day after day the newspapers carried reports of the home-coming: the procession from Portsmouth to London of thirty-two wagons laden with silver; the feting of Anson and his men; details of the prizemoney and the dispute over its allocation.[86] A book written by 'John Phillips' (allegedly an officer on the expedition) was rushed through the press in a matter of weeks; another narrative appeared in instalments in *The Universal Spectator*; and in 1745 Pascoe Thomas's lively firsthand account, *A True and Impartial Journal of a Voyage to the South Seas*, was published.

---

[85]Letter in possession of late Commander C.G. Pitcairn Jones; printed in Glyndwr Williams, ed., *Documents relating to Anson's Voyage round the World 1740–1744* (London, The Navy Records Society, 1967), p. 152.
[86]*Ibid.*, pp. 233–7.

Some were able to look beyond the immediate excitement of the *Centurion*'s return, and consider the long-term implications of Anson's experiences in the Pacific. In his revised edition of Harris's collection of voyages first published in 1705, that prolific writer on mercantile subjects, John Campbell, included an account of Anson's voyage. Campbell was an enthusiastic advocate of overseas enterprise in all parts of the globe, and he drew from the voyage evidence of the opportunities awaiting Britain in the Pacific. His detailed arguments resembled those put forward by Hutchinson and Naish in 1739, and his general sentiments were summed up in his warning that 'History affords us no instance of a maritime power that remained long at a stay. If we do not go forward, we must necessarily go backwards'.[87] More was heard on this theme when the long-awaited official account of the enterprise, *A Voyage round the World by George Anson*, appeared in May 1748. The book was a bestseller, and before the end of the year was in its fifth edition. Ostensibly written by Richard Walter, chaplain of the *Centurion*, the volume's literary style owed much to Benjamin Robins, an experienced pamphleteer of the day, but without doubt the opinions expressed in the account were those of Anson, who was now reaching a dominant position in the conduct of naval affairs. In 1745 he was appointed to the Board of Admiralty; he was promoted successively rear-admiral, vice-admiral and (in 1748) admiral; he was created a peer in 1747 after his victory over the French fleet at Cape Finisterre; and in 1751 he became first lord of the Admiralty.

Anson exercised close control over the writing of the *Voyage*, which in its general chapters contained a partisan analysis of Spanish power in the Pacific.[88] It urged that the Falklands (sighted by Rogers and Frezier, though not by Anson) should be surveyed as a preliminary step towards the establishment of a British base near the Cape Horn entrance into the Pacific; and it revived the plan of Narborough's expedition for the exploration of the west coast of Patagonia between the Strait of Magellan and the most southerly Spanish settlements, with an eye to finding a more convenient harbour than Juan Fernandez. Then followed a highly optimistic account of 'what might have been expected from our squadron had it arrived in the South-Seas in good time', which led a critical Horace Walpole to remark: 'He sets out with telling you that he had no soldiers sent with him but old invalids without legs or arms; and then in the middle of the book there is a whole chapter to tell you, what they would have done if they had set out two months sooner; and that was no less than conquering Peru and Mexico with this disabled army'.[89] Walpole was no friend

---

[87]John Campbell, *Navigantium atque Itinerantium Bibliotheca: or, a compleat Collection of Voyages and Travels* (London, 1744–8), I, 364–5.
[88]*A Voyage round the World . . . by George Anson*, pp. 90–4, 279–89.
[89]W.S. Lewis, ed., *The Yale Edition of Horace Walpole's Correspondence*, IX (New Haven, 1941), p. 55.

of Anson's, but there is some substance in his jibe. If Valdivia had been taken, 'we should immediately have been terrible to the whole kingdom of Chili, and should doubtless have awed the most distant parts of the Spanish Empire in America'. Captured Spanish letters, the official account insisted, revealed a situation of hopeless decadence and confusion along the entire Pacific seaboard: resentful Creoles, 'universally discontented' Indians, defenceless ports, and 'mutual janglings amongst the Governors'. The fall of Valdivia would have set off a full-scale Indian uprising in· Chile, which would have spread to Peru, and soon become 'a general insurrection' sweeping through Spanish America, and giving Anson's force the opportunity to control the coasts and by implication the entire continent.

There is a strong element of wishful thinking in all this, but developments in the next year showed Anson's seriousness of purpose. Early in 1749, the first year of peace, a naval expedition was planned which was to survey the Falklands and then pass into the South Seas, calling at Juan Fernandez on the way. British assurances about the scientific nature of the voyage, and even the cancelling of the second part of the enterprise, failed to mollify the Spaniards, understandably touchy about Anson's intentions. As the Spanish first minister Carvajal pointed out to the British ambassador Benjamin Keene, 'he hoped we would consider what air it would have in the world to see us planted directly against the mouth of the Straits of Magellan, ready upon all occasions to enter into the South Seas'.[90] The Spanish concept of the Pacific as *mare clausum* died hard, and the British government was forced to recognise the strength of Spanish feelings. Its anxiety not to upset the delicate negotiations in progress on the *asiento* and other issues led the Duke of Bedford to instruct the Admiralty to drop the proposed expedition, and so the dispute over the Falklands was postponed for fifteen years. As in 1711, plans for distant ventures had been halted as soon as they conflicted with the requirements of diplomacy nearer home, and not until the closing years of the Seven Years War did Anson and his colleagues find an opportunity to launch an assault against Spain's overseas empire.

Anson's expedition forms an appropriate conclusion to a survey of English interest in the South Seas in the late Stuart and early Hanoverian period. If in its origins it summed up the aspirations of past generations of projectors and merchants, its grim experiences revealed the difference between the easy theories of the armchair strategists and the realities of a Pacific voyage under stress. Its sailing instructions illustrate a fallacy which was never overcome in the various South Seas projects put forward after Narborough's voyage. At no time was proper thought given to the problem

[90]Extracts from the correspondence of Keene and Bedford in 1749, now in the Library of Congress, Washington, are printed in Julius Goebel, *The Struggle for the Falkland Islands* (New Haven, 1927), pp. 196–201.

raised by St John in 1711 when he pointed out that 'the prospects of opening a new trade with the Spaniards and of attacking their colonies at the
same time tended to be repugnant one to another'.[91] Since Spain, regard-
less of internal distress and disorganisation, showed little inclination to
abandon its exclusionist policies, Britain could gain commercial privileges
along the Pacific seaboard of South America only by force. No administration seriously considered either risking war by attempting this in peace-
time, or diverting scarce resources to so distant a theatre once hostilities
were declared. The diplomatic implications of such a move, the logistic
problems involved, and the suspicion that the acquisition of remote
regions of Spanish America might bring not a golden inheritance but a
sea of troubles, were enough to make any government hesitate.

Yet if the wilder hopes of the theorists were disappointed, at a less
dramatic level much was gained. Though knowledge in England of the
coasts of the eastern Pacific remained hazy, the area was no longer the
terra incognita it had been before 1670. The published accounts of the
voyages, maps, pamphlets, and newspaper comment, whatever their
deficiencies, had brought the South Seas within the broadening horizons
of the literate public. The lands and seas beyond Cape Horn were not
only the realm of privateers and traders; they provided the setting for
some of the most popular fiction and satire of the period. Gulliver's travels
took him to the Pacific, where Lilliput was situated north of Van Diemen's
Land, and Brobdingnag somewhere east of Japan. Voltaire's *Alzire*
was given a Peruvian background. Defoe's *Robinson Crusoe*, though set in
the Caribbean, owed much to the story related by Woodes Rogers of the
marooning of Alexander Selkirk on Juan Fernandez.[92]

In the second half of the century, British interest in the Pacific was to be
at once wider and deeper. It became truly oceanic; attention turned to
unknown areas rather than to settled coasts; the insistent quest for knowledge became a motive as important as more material considerations. But
continuity remained. To listen to Dalrymple on the dazzling prospects
of the undiscovered southern continent — 'the scraps from this table
would be sufficient to maintain the power, dominion, and sovereignty of
Britain, by employing all its manufactures and ships'[93] — is to hear again
the voices of Defoe and Bowrey on the South Seas trade. Cornish's capture
of Manila in 1762, Anglo-Spanish rivalry over the Falklands, the search
for new markets and bases by Cook and his successors, the achievement
of British merchants in gaining access to the markets of Spanish America
during the upheavals of the Napoleonic Wars — all were foreshadowed
by the discussions of 1711 and 1739, and by the arguments of a long line

[91]BM, Portland Loan, 29/288.
[92]See Rogers, *A Cruising Voyage*, pp.
[93]A. Dalrymple, *A Collection of Voyages to the South Seas* (London, 1770–1),
I, p. xxix.

of advocates of Pacific expansion from Dampier to Anson. The belief that British interest in the Pacific dates only from 1763 springs from a confusion between intention and achievement, a reluctance to recognise (if we may use the terminology of the historians of a later period of European expansion) the role of unofficial agents of imperialism. In terms of tangible exploration, trade and settlement the sporadic incursions of English adventurers into the South Seas between 1670 and 1750 were of negligible importance; but in terms of interest roused, speculation excited, and projects advanced, they form the essential preliminary to the upsurge of British activity in the Pacific in the late eighteenth century.

4.

PETER BURROUGHS

The Canadian rebellions in British politics

Few historians would any longer describe the early and mid-Victorian period as an age of anti-imperialist sentiment in England. But if the assault of revisionist criticism has effectively demolished the old orthodoxy, and the familiar landmarks erected by C.A. Bodelsen and R.L. Schuyler are now in ruins, a new synthesis has yet to emerge. In the task of reconstruction, it would be futile to repeat the errors of the past. A reassessment of British attitudes to empire should not therefore aim at delineating the prevailing mood of the age or at forging a consistent, enduring outlook from the diverse, conflicting views of individuals or amorphous groups. Imperial history in the nineteenth century has suffered long enough from grand hypotheses and a preference for armchair theorising on the basis of inadequate evidence. Designs sketched by creative architects may appeal to the imagination, but a house cannot be constructed until the bricks have been made. Imperial historians must go back to the sources in order to discover what contemporaries actually said and wrote, as distinct from the views attributed to them by later writers, and by dint of hard, grinding toil in archives compile a wealth of case studies dealing with specific topics, particular themes, various geographical areas. Only when this essential groundwork has been done can the lingering myths and accumulated misconceptions of the past be replaced by a deeper appreciation of British attitudes to empire in the Victorian era.

Greater care must also be exercised than in the past in interpreting contemporary comment. Bodelsen and Schuyler set out to prove a case: they expounded their doctrine of anti-imperialism by selecting from a limited range of sources evidence that corroborated a preconceived thesis. This technique not only obscured the bewildering, fascinating variety of English attitudes, but also ignored the difficulties involved in subjecting an unwieldy mass of opinion and prejudice to coherent analysis. No allowance was made for the context of remarks — the occasion, the topic under discussion, the audience addressed, the purpose sought. Historians failed to appreciate that much of what politicians said in public debate about the empire was rhetoric and should not be taken at its face value. Most significantly, the views of Englishmen on colonial affairs were inextricably related to the political preconceptions and party interests that animated British politics. The tendency of writers to treat Britain's imperial and domestic history as separate, self-contained areas of historical inquiry is particularly regrettable on an issue where contemporary attitudes are not fully intelligible if divorced from the domestic context. There was no such thing as an objective appraisal of colonial questions; quite apart from the remoteness and unfamiliarity of conditions overseas, imperial questions were handled according to the exigencies of English politics and interpreted in the light of ingrained political principles fashioned by the British experience.

These considerations can be aptly illustrated by an analysis of the reactions of Englishmen to the Canadian rebellions in 1837. In time of peace the early Victorians tended to take colonies for granted, but at a time of imperial crisis views were aired and prejudices displayed that might be left unexpressed at calmer moments. Events in Canada raised basic issues concerning the empire and imperial relations which were vigorously debated, for a few months at least, by Englishmen who were certainly not indifferent to the immediate outcome of a colonial revolt. Public interest was further stimulated by the potential repercussions of the Canadian crisis, for the rebellions injected a new issue into domestic politics and provided fresh ammunition for Tory and radical critics of the Whig ministry of the day. 'Canadian affairs are all the rage', commented one newspaper in January 1838. 'In parliament or out of it the almost sole topic of discussion is the proposed ministerial mode of dealing with our dissatisfied colonists in the Canadas.'[1]

As was the case with the more enduring debate in Britain concerning the character and relevance of American democracy,[2] the response of Englishmen to the Canadian rebellions and to differing Canadian concepts of politics and society reflected the political principles, temperaments, and interests of the individuals concerned. Such reactions therefore throw considerable light on the nature of early Victorian radicalism, Whiggery, and Toryism. The radical Henry Warburton warned fellow parliamentarians that 'We must not judge of the feelings and principles of the inhabitants of other countries by our own feelings and principles',[3] but in practice these cautions were thrown to the winds, as the preconceptions and emotions of British politicians of every persuasion were made explicit in a debate over a sufficiently remote controversy in a colony. Stereotypes of the colonist and the North American, the demagogue and the patriot, could be used to illustrate and fight a whole range of universal battles: the contests between democracy and aristocratic government, between

---

[1] *Whitehaven Herald*, 27 Jan. 1838.
[2] For a most illuminating discussion of this theme, D.P. Crook, *American Democracy in English Politics 1815–1850* (Oxford, 1965).
[3] *Hansard*, 3rd series, 39, 22 Dec. 1837, 1472.

popular rights and prescriptive authority, between innovation and tradition, between American and British values. The conflict of political philosophies at home could be energetically but safely fought out on a distant Canadian battleground. By the use of analogy and comparison, radicals might by implication attack the inegalitarian structure of British society, the power of the aristocracy, and the perfection of the constitution without the danger of provoking undue hostility or being charged with subversion. Similarly, Whigs might quietly defend their vested interests in a hierarchical society and a balanced constitution, while Tories could voice their contempt for innovation and their fear of democracy. Consequently, English observers tended to see what they wanted to see in the Canadian crisis; events and conditions in Canada were interpreted to square with settled convictions and adapted to serve the needs of party propaganda.

In line with their advocacy of American democracy, English radicals sympathised with the aspirations of the Canadian rebels as the champions of popular government and individual liberty engaged in a struggle against oligarchy and oppression. The fundamental issues of political principle raised by the colonial dispute were ideally designed to arouse the passionate concern of the extremist, doctrinaire wing of reformers, the philosophic radicals, whose spokesmen in parliament constituted the most vehement and persistent critics of the government's Canadian policy, though they were supported in this campaign by newspapers that reflected other facets of radical opinion.[4] At the other political extreme, Tories denounced the rebels as agitators or disloyal French-Canadian Catholics out to subvert legitimate political authority and imperial rule. In the centre the spectrum of Whig opinion ran the gamut from conservative through ministerial to liberal. The Whigs afforded the most objective interpretation of events in Canada, because detachment seemed unlikely to endanger their political interests, and because they tended by tradition and temperament to be calmly pragmatic in outlook, displaying what John Stuart Mill called 'the ordinary Whig aversion to strong opinions on either side'.[5] Not every issue raised by the Canadian rebellions was susceptible to exploitation for British party purposes, least of all matters concerning the future unity or disintegration of the empire, and the variety of attitudes precludes a rigid application of a threefold categorisation. Nevertheless, the reactions of Englishmen to events in Canada and the political capital made out of the crisis of 1837–38 suggest the limitations of accepting too

---

[4]For the philosophic radicals, see J. Hamburger, *Intellectuals in Politics: John Stuart Mill and the Philosophic Radicals* (New Haven, 1965). In 1834 the radical J.A. Roebuck, MP for Bath, was appointed agent of the assembly of Lower Canada.

[5][J.S. Mill], 'Lord Durham and the Canadians', *London and Westminster Review*, XXVIII (Jan. 1838), 518.

uncritically the view that 'The spectrum of opinion on colonial policy was much narrower than the language of partisan politics would seem to indicate'.[6] Certainly, attitudes to colonial questions grew out of, and remained firmly rooted in, the English political experience and the exigencies of domestic politics.

Reports of an insurrection in Lower Canada first began to reach England in mid-December 1837. Initial reactions in the press and in parliament reflected general uncertainty and apprehension, since it was not clear how extensive or widely supported the revolt would prove to be, and at a time of year when the St Lawrence was frozen Englishmen were dependent for early news of events in Canada on American newspapers whose reports were far from impartial. No one at first knew whether the rebellion was confined to the French inhabitants of Lower Canada or whether they had been joined in arms by British settlers. Since Englishmen assumed that Upper Canada would remain loyal and peaceful, their apprehensions were naturally increased when official reports confirmed that an uprising had occurred in the upper province. There were also disquieting rumours of impending American intervention, if only by restless republicans on the border, and the danger that the disturbances in the Canadas might lead to war with the United States was anxiously debated by the British public during the coming months. The paucity of information concerning the actual state of affairs in the Canadas did not discourage Englishmen from expressing their hopes and fears, advising the government on the appropriate methods of dealing with the situation, and speculating on the likely outcome of events. Moreover, because individual views on these initial questions were largely predetermined by the political outlook and preconceptions of the observer, expectations were savoured and predictions of the desired results were made by radicals and Tories with more confidence than available information warranted; only the Whigs allowed themselves the luxury of nagging doubts.

English radicals rushed to champion the insurgents' cause because they believed that the Canadian dispute involved universal principles. Here was an oppressed people claiming their political rights and attempting to overthrow the tyranny of a local oligarchy backed by imperial authority. Since the cause of freedom was at stake and the whole of British North America appeared to be in a ferment of discontent, radicals anticipated a widespread uprising that would engage the active support of the entire colonial population. Whigs and Tories therefore grossly deceived themselves and fatally underrated the difficulties and dangers of the situation

[6]J.S. Galbraith, 'Myths of the "Little England" Era', *American Historical Review*, LXVII (1961), 42.

when they dismissed the rebellions as the work of a few misguided agitators. The government should recall the contest with the Thirteen Colonies and the futility of a policy of coercion when Britain was last confronted with a popular insurrection in a vast country on the other side of the Atlantic. Regrettably, ministers seemed bent on repeating the folly of their predecessors, and thus being 'held up to the scorn and execration of posterity, as the men who, with the example of the struggle for American independence before their eyes, plunged England into a disgraceful and disastrous war, for the purpose of chastising a colony which they had themselves, by their own incompetence, injustice, and misgovernment, forced into open rebellion'.[7]

While British arms had been defeated on the earlier occasion, radicals noted that the Canadian rebels might expect assistance from American sympathisers, and the very real danger that Britain might thereby become embroiled in war with the United States appeared a compelling reason why the government should pause before it embarked on a reckless attempt to put down the Canadians by force. Radicals expected, yet feared, that armed bands of American citizens would cross over the border into Canada, not only animated by a love of adventure and tempted by the promise of rich lands, but determined to drive the last relics of monarchy from the North American continent and so complete the victory of democracy in the New World. Americans would regard the Canadian struggle against the despotic rule of England as a repetition of their own glorious fight for freedom and independence, and in the face of popular excitement the federal government of the United States would be powerless to prevent its citizens from intervening on behalf of the Canadian insurgents. The recent incursion of Americans into Texas was cited by the radicals as a warning of what Britain might expect in the event of a struggle for Canada.[8]

With these dangers in prospect and before repressive measures were adopted to assert British supremacy, radicals urged the government and Englishmen generally to assess the costs and benefits of successfully crushing the Canadian uprisings. If the authorities were eventually triumphant in an inglorious campaign against colonial liberties, only a military occupation financed by the British taxpayer could effectively secure the obedience of discontented colonists awaiting the first opportunity to seek revenge.[9] But what kind of tranquillity, the radicals enquired, would be gained at the point of a bayonet? British rule could not be indefinitely upheld by a tyrannical regime, particularly in a colony bordering on

---

[7]John Leader, *Hansard*, 39, 22 Dec. 1837, 1445; also Warburton, *ibid.*, 1477; *Leeds Mercury*, 30 Dec. 1837; *Philanthropist* (Birmingham), 28 Dec. 1837; *Leicestershire Mercury*, 6 Jan. 1838; [J.A. Roebuck], *Canadian Portfolio*, (London, 1838), p. 2.
[8]*Canadian Portfolio*, pp. 47–8; Sir William Molesworth, Leader, *Hansard,* 39, 22 Dec. 1837, 1465–6, 1439; *Hull Advertiser*, 26 Jan. 1838; *Bristol Mirror*, 3 Feb. 1838.
[9]Leader, George Grote, *Hansard*, 39, 22 Dec. 1837, 1442, 1485; *Liverpool Chronicle*, 30 Dec. 1837; *Kent Herald*, 4 and 25 Jan. 1838; *Gateshead Observer*, 13 Jan. 1838.

the United States. Moreover, the commercial advantages which Britain was supposed to derive from the possession of Canada would be severely impaired by war and the subsequent legacy of bitterness and hostility; certainly they were not 'worth purchasing at the cost of eternal coercion and an unceasing struggle to put down the feelings of the great mass of the Canadian people'.[10]

Repressive measures in the colony and war with the United States would have wider repercussions which the radicals were anxious to avoid. Sir William Molesworth referred to 'the baneful prejudices, the odious antipathies, which it will produce amongst nations, whose mutual interest it is to cultivate kindly feelings towards one another'.[11] Radicals were particularly concerned about Anglo-American relations, where half a century had hardly obliterated the legacy of bad feeling generated by the war of independence, and they deeply regretted that a new source of friction now threatened to destroy a growing sense of amity and mutual respect that had recently begun to develop between the two countries. They fervently wished to promote this cordiality, both as admirers of American democracy and as the advocates of democratic institutions in Britain. Such was the close interrelationship of colonial and domestic policies that the vindication of despotic principles of government in Canada might be used by ministers 'as a fulcrum for the lever of oppression at home'.[12] At the very least, Molesworth explained,

> a war invariably appeals to the vilest passions of a nation — to its worst national vanities, and tends, for a time, to put a stop to all improvements; and many who fear the march of improvement will, I doubt not, gladly seize upon such an opportunity as the present with the hope of occupying by war the national mind, and turning it away from the consideration of reform.[13]

So evil would be the consequences of warfare in North America that radicals concluded that a British victory over the Canadians would be purchased at too dear a price, and many expressed the hope that if the government resorted to force, British troops might be defeated by the Canadian patriots. 'May all that disgrace attend the British arms', declared the *Leicestershire Mercury*, 'which is demanded at the hands of justice by the iniquity of the British cause!'[14] Such unpatriotic sentiments were bitterly denounced as treason by Tories and Whigs. Molesworth was severely censured for his outspoken views, which apparently strained

---

[10]Grote, *Hansard*, 39, 22 Dec. 1837, 1485. Also Thomas Wakley, *ibid.*, 1505; *Canadian Portfolio*, p. 121; *Hull Advertiser*, 12 Jan. 1838.
[11]*Hansard*, 39, 22 Dec. 1837, 1466.
[12]*Leeds Times*, 30 Dec. 1837. Also *Leicestershire Mercury*, 6 and 13 Jan. 1838; *Birmingham Journal*, 6 Jan. 1838; *London Dispatch* 24 Dec. 1837.
[13]*Hansard*, 39, 22 Dec. 1837, 1467.
[14]*Leicestershire Mercury*, 6 Jan. 1838; also *Leeds Mercury*, 30 Dec. 1837; *Birmingham Journal*, 30 Dec. 1837.

to the limits the patience and language of the House of Commons. If war broke out, he proclaimed:

> I should more deplore success on the part of this country than defeat; and though as an English citizen I could not but lament the disasters of my countrymen, still it would be to me a matter of less poignant regret than a success which would offer to the world the disastrous and disgraceful spectacle of a free and mighty nation succeeding by force of arms in putting down and tyrannising over a free though feebler community struggling in defence of its just rights . . . if unhappily a war does ensue, may speedy victory crown the efforts of the Canadians, and may the curses and execrations of the indignant people of this empire alight on the heads of those Ministers, who, by their misgovernment, ignorance, and imprudence, involve us in the calamities of civil discord, and expend our national resources in an unholy struggle against liberty.[15]

With such fundamental issues at stake and such pernicious consequences in view, the small group of Canadian sympathisers in the House of Commons appealed for support beyond parliament to the friends of democracy and liberty among the British public. The dispute was no longer a colonial affair, but a controversy between the government and people of England. One commentator suggested that the 'treatment of the Canadian question will be a kind of test as to the advance of civilization in this country',[16] and radicals were confident that English opinion, if it could be effectively aroused, would be sufficiently enlightened to support the colonists' cause. The 'people of England', John Leader optimistically announced, 'would not sanction a crusade against the constitutional rights of a free colony', nor would they consent to a wasteful expenditure of blood and treasure in order to gratify the government's love of colonial dominion or keep the colonists in unwilling subjection.[17] To promote a popular campaign meetings were organised throughout the country, at which resolutions were passed denouncing the ministry and expressing solidarity with the Canadian patriots, and petitions were presented to parliament by such radical and working-class groups as the London Working Men's Association.[18] Nevertheless, events were to show that the

---

[15]*Hansard*, 39, 22 Dec. 1837, 1467. Molesworth told his mother that 'I am the theme of very general execration for which I don't care a dam.' 10 Jan. 1838, Pencarrow Papers, II, f. 36.

[16]*Kent Herald*, 4 Jan. 1838.

[17]*Hansard*, 39, 22 Dec. 1837, 1437; also Molesworth, Warburton, Wakley, *ibid.*, 1467, 1478, 1505–6; *Leeds Times*, 30 Dec. 1837; *Manchester Times*, 13 Jan. 1838.

[18]One of the most notorious meetings was held in London at the Crown and Anchor Tavern, 4 Jan. 1838, at which Molesworth, Leader, and Joseph Hume raged against the ministry. Reported in *The Times* and other papers, 5 Jan. 1838. For the petitions presented by William Lovett's London Working Men's Association against Whig policy in Canada in 1837–8 and an Address to the Canadian People, *Life and Struggles of William Lovett*, ed. R.H. Tawney (London, 1967 edn), pp. 84–91, 124.

radicals' estimate of the effectiveness of outraged protests from the English public was as false as their prediction of the dire consequences that would result from the vigorous suppression of the rebellions.

At the opposite extreme of the British political spectrum, Tories responded to events in Canada with a forthright denunciation of rebellion against legitimate authority and a demand that the uprisings should be crushed by an energetic display of force. 'If there be any justice in England', thundered the *Liverpool Mail*, 'it will be disgraced and polluted if these men be not severely punished. If the QUEEN's name and authority are not to be trampled upon with impunity, these miscreants, and all their leaders and abettors, must be made a fearful example of.'[19] Punitive measures constituted the Tory prescription for restoring tranquillity in the Canadas and upholding British authority, and until this essential task had been successfully accomplished, no attention need be given to investigating the sources of colonial dissatisfaction or framing constructive remedies. Retribution before redress remained the Tory precept; concessions must not be made at the point of a sword, and there might be dangerous repercussions for government if malcontents in Britain or elsewhere in the empire were encouraged by mistaken leniency on this occasion to seek their objectives by an appeal to force.

As part of their spirited response Tories charged the Whig ministry with having precipitated the outbreak of civil discord by a failure to adopt timely, determined measures. The uprisings were the predictable result of habitual vacillation, as ministers had watched 'in silence and inactivity, the open and unmasked process by which treason in Canada was gradually ripening into rebellion'.[20] Assiduous, artful agitators, instead of being suppressed, had been humoured and petted, as contempt for lawful authority and British power was nurtured by a misguided policy of conciliation. 'Soft words, and persuasive arguments, and liberal professions', explained one newspaper, 'have only sharpened the daggers drawn against us.'[21] The Whigs were known to be inveterate procrastinators, but this criminal inactivity was attributed by the Tories to the ministry's degrading subjection to a knot of parliamentary radicals in league with the revolutionary

[19]*Liverpool Mail*, 19 Dec. 1837. Also *Plymouth Herald*, 30 Dec. 1837; *Leicester Herald*, 13 Jan. 1838; Sir R.H. Inglis, W.P. Borthwick, *Hansard*, 39, 22 Dec. 1837, 1486, 1494.

[20]*Morning Post* (London), 25 Dec. 1837. Also *Morning Herald* (London), 28 Dec. 1837 and 1 Jan. 1838; *Wheeler's Manchester Chronicle*, 30 Dec. 1837, *Sunderland Beacon*, 10 Jan. 1838; *Berwick and Kelso Warder*, 20 Jan. 1838; *Liverpool Courier*, 24 Jan. 1838; *Standard* (London), 5 Feb. 1838; *Hints on the Government of Canada, for the consideration of members of parliament* (London, 1838), pp. 4–5; Borthwick, Lord Aberdeen, *Hansard*, 40, 17 Jan. 1838, 118, and 2 Feb. 1838, 652.

[21]*Liverpool Mail*, 26 Dec. 1837. Also *Cumberland Pacquet*, 2 Jan. 1838; *The Times*, 15 Jan. 1838; *Cambridge Chronicle*, 27 Jan. 1838; *Liverpool Courier*, 28 March 1838.

leaders of the colonial assemblies. The radicals' votes were considered vital to keep the government in office, and in order to avoid offending Leader, Molesworth, Joseph Hume, and others, sedition had been condoned in Canada, just as England's interests had been sacrificed in Ireland to retain the votes of Daniel O'Connell and his Irish supporters.[22]

The related matter of military precautions formed a contentious issue in parliament. The government frankly admitted in the House of Commons that, at least since the passage of Lord John Russell's Resolutions in March 1837, it had been aware that malcontents in Lower Canada might resort to arms. But apart from the transfer of troops from the Maritimes, no steps were taken to send reinforcements from Britain until the rebellions occurred and the St Lawrence was frozen. Ministers had apparently ' "stood at ease", or slept, like Lord GLENELG, in profound tranquillity, until the thunders of the Canadian "Lexington" disturbed their repose'.[23] Tories threatened to impeach the ministry for leaving the colonies in a defenceless state when protests against the Resolutions had been expected and the revolt had taken no one by surprise. The dispatch of adequate troops would have demonstrated a resolution to maintain British rule, checked the temptation to rebel, protected the lives and property of loyal citizens, and prevented much unnecessary violence and bloodshed.[24]

While they doubted the capacity of the present ministry to deal firmly with the crisis, Tories unhesitatingly and patriotically predicted the speedy defeat of the insurgents and the vindication of British authority. Unlike contemporaries of other political persuasions, Tory confidence in the outcome was not shaken by memories of the American Revolution, an event of an entirely different character and order of magnitude. Tories belittled the rebellions as minor affrays worked up by wily demagogues playing on the passions and prejudices of an ignorant population. The ample resources of British power, backed by the overwhelming loyalty of English Canadians in both provinces, would be more than a match for such feeble ebullitions.[25]

Tory commentators also severely censured the parliamentary radicals for the effrontery of championing revolt, bloodshed, and treason on the floor of the House of Commons. While Tories had 'long been convinced

---

[22]*Manchester Courier*, 23 Dec. 1837; *Birmingham Advertiser*, 28 Dec. 1837; *The Times*, 20 and 23 Dec. 1837; *Newcastle Journal*, 27 Jan. 1838; *Leeds Intelligencer*, 20 Jan. 1838; *Bath Post*, 3 Feb. 1838; *Leicester Herald*, 10 Feb. 1838; *Hints on the Government of Canada*, pp. 4, 6
[23]*Morning Herald*, 1 Jan. 1838.
[24]Borthwick, Earl of Ripon, William Gladstone, Sir Robert Peel, Lord Wharncliffe, *Hansard*, 40, 17 Jan. 1838, 115, 18 Jan. 1838, 231–4, 23 Jan. 1838, 438, 457–8, and 2 Feb. 1838, 705; *The Times*, 28 Dec. 1837; *Leicestershire, Nottinghamshire, and Derbyshire Telegraph*, 6 Jan. 1838; *West of England Conservative* (Plymouth), 31 Jan. 1838; *Hints on the Government of Canada*, pp. 21–3.
[25]*Morning Post*, 25 Dec. 1837; *Liverpool Journal*, 23 Dec. 1837; *Albion* (Liverpool), 25 Dec. 1837; *Bath Post*, 6 Jan. 1838.

that loyalty and Radicalism are incompatible',[26] the latest expression of unpatriotic, traitorous sentiments provoked a flood of outraged indignation. 'To hear men who owe allegiance to the Queen of England', protested a Tory paper in a typical outburst, 'exulting in the success of rebels, glorifying in the civil war, and expressing their joy at . . . the anticipated defeat of Her Majesty's forces, and the immediate separation of the Canadas from this country, is insufferably insolent and disgusting.'[27] An obsessive concern with patriotism always formed a distinctive part of the Tory outlook and an identification with national interests offered a congenial contrast to the unpatriotic internationalism of the radicals. Tories had long believed that it was 'the very core of the Radical party to overturn the Colonial supremacy of Great Britain', and the disgraceful exhibition of Molesworth and others revealed as clearly as daylight that the parliamentary radicals had treacherously fomented the spirit of disaffection in Canada. Here were the real authors of the uprising in whose hands Louis Papineau had been no more than a foolish puppet.[28]

The radicals were further denounced by Tories for advocating the insidious, dangerous view that colonists could throw off their allegiance to the British crown whenever they wished and whatever the pretext. Acceptance of this novel doctrine would mean that government at home or overseas had no right to demand of its subjects any obedience which was not voluntarily given; it would subvert all established ideas of law and order, sovereignty and subjection, on which government should properly be based. Tory hostility to democracy and innovation was reflected in this defence of the claims of legitimate authority and Britain's national institutions of crown, aristocracy, and empire, as well as in an attack on a theory of natural rights or 'some ideal notion of liberty'.[29] It was the duty of Tories 'to check the ravings of the democratic frenzy, and bestow the merited chastisement upon the teachers of the execrable doctrine in which none but the enemies of England — of constitutional

[26]*Leicester Herald*, 6 Jan. 1838.
[27]*Liverpool Mail*, 26 Dec. 1837. Also C. Lushington, G.F. Young, *Hansard*, 39, 22 Dec. 1837, 1445, 1478–9; *Morning Post*, 23 Dec. 1837; *Standard*, 23 Dec. 1837; *Morning Advertiser* (London), 25 and 27 Dec. 1837; *Morning Herald*, 30 Dec. 1837; *Observer* (London), 31 Dec. 1837; *The Times*, 5 and 26 Jan. 1838; *Cambridge Chronicle*, 6 Jan. 1838; *John Bull*, 7 Jan. 1838; *Cheltenham Journal*, 8 Jan. 1838; *Bristol Gazette*, 10 Jan. 1838; *Preston Pilot*, 13 Jan. 1838; *Bath Herald*, 13 Jan. 1838; *Plymouth and Devonport Weekly Gazette*, 25 Jan. 1838; *Leicester Journal*, 26 Jan. 1838; *Norwich Mercury*, 3 Feb. 1838; *The Canadian Controversy; its origin, nature, and merits* (London, 1838), pp. 60–1.
[28]*Northampton Herald*, 10 Feb. 1838; also *Plymouth Herald*, 30 Dec. 1837; *Albion*, 1 Jan. 1838; *Bath Post*, 6 Jan. 1838; *Devonport Telegraph*, 13 Jan. and 17 Feb. 1838; *Coventry Standard*, 19 Jan. 1838; *Norfolk Chronicle*, 20 Jan. 1838; *Globe* (London), 25 Jan. 1838; *Hull Packet*, 26 Jan. 1838; *Stockport Advertiser*, 2 Feb. 1838; *Hints on the Government of Canada*, pp. 7–9.
[29]*Liverpool Mail*, 26 Dec. 1837; also *Whitehaven Herald*, 5 Jan. 1838; *Bath Post*, 10 Feb. 1838.

liberty, and of civilisation itself, could rejoice'.[30] In this task, Tories comforted themselves with the thought that the British public would display a thorough contempt for the unnatural sentiments of the philosophic radicals, those drawingroom revolutionaries 'who sympathise with every accession of democratic power, with every step towards republicanism and anarchy'.[31] Tories therefore confidently rejected the prediction that the English people would rush to the defence of Canadian rebels, and when events fully vindicated this confidence, caustic comparisons were drawn between the earlier boasts of the radicals and their subsequent shamefaced moderation.

The Whigs were uncomfortably caught in the crossfire between these two hostile outspoken extremes, and were thus subject to the criticisms of both for pursuing a policy that attempted to combine firmness with conciliation and steer between the twin hazards of retribution and surrender. Neither the exigencies of domestic politics nor the demands of their political philosophy required the Whigs to champion or to vilify the insurgents, while the responsibilities of office similarly encouraged ministers to persevere with a moderate, forbearing approach to the crisis. On some points Whigs found themselves in agreement with the Tories. With a preference for political gradualism and an inbred respect for the British constitution, the Whigs believed that the colonists had no excuse for resorting to force to redress grievances that could have been remedied through constitutional channels. While this response reflected the Whig temperament and tradition, it also provided an effective argument to vindicate past policy at a time when the ministry came under attack for its handling of Canadian disputes and for having precipitated the rebellions. Like their Tory critics, the Whigs blamed agitators for the uprisings and emphasised the restricted nature of the unrest; this had long been the explanation of colonial dissatisfaction favoured by Whig ministers in the years before discontent erupted into violence. Moreover, as the government of the day, the Whigs had a particular responsibility to put down colonial revolts wherever they challenged imperial authority. No ministry would be worth its salt or could hope to remain in office if it did not display a confident determination to suppress the rebellions with speed and vigour. If Britain 'took a timid and pusillanimous tone', Russell further pointed out, 'we should invite the aggression of foreign Powers' and should 'become accomplices in our own fall and degradation'.[32]

Once the outbreaks were extinguished, however, the Whigs expressed no desire for retribution and little sympathy for the vindictive sentiments that came so naturally to Tories. The Liverpool *Albion* welcomed the unanimity with which the press seemingly condemned the conduct of the

[30]*Morning Herald*, 2 Jan. 1838.
[31]*Bath Post*, 6 Jan. 1838.
[32]*Hansard*, 39, 22 Dec. 1837, 1501.

Canadians, but it noted a difference of approach between the two major parties. While the Tories 'appear to thirst for blood, and to desire the extermination of a misguided people, because they are capable of resisting power', the Whigs, 'when about to wield the rod, seem to remember, that the Canadians are fellow-men and fellow-citizens, whom, although they are obliged to chasten, they wish to bring back into the social circle'.[33] Ministerial supporters tended to regard the colonists as temporarily deluded by demagogues, and once the fighting was ended, the government had a duty to exercise generosity and recognise the political rights of the Canadians. The Tories, commented the *Welshman*, 'are as happy as ducks in a shower at this opportune bit of warfare', but Whigs rejected the argument that tranquillity in Canada depended on hanging every agitator and the security of British rule on proscribing the colonists' constitutional liberties.[34]

As might be expected of a party that spanned the central ground of politics, not all Whigs agreed that the government had handled the developing crisis in the most efficacious manner;[35] but there was unanimous rejection of the Tory charge that the ministry had not sufficiently anticipated the outbreak of violence in Canada and provided the colony with an adequate military force to meet the emergency. 'To anticipate rebellion', explained the *Courier*, 'is natural to the Tories who will govern only by the sword; but it would have been unnatural in the Whigs, whose principles of government are founded on the willing assent and obedience of the people.' With a reputedly loyal, peace-loving population in Canada, Whig ministers 'had no reason to feel the Tory fears, or act on Tory principles'.[36] Moreover, if the Russell Resolutions had been followed by the dispatch of troops and military preparations, aspersions would have been cast on the loyalty of colonists and popular unrest encouraged. Far from helping to settle disputes amicably, such an action would have afforded the Canadians an additional pretext, if not a full justification for revolt. 'It was something to have robbed revolt of all justification', applauded Edward Lytton Bulwer. 'Had you sent out troops as the heralds and carriers of your resolutions — had you by that parade of power, justly irritated the pride of men to whom you have communicated the jealous English spirit of liberty and honour ... you would have procured for them the popular sympathy of England' and the United States.[37] The Whigs further

---

[33]*Albion*, 1 Jan. 1838.

[34]*Welshman* (Carmarthen), 12 Jan. 1838; also *Courier* (London), 28 Dec. 1837.

[35]The *Liverpool Mercury*, 29 Dec. 1837, for example, criticised the lack of expedition in remedying colonial complaints, whereas the *Globe*, 2 Jan. 1838, regretted the irresolution shown in asserting British authority in Canada.

[36]*Courier*, 9 Jan. 1838; also *Philanthropist*, 28 Dec. 1837 and 8 Feb. 1838; *Sun* (London), 27 Dec. 1838; *Berwick Advertiser*, 13 Jan. 1838; *Glasgow Herald*, 19 Jan. 1838.

[37]*Hansard*, 40, 23 Jan. 1838, 397; also Glenelg, Melbourne, *ibid.*, 18 Jan. 1838, 172–3, 221; *Courier*, 20 Jan. 1838.

contended that Britain could not have quashed a widespread uprising by thousands of disaffected Englishmen determined to resist imperial authority, and military measures would have given the Canadian agitators the following they had so conspicuously lacked. The outcome of events appeared to vindicate the wisdom of the decision not to send additional troops, a decision that was broadly endorsed by the unrivalled military expertise of the Duke of Wellington, much to the Whigs' delight.[38] On this issue at least they seemed to have the better of the argument, and it strengthened their resolve to continue to approach the uncertain progress of events in Canada in a spirit of generous forbearance.

When Englishmen came to examine the causes and justification of the Canadian rebellions, there was scope for a considerable variety of views on particular issues but a fundamental division of opinion emerged between the radicals, who thought that the sum of colonial grievances justified an appeal to arms, and the broad mass of Tories and Whigs, who with differing emphases dismissed the uprisings as wholly unwarrantable. To the radicals, the controversy in the Canadas represented a political struggle between liberty and oppression, between democracy and aristocracy. The crisis could not be treated in isolation as a matter unconnected with British politics or remote from the interests of mankind, since it was a manifestation of a universal, continuing conflict over whether government should serve the interests of the few or the welfare of the many.[39] Like the earlier dispute with the American colonies, with which radicals persistently drew a parallel,[40] the Canadian struggle raised fundamental principles of concern for the people of communities throughout the civilised world.

The history of the Canadas had for years past witnessed a continuous struggle by the colonists to rid themselves of 'the unjust and insulting dominancy of the most wretched and contemptible of cliques that ever goaded and irritated a people'.[41] This insolent, domineering, irresponsible oligarchy of local tyrants controlled the councils, monopolised provincial patronage in the interests of its sycophants, and won over or cowed successive governors by threats to secure the recall of any administrator who displayed an inconvenient inclination towards impartiality or independence.[42]

[38]Lord Howick, E.S. Cayley, Sir George Grey, Glenelg, Wellington, *Hansard*, 40, 16 Jan. 1838, 85, 17 Jan. 1838, 111, 145, and 18 Jan. 1838, 171–2, 226–7.
[39]*Leeds Times*, 30 Dec. 1837; *Leicestershire Mercury*, 13 Jan. 1838; *Canadian Portfolio*, p. 150.
[40]D.W. Harvey, Hume, W.D. Gillon, *Hansard*, 39, 22 Dec. 1837, 1503–4, 40, 17 Jan. 1838, 134, 23 Jan. 1838, 526; *Spectator*, 30 Dec. 1837; *Liverpool Chronicle*, 30 Dec. 1837; *Bolton Free Press*, 6 Jan. 1838; *Northern Liberator* (Newcastle), 6 Jan. 1838; *Liverpool Mercury*, 12 Jan. 1838; *Canadian Portfolio*, pp. 3–4.
[41]*Northern Whig* (Belfast), 20 Jan. 1838.
[42]*Philanthropist*, 28 Dec. 1837; *North Wales Chronicle*, 9 Jan. 1838; *Cheltenham Free Press*, 27 Jan. 1838.

Although the colonies indeed possessed representative institutions, radicals believed that maladministration and injustice tended to thrive under the existing colonial system. Even if their intentions had been worthy, the imperial authorities could not 'prevent in so distant a colony as Canada the possession of power which might be turned to the private purposes of a small knot of individuals, of a little oligarchy, who govern under the name of the colonial office'.[43]

For reformers in Britain and Canada, the character and activities of the legislative council came to personify the evils of Canadian government and constitute the major, basic cause of rebellion in both provinces. According to the British architects of the constitution of 1791, the legislative council, as the upper house of a bicameral legislature, was designed to occupy a similar position to the House of Lords. Its members were regarded as an incipient colonial aristocracy whose political independence and social standing might provide stability in a country where politics were apt to be influenced by democratic or republican sentiments, as earlier experience with the American colonies seemed to show. Far from acting with impartial independence, however, the nominated legislative council had resolutely and scornfully thwarted the wishes of the people's representatives by obstructing the progress of all legislation passed by the assembly that did not harmonise with the selfish interests of the ruling junta.[44] Moreover, the materials for constructing an aristocracy in Canada simply did not exist; there was no class of inhabitants with sufficient wealth, rank, or distinction to constitute an aristocratic upper house that would carry political weight or command popular respect, and none could be created by legislative enactment in a country noted for its equal distribution of wealth. Whatever might be thought in England of the House of Lords, John Arthur Roebuck argued that an 'aristocracy is a social distinction; it is the growth of ages; it results from ancient national peculiarities, it cannot be brought into existence at a moment . . . you cannot force an aristocracy as you would force a cucumber'.[45] It was hardly surprising, therefore, that the contemptible mushroom aristocracy of Canada with its airs and pretensions had long been an abomination, or that the attempt to impose on the colonists institutions incompatible with local conditions had produced widespread discontent. British radicals drew the congenial conclusion, however, that the 'state of society in the colony. . . was essentially favourable to democratic institutions'.[46] With the ever-

---

[43]Grote, *Hansard*, 40, 16 Jan. 1838, 63; also Roebuck, defeated in the election of 1837, speaking before the bar of the House of Lords on behalf of Lower Canada, 5 Feb. 1838, *ibid.*, 736; *Manchester Times*, 13 Jan. 1838.
[44]Molesworth, *Hansard*, 39, 22 Dec. 1837, 1456; *Manchester and Salford Advertiser*, 27 Jan. 1838; *Examiner* (London), 31 Dec. 1837; 'Lord Durham and the Canadians', *London and Westminster Review*, XXVIII, (Jan. 1838), 522–3.
[45]*Hansard*, 40, 5 Feb. 1838, 747–8; also *Planet* (London, 31 Dec. 1837).
[46]Warburton, *ibid.*, 25 Jan. 1838, 479.

present example of the neighbouring United States and the contagious American love of liberty, radicals looked with hope and confidence to the eventual triumph of popular institutions in Canada.

As a means of remedying the present situation, radicals endorsed the insistent colonial demand that the legislative council should be made elective. They rejected the common accusation that the Canadians had taken up arms to accomplish a minor constitutional principle or vindicate 'merely a philosophical and abstract opinion'; few men would jeopardise their lives by going to war unless they were impelled by substantial, persistent, practical grievances.[47] As a fundamental source of colonial afflictions, only an organic change in the legislative council would effectively destroy the power of the oligarchy and enable the upper house to fulfil honestly and acceptably the constitutional functions assigned it. The British government had acknowledged the deficiencies of the council, but with the failure to reform it satisfactorily by better appointments, the colonists had naturally turned to a system of elective councils under which the Americans had long flourished.[48] Far less prominence was given by the radicals to the demand for a colonial executive responsible to the local assembly. With the publication of Lord Durham's Report in 1839 'responsible government' became the major plank in the programme of radicals and reformers, but Canadian assemblies had hitherto given pride of place in their catalogue of grievances to requests for an elective legislative council, and this was particularly true of Lower Canada which remained for Englishmen of all political persuasions at the forefront of the present crisis. For the moment, therefore, British radicals maintained that colonial governments might most effectively be brought into harmony with the interests of the people by giving the same party a majority in both houses of the legislature.

In view of the radicals' unshakable conviction that colonial controversy had political causes, the same reasoning might be applied equally to Lower and Upper Canada, even though the assembly in the former province was dominated by French Canadians. Such a view neglected the tendency of the English minority to regard the upper house as a defender of its sectional interests; but radicals rejected the argument that an elective council could not be conceded in a colony where the inhabitants were divided by ethnic and religious distinctions, lest it lead to the triumph of the French party at the expense of English settlers.[49] Precisely

---

[47]Harvey, *ibid.*, 39, 22 Dec. 1837, 1502–3; also *Birmingham Journal*, 6 Jan. 1838; *Bradford Observer*, 8 Feb. 1838.

[48]Grote, Roebuck, *Hansard*, 40, 16 Jan. 1838, 61–2, and 5 Feb. 1838, 749. Charles Villiers also pointed to municipal reform in Britain and the Whig ministry's advocacy of popular control as the basis of local government, *ibid.*, 25 Jan. 1838, 522.

[49]Hume, *ibid.*, 16 Jan. 1838, 44; 'Lord Durham and the Canadians', *loc. cit.*, 524–5.

the same excuse was used to deny Ireland good municipal government, and radicals generously insisted that in both countries the people should enjoy equal rights as individuals irrespective of religious or cultural differences. Charles Villiers rightly, if somewhat naively, asserted 'that it was by recognising these distinctions by law that they were perpetuated; and that it was by making the law equal, and not in recognising such difference, that it was found, that they merged in the common interest, and that one race and one religion, instantly trusted and lived in communion with the other'.[50]

Since the radicals interpreted the dispute in Lower Canada as a controversy over political principles, they strenuously denied the assertion of Tories and Whigs that it could be attributed to ethnic or national antagonisms. 'The struggle', protested the *Spectator*, 'is pronounced to be one between the French and English inhabitants; while it is in reality a struggle between the majority contending for right and liberty, and the minority contending for despotism and the wrong of which it is in the profitable enjoyment.'[51] Here was a typical example of the kind of specious argument maliciously invented and assiduously propagated by opponents of the Canadian people as a pretext for rejecting demands that were so plainly based on principles of justice that every unprejudiced Englishman would otherwise at once endorse them. While there was indeed an English party in Lower Canada, radicals explained that its only resemblance to the majority of British settlers was the English tongue. Like the Orange faction in Ireland, this clique of cunning, unscrupulous men sought to retain power by disgracefully exploiting national antipathies and appealing to odious passions and mischievous prejudices. Molesworth 'felt ashamed and humiliated that in this, the nineteenth century, he should have to combat and denounce antipathies arising out of the difference of race', but a real danger existed that this insidious propaganda might encourage the British government to undertake a crusade against political liberty in the colony on the pretext that the disgruntled colonists were French by descent and Catholic by religion.[52]

Radicals also pointed to the earlier cooperation and amity amongst Canadians from different ethnic backgrounds. British members had been returned to the assembly from French-speaking areas of the province and many had regularly voted with the popular party.[53] It was simply playing on unreasonable fears to assert that concessions to the lower house or the withdrawal of British protection would mean the surrender of English

---

[50]*Hansard*, 40, 25 Jan. 1838, 523.
[51]*Spectator*, 30 Dec. 1837; also *Leeds Times*, 30 Dec. 1837; *Star in the East* (Wisbech), 6 Jan. 1838; *Manchester and Salford Advertiser*, 6 Jan. 1838.
[52]*Hansard*, 40, 23 Jan. 1838, 381–2; also *Planet,* 31 Dec. 1837.
[53]It was also noted English and Irish settlers had been involved in a rebellion that was not exclusively confined to the French party. *Birmingham Journal*, 6 Jan. 1838; *Bristol Mercury*, 6 Jan. 1838; *Canadian Portfolio*, p. 150.

colonists to the tyranny and prejudices of the French.[54] The assembly had not acted capriciously in the past; there was no reason why responsible political leaders like Papineau should show hatred or malice towards English inhabitants in the future. The radicals condemned the prevalence of anti-French sentiments, the depreciation of French culture, and the tendency to treat the French Canadians as 'aliens in blood, aliens in language, and aliens in religion'.[55] In their defence of the colonists against the common but malevolent charge of being 'a bigoted and ignorant people, stupidly and slavishly attached to ancient and barbarous feudal customs and privileges',[56] radicals criticised both the misconception of the *habitant* as a European serf and the fallacy of equating education with the ability to read and write. As his own master, the small agricultural proprietor in North America acquired the habit of independent thought and action, which made him disinclined to show a blind obedience to the authority of seigneur and priest or to the propaganda of demagogues.[57]

Similarly, when the radicals turned from explaining the causes of colonial unrest to justifying the actions of the Lower Canadian assembly, they felt compelled to reject a variety of disparaging assertions. To deaden English sympathies, Roebuck complained, the 'wildest stories, the foulest calumnies, have been unhesitatingly used to blacken the character of the Assembly, and to induce the people of this country to look upon them as a factious set of unprincipled demagogues'.[58] It was false to claim that agitators had stirred up discontent; this had long been widespread amongst the inhabitants and the assembly faithfully reflected the popular unrest.[59] Furthermore, contrary to Tory allegations, the assembly's demands were reasonable and fully in accord with British parliamentary precedents. Like all popular bodies, the Lower Canadian legislature might occasionally have acted doggedly, even domineeringly, but it was both a legitimate aspiration and an effective means of remedying long-standing abuses for the lower house to appropriate provincial revenues and influence the composition and policies of the colonial executive.

For many years the Canadians had patiently petitioned for the redress of certain notorious fully documented grievances, trusting to the justice of their case and the generosity of England. But while some grievances were acknowledged, colonial demands were neglected or treated as unreasonable. Eventually, in despair at the fruitlessness of supplication

---

[54]Edward Baines, Villiers, *Hansard*, 40, 25 Jan. 1838, 512, 525; *Leeds Mercury*, 6 Jan. 1838; 'Lord Durham and the Canadians', *loc. cit.*, 525, 529–30.

[55]*Spectator*, 30 Dec. 1837; *Weetily Dispatch* (London), 7 Jan. 1838.

[56]Molesworth, *Hansard*, 40, 23 Jan. 1838, 382. Also Gillon, *ibid.*, 25 Jan. 1838, 528; *Canadian Portfolio*, p. 61; 'Lord Durham and the Canadians', *loc. cit.*, 525–6.

[57]Roebuck, *Hansard*, 40, 5 Feb. 1838, 763–4.

[58]*Ibid.*, 737.

[59]Warburton, *ibid.*, 25 Jan. 1838, 477; *Leicestershire Mercury*, 13 Jan. 1838; *Canadian Portfolio*, p. 2.

and remonstrance, the Lower Canadian assembly was compelled to resort to the legal power of refusing to vote money for the local administration until certain demands were met. According to the constitution granted by England in 1791, the lower house indisputably possessed the right to vote or withhold supplies at pleasure, and the imperial authorities were not competent to judge whether that right had been exercised at the proper time or in the proper manner. As Roebuck pointed out, 'we gave them with our eyes open a discretionary power, and we are not justified in quarrelling with their use of it'. The radicals therefore denied the charge that the assembly had wantonly abused its power of the purse to accomplish an organic reform in the legislative council and then sought to destroy the constitution of the province when its demands were not conceded.[60]

With this vindication of the assembly's right to stop the supplies, radicals went on to argue that it was the British government that had first violated the Canadian constitution. When the lower house persisted in its chosen course of action, ministers transformed this into a plea of unmanageableness, and on that pretext persuaded parliament in March 1837 to endorse a string of uncompromising resolutions which not only rejected colonial demands for reform but violated and made a mockery of the provincial constitution. The assembly's capacity for self-defence was destroyed with the suspension of its constitutional right to refuse the supplies, and insult was added to injury by the British government's decision to appropriate funds in the colonial treasury for arrears of official salaries in direct opposition to the wishes of the lower house.[61] In the view of the radicals, Russell's Resolutions were 'the first, the most flagrant, violent, breach of the constitution', accomplished by the very people whose primary duty should have been to ensure that the constitution was strictly upheld.[62] Here was an indefensible 'act of pure despotism', a *rank, barefaced, impudent robbery'*, that had not the remotest connection with the questions of whether an elective council should be conceded or whether the assembly had acted wisely in stopping the supplies.[63]

By this reckless attempt to coerce the Canadians, the radicals charged, the British government had driven the colonists in desperation at the futility of peaceful petitioning to the last resource of free men: that of asserting their rights and defending their liberties with their arms. In answer to the accusation that the colonists had rebelled without cause,

---

[60]*Hansard*, 40, 5 Feb. 1838, 749–50; also Leader, Hume, *ibid.*, 39, 22 Dec. 1837, 1432, 40, 17 Jan. 1838, 138; *Spectator*, 27 Jan. 1838; *Nottingham Review*, 2 Feb. 1838; *Bradford Observer*, 8 Feb. 1838; 'Lord Durham and the Canadians', *loc. cit.*, 515–16.

[61]Leader, Hume, Dillon Browne, Gillon, *Hansard*, 39, 22 Dec. 1837, 1432, 1444–5, 1447, 40, 17 Jan. 1838, 120, 25 Jan. 1838, 526; *Examiner*, 31 Dec. 1837.

[62]Roebuck, *ibid.*, 40, 5 Feb. 1838, 754; also *Somerset County Gazette*, 30 Dec. 1837; *Bath Guardian*, 13 Jan. 1838; *Canadian Portfolio*, pp. 19–20; 'Lord Durham and the Canadians', *loc. cit.*, 514–15.

[63]*Northern Whig*, 20 Jan. 1838, and *Birmingham Journal*, 30 Dec. 1837.

radicals maintained that in British aggression could be found sufficient ground for the revolt of a civilised people, if any justification had ever existed for claiming the common rights of humanity.[64] Britain had confronted the Canadians with an inescapable dilemma:

> either to submit to the resolutions and be slaves, or to resist them and run the risk of civil war. In this dilemma, they made that choice which would be made by every people who had once enjoyed any portion of freedom — they determined on resistance. They would have been despicable, and the English people would have been the first to despise them, if taking the other alternative, they had tamely submitted to injustice and oppression.[65]

There were times when opposition to tyranny became a virtue as well as a necessity. In defence of the principles of a free constitution, Molesworth claimed 'not only was rebellion justifiable, but resistance became the sacred and imperious duty of freemen — a duty which all who belonged to our race, whether on this or the other side of the Atlantic — all in whose veins English blood had circulated, had never failed to fulfil'.[66] Faced with the same threat, Englishmen would have acted precisely as the Canadians had done; where did the colonists learn to resist despotism the radicals enquired, if not from their British heritage? Moreover, was a country that supported the struggles for freedom in Greece, Belgium, Poland, and South America prepared to deny assistance to Canada? Would Englishmen refuse the Canadians, to whom they had already granted considerable liberty, the right of enjoying all the advantages that arose out of popular institutions? 'If there is any general principle of human right and liberty on which Englishmen are agreed', proclaimed the *Leeds Mercury*, 'it is this, that a nation has a right to choose its own government.'[67] Radical newspapers like the *Bradford Observer* insisted that the wishes of the Canadians should be paramount because the will of the people was the ultimate sovereignty, and this argument applied as much to a colony as to any other country. Britain did not have the right, on the grounds of conquest or imperial superintendence, to determine what form of government was best for Canadians.[68]

Indeed, according to the radicals, whether Englishmen thought colonial claims reasonable and colonial actions justified was largely beside the point: the crucial matter was what the colonists themselves thought and

---

[64]Hume, *Hansard*, 40, 16 Jan. 1838, 54; *Spectator*, 23 Dec. 1837; *Leeds Times*, 30 Dec. 1837 and 27 Jan. 1838; *Gateshead Observer*, 30 Dec. 1837; *Northern Liberator*, 6 Jan. 1838; *Liverpool Mercury*, 19 Jan. 1838; *Nottingham Review*, 26 Jan. 1838; *Cheltenham Free Press*, 27 Jan. 1838.

[65]Leader, *Hansard*, 39, 22 Dec. 1837, 1433.

[66]*Ibid.*, 1457; also Hume, *ibid.*, 1449, and 40, 17 Jan. 1838, 130; *Somerset County Gazette*, 30 Dec. 1837; *Liverpool Chronicle*, 13 Jan. 1838.

[67]*Leeds Mercury*, 30 Dec. 1837.

[68]*Bradford Observer*, 8 Feb. 1838; also *Leeds Times*, 6 Jan. 1838.

resolved to do about their predicament. The outcome of the uprisings would in any case determine the reputation of the act: if defeated, the colonists would be denounced as rebels; if triumphant, history would praise them as patriots who spurned tyranny and nobly threw off the yoke of an imperial power that dared to trample on their constitutional rights.[69] Yet radicals took comfort from the thought that even the speedy defeat of the insurgents in Canada would not necessarily mean that their cause had been wholly unjustifiable. The shock of the rebellions might also for the first time successfully focus public attention in England on the causes of Canadian discontent and on the evils of the colonial system in a way that peaceful protest and constitutional remonstrance had signally failed to do; that result would be a tangible gain.[70]

In contrast to the radicals, Tories and Whigs argued that the colonists were not justified in resorting to rebellion, though the arguments used to reach this common conclusion were not identical. Tories denied that the Canadians suffered from any practical grievances. No valid reason or colourable pretext for an appeal to arms could exist in a colony where there was no repression, where persons and property were secure, and where the law was duly administered. 'Nowhere', asserted G.F. Young, 'in the pages of history, was there recorded a single instance of a revolt having taken place with so little even of the shadow of a justification upon the part of the insurgents.'[71] Far from suffering from grievances, the Canadians gained positive benefits from British rule: they were afforded ample protection free of cost and they enjoyed the 'most perfect religious and social freedom'. The revolts savoured more of colonial ingratitude than imperial oppression.[72]

The Whigs arrived at similar conclusion by a more moderate and sympathetic route. They were prepared to admit that the colonists suffered to a greater or less degree from certain genuine grievances, such as the abuse of patronage and the unsatisfactory composition of the legislative council; but these minor irritations did not warrant a recourse to rebellion, an

---

[69]*Preston Observer*, 6 Jan. 1838; *Liverpool Mercury*, 19 Jan. 1838; *Star in the East*, 20 Jan. 1838; Hume, *Hansard*, 40, 17 Jan. 1838, 133.

[70]*Spectator*, 6 Jan. 1838; *Leicestershire Mercury*, 13 Jan. 1838; *Bath and Cheltenham Gazette*, 20 Feb. 1838.

[71]*Hansard*, 40, 25 Jan. 1838, 509; also Gladstone, Borthwick, W. Clay, Aberdeen, *ibid.*, 39, 22 Dec. 1837, 1454, 40, 17 Jan. 1838, 117, 125, and 2 Feb. 1838, 649; *Manchester Guardian*, 27 Dec. 1837; *Leeds Intelligencer*, 30 Dec. 1837; *Cumberland Pacquet*, 2 Jan. 1838; *Newcastle Journal*, 20 Jan. 1838.

[72]*Morning Advertiser*, 9 Jan. 1838; also Sir James Carnac, *Hansard*, 40, 16 Jan. 1838, 58; *Wheeler's Manchester Chronicle*, 30 Dec. 1837; *Cheltenham Journal*, 1 Jan. 1838; *Liverpool Courier*, 3 Jan. 1838; *Albion*, 25 Dec. 1837; *Welshman*, 2 Feb 1838; *Hints on the Government of Canada*, p. 30; *A Plain Statement of the Quarrel with Canada; in which is considered who first infringed the constitution of the colony* (London, 1838), pp. 4–5.

extreme step that did not appeal to Whig constitutionalists.[73] Given the sedulous, persevering desire of recent ministries to remove abuses and meet the wishes of colonists, the political problems of the Canadas could with patience and reasonableness on both sides have been resolved within the framework of the existing constitution. Yet the assemblies, particularly that of Lower Canada, had responded to imperial concessions and a genuine spirit of conciliation by inventing imaginary grievances and resorting to extreme demands designed to throw off the authority of the mother country. Such an irrational reaction was unlikely to elicit for the rebels much sympathy from patriotic Englishmen. Whigs felt obliged to avow their hostility to arbitrary power and their support for all people struggling for political rights, but this avowal generally prefaced the declaration that the Canadians had not made out a sufficiently convincing case to bring them within the pale of British sympathy.[74] In striking contrast to the American Revolution, Whigs and Tories agreed that the Canadian rebellions did not involve the noble cause of liberty and were '*not* consecrated by any great principle pervading society, — which is the only justification of resistance to government'.[75]

As a further part of their common ground, Tories and Whigs traced the origins of the uprisings to the selfish ambitions of agitators. In Lower Canada a 'few factious scoundrels' led by Papineau had 'managed, by lying and delusion, to inflame an ignorant populace into outrage and sedition'.[76] This comforting explanation was reinforced when news reached England of the limited nature of the revolts. Contrary to some initial reports and the boasts of radicals, open disaffection in the province had been confined to the Montreal area and English settlers had everywhere remained loyal. Even the vast majority of French Canadians had lived up to their reputation for docility and displayed little open aversion to British rule; the *habitants'* only crimes had been those of gullibility and gross ignorance of their true interests.[77] In Upper Canada, the rebels could not plausibly claim to be the champions of popular grievances,

[73]Russell, Glenelg, *Hansard*, 40, 16 Jan. 1838, 11–12, and 18 Jan. 1838, 165; *Wisbech Gazette*, 13 Jan. 1838, *Huntingdon, Bedford, and Peterborough Gazette*, 13 Jan. 1838; *Devonport Telegraph*, 13 Jan. 1838; *Nottingham and Newark Mercury*, 20 Jan. 1838; *Coventry Herald*, 26 Jan. 1838.

[74]Glenelg, Melbourne, Lord Lansdowne, *Hansard*, 40, 18 Jan. 1838, 167, 218, 238; *Canadian Controversy*, p. 32; *Liverpool Journal*, 23 Dec. 1837; *Morning Chronicle* (London), 25 Dec. 1837; *Sun*, 29 Dec. 1837; *Courier*, 3 Jan. 1838; *Dublin Evening Post*, 20 Jan. 1838; *Philanthropist*, 25 Jan. 1838.

[75]*Preston Chronicle*, 20 Jan. 1838; Also *Morning Chronicle*, 12 Jan. 1838.

[76]*Liverpool Courier*, 30 Jan. 1838; also Peel, Wellington, Russell, *Hansard*, 40, 16 Jan. 1838, 78, 18 Jan. 1838, 225, and 26 Jan. 1838, 547; *Courier*, 23 Dec. 1837; *Naval and Military Gazette*, 30 Dec. 1837 and 13 Jan. 1838; *Cambridge Chronicle*, 6 Jan. 1838; *Sunderland Beacon*, 17 Jan. 1838; *Liverpool Times*, 30 Jan. 1838.

[77]Grey, Young, Peel, Aberdeen, *Hansard*, 39, 22 Dec. 1837, 1468, 1479–80, 40, 16 Jan. 1838, 79, 2 Feb. 1838, 649; *Liverpool Courier*, 10 Jan. 1838; *Canadian Controversy*, pp. 40–1.

because the outbreak was easily suppressed by the unassisted efforts of the people. Englishmen cursorily dismissed the disturbances in the upper province as a feeble gesture by a few misguided hotheads and anticipated no threat to British rule from a colony where the inhabitants were over-whelmingly British in origin and therefore unquestionably loyal to the imperial connection. Elsewhere in British North America colonists had at numerous public meetings recorded their decided attachment to the British constitution and the mother country.

In the view of Tories and Whigs, the designs of agitators were reflected in the outrageous pretensions of the Canadian assemblies. Not content with the exploitation of their own rights and privileges, the lower houses had wanted to encroach on those of the other branches of the local legisla-tures by the creation of elective legislative councils, a usurpation of power that would have violated the provincial constitutions. Whigs stressed the need for a division of powers to keep the elements of monarchy, aristocracy, and democracy in a proper equilibrium; if one was allowed to preponderate, the rights of the rest would be invaded and the balance of the constitution overthrown. One branch of the legislature did not have the right to seize the authority and destroy the independence of another branch, thus making itself the sole repository of the power of the state.[78] The demand for an elective council, especially when coupled with that for a responsible executive, appeared a covert attempt to establish the constitution for an independent state rather than a means of removing practical grievances.

Furthermore, Whigs and Tories noted that when the British govern-ment rejected these pretensions, the Lower Canadian assembly wantonly employed its power of the purse to embarrass public affairs and bring the local administration to a halt. Like its analogue, the British House of Commons, the provincial lower house possessed the right to stop the supplies, but neither body was entitled to abuse that power. 'The pri-vileges of a popular assembly', the *Standard* explained, 'are, like the pre-rogatives of the Crown, given, in the first place, to be used in carrying on the ordinary government; in the next place, for *defence*, but never for *aggression*.' The provincial assembly had violated both criteria: it had thrown the whole machinery of government into disorder and had un-constitutionally used its financial powers for an attack on the authority of other branches of the legislature.[79] Financial control had not been given to colonial assemblies 'to enable them to refuse those supplies when they could not carry any political object on which they had set their hearts', and certainly not as a weapon to accomplish organic changes in the

---

[78]Carnac, Lord Mansfield, Melbourne, *Hansard*, 40, 16 Jan. 1838, 57, 8 Feb. 1838, 855, and 2 Feb. 1838, 687; *Globe*, 25 Dec. 1837; *Liverpool Mail*, 19 Dec. 1837.
[79]*Standard*, 11 Jan. 1838; also Lansdowne, Sugden, *Hansard*, 40, 18 Jan. 1838, 240, 23 Jan. 1838, 414; *Plain Statement of the Quarrel with Canada*, pp. 11–12.

constitution of 1791.[80] It was not a legitimate exercise of its constitutional privileges, Sir E.B. Sugden asserted for the assembly to refuse the supplies for 'an indirect purpose, not for the redress of any wrong, but for the assertion of a right which did not belong to them, and which, if conceded, would destroy the connexion between this country and the Canadas'.[81]

Critics of the assembly therefore concluded that its leaders, and not the British government, had first violated and suspended the Canadian constitution.[82] According to this process of reasoning, the ministry's threatened appropriation of provincial revenues represented the resumption of a privilege that had been abused. In an extremity the imperial authorities had been forced to intervene in order to restore the operation of government and rescue public officials from financial embarrassment. This intervention, Russell argued, 'was no act of oppression upon our part; it was not a measure of finance, but a measure of defence', to prevent the continued refusal of supplies for four years from throwing the colony into anarchy.[83]

Among the specific demands of the colonial agitators, both Whigs and Tories singled out for special criticism the proposal for an elective legislative council. Few English observers discerned any positive merits in the present Canadian upper houses or applauded the way they had discharged their functions,[84] and most agreed that the attempt to establish aristocratic chambers in the Canadas had been unrealistic. Nevertheless, there was a fear that elective councils would have deleterious consequences for the internal administration of the provinces. The upper house would thereby become a mere echo of the assembly and thus the agency of a faction, 'not an engine of popular Government, but a tool of factious greediness and ambition'.[85] The ability of the executive to hold a balance between com-

---

[80]Lansdowne, *Hansard*, 40, 18 Jan. 1838, 239; also Clay, Peel, *ibid.*, 17 Jan. 1838, 125, and 23 Jan. 1838, 447.

[81]*Ibid.*, 23 Jan. 1838, 414; also *The Times*, 5 Jan. 1838; *Preston Chronicle*, 27 Jan. 1838; *Canadian Controversy*, pp. 49–50; *Plain Statement of the Quarrel with Canada*, pp. 8–11; *Canada. From the Foreign Quarterly Review*, XLI (London, [1838]), pp. 15–18.

[82]Russell, *Hansard*, 40, 16 Jan. 1838, 27; *Coventry Standard*, 2 Feb. 1838; *Globe*, 25 Dec. 1837.

[83]*Hansard*, 39, 22 Dec. 1837, 1499; also Peel, Melbourne, *ibid.*, 40, 23 Jan. 1838, 477, and 2 Feb. 1838, 687; *Morning Chronicle*, 27 Dec. 1837; *Huntingdon, Bedford, and Peterborough Gazette*, 13 Jan. 1838; *Liverpool Times*, 30 Jan. 1838; *Canadian Controversy*, p. 47; *Plain Statement of the Quarrel with Canada*, p. 12.

[84]Gladstone wholeheartedly defended the legislative council and denied that any charges against them had been substantiated. *Hansard*, 40, 23 Jan. 1838, 425–6. Another commentator considered an aristocratic chamber valuable for moderating democracy and giving due weight to the property and intelligence of the upper classes, especially in a colony where the electoral system favoured the uneducated masses. *Canada. From the Foreign Quarterly Review*, p. 31.

[85]*The Times*, 27 Jan. 1838; also *Wheeler's Manchester Chronicle*, 30 Dec. 1837; *Evening Packet* (Dublin), 25 Jan. 1838; *A Few Words on the Subject of Canada* (London, 1837), pp. 16–17.

peting interests, administer impartial justice, and defend the rights of person and property would be seriously undermined. This argument applied with particular force to Lower Canada, where the population was divided into antagonistic ethnic groups and where English settlers regarded the legislative council as a constitutional bulwark for the defence of their interests against the power of a French assembly. 'I am against the elective principle in the Council', confessed Thomas Spring Rice, 'thinking it would make Papineau supreme, & enable him to tyrannise over the British Canadians', or at least provoke a civil war.[86]

These arguments were decisively reinforced by British domestic and imperial considerations. An elective council, with its close similarity to the republican institutions of the United States and its democratic over-tones, was anathema to Whigs and Tories with their deep respect for monarchy and the British constitution. Not only should the institutions of the mother country be encouraged throughout the empire, but, more crucially, an elective upper house in Canada might be used as a precedent or additional argument for a reform of the House of Lords. This was a sensitive issue in domestic politics at a time when the Lords were under fire for adopting what radicals and many moderate Whigs regarded as a partisan, obstructionist attitude towards the legislative proposals of the Whig ministry. Tories therefore were not surprised to find the demand for an elective council supported by radicals and other 'disaffected and grovelling blockheads in Britain', who ardently wished to destroy the House of Lords as the principal obstruction to the spread of republican and revolutionary ideas.[87]

A more widespread and decisive criticism was that an elective council would be incompatible with the maintenance of British supremacy in a colonial dependency and with the relationship that must exist between colony and parent state. Whether or not Lower Canada and the other North American provinces eventually became independent communities, for the moment the protection of British interests and the responsibility for defending Canada gave the metropolitan government a right of control. If an elective council was conceded, imperial authority would be fatally undermined because the Canadians would then in practice possess 'the power of choosing, when it may be the most convenient for them, to abrogate every vestige of the Sovereignty claimed by England, under the

---

[86]Rice to Howick, 5 Jan. 1838, Grey Papers 1 Monteagle. Edward Ellice thought that an elective council might have been conceded in Upper Canada, but in the lower province this reform would have meant an abandonment of British settlers and domination of the St Lawrence navigation by the French. Ellice to Russell, 7 Jan. 1838, Russell Papers, PRO 30/22/3A, f. 43. Also *Manchester Courier*, 30 Dec. 1837; *Liverpool Times*, 2 Jan. 1838; *Durham Advertiser*, 5 Jan. 1838; *Canadian Controversy*, pp. 38–40.

[87]*Liverpool Mail*, 19 Dec. 1837; also *Cheltenham Journal*, 1 Jan. 1838; *Hints on the Government of Canada*, pp. 17–18.

triple right of conquest, treaty, and possession'.[88] The Canadas would to all intents and purposes at once become totally independent of Britain, for a 'Legislative Council which should harmonize with M. PAPINEAU must be one which, so far as in it lay, would dissolve the whole frame of civil government in the province, throw off the supremacy of Queen VICTORIA's crown, and dismember the British empire'.[89]

The validity of these conclusions was reinforced by the belief that the contemporaneous demand for an executive council responsible to the assembly, and removable at the pleasure of the lower house and not of the crown, was equally inconsistent with the preservation of British authority. *The Times* maintained that 'these two claims together amount to an entire overthrow of the relations between a colonial dependency and the parent state'.[90] Although most Englishmen failed to appreciate the precise character of responsible government as it was demanded by Canadian reformers, cabinet government as practised in Britain could not be conceded to a subordinate colony, because the governor, as representative of the crown, could not be responsible to the assembly for his actions and at the same time carry out orders from his superiors in London. With a local executive dependent on the majority in the assembly, laws might be passed that ran directly counter to the honour of the crown or to the interests of Britain. In these circumstances, the assembly would be no longer a colonial but an independent legislature.[91]

The conclusion drawn by most critics of the Lower Canadian assembly was that the extremists wished to monopolise political power in order to throw off colonial dependence and demolish the last remnants of imperial authority, an objective finally made explicit with the outbreak of rebellion.[92] The assembly's leaders had not been genuinely interested in constitutional reform; their claims had been fraudulently designed to attain an unacknowledged, disguised objective that had nothing to do with remedying the grievances of the Canadian people.[93] Not surprisingly, the greater the British government's willingness to remove abuses and make concessions, the more extreme and clamorous the demands of the popular party had

[88]*Sun*, 29 Dec. 1837.
[89]*The Times*, 25 Jan. 1838; also Aberdeen, Lord Ashburton, *Hansard*, 40, 2 Feb. 1838, 663, and 8 Feb. 1838, 848; *Devonport Telegraph*, 13 Jan. 1838; *Morning Herald*, 3 Feb. 1838; *Few Words on the Subject of Canada*, pp. 15–17.
[90]*The Times*, 15 Jan. 1838; also Melbourne, *Hansard*, 40, 2 Feb. 1838, 687; *Morning Chronicle*, 23 Dec. 1837; *Canadian Controversy*, pp. 32–3.
[91]Russell, Sugden, *Hansard*, 39, 22 Dec. 1837, 1499, and 40, 23 Jan. 1838, 409–10; *Bath Post*, 6 Jan. 1838.
[92]Glenelg, *Hansard*, 40, 18 Jan. 1838, 167; *Morning Chronicle*, 23 and 28 Dec. 1837; *The Times*, 23 Dec. 1837; *Globe*, 2 Jan. 1838; *Caledonian Mercury* (Edinburgh), 20 Jan. 1838; *Northampton Mercury*, 20 Jan. 1838; *Morning Herald*, 3 Feb. 1838; *Canadian Controversy*, pp. 59–60.
[93]Russell, Cayley, Wharncliffe, *Hansard*, 39, 22 Dec. 1837, 1499, 40. 17 Jan. 1838, 111, and 2 Feb. 1838, 702; *Plymouth and Devonport Weekly Journal*, 4 Jan. 1838; *Atlas* (London), 7 Jan. 1838.

become. 'The truth was', Lord Glenelg confessed, 'that the leaders of the House of Assembly were not disposed to acquiesce in any proposition which did not involve a surrender of the province.'[94] Now that the hidden purposes of Canadian agitation had become fully apparent, many Whigs could find less sympathy for the colonists than had earlier been possible when popular rights had seemingly been at stake.

Those Englishmen who rejected the desirability of colonial independence argued that the Canadian rebels had failed to appreciate the true nature of imperial relations. The British empire was not 'a loose federation of separate states, like that of the American Union', nor did 'the British constitution recognise, either at home or in the colonies, assemblies co-ordinate — co-extensive in powers with the Imperial Parliament'. On the contrary, the 'colonial connexion supposes some degree of dependence, some degree of supremacy in the old, of subordination in the young, community. This is what is not understood by the simple *habitants*; their crafty leaders have persuaded them they can eat their cake, and have it too—be subjects, and masters.'[95] In a dependency where British capital was extensively invested, where British emigration and commerce had introduced new sources of wealth, and where the inhabitants were not required to defend themselves, British rule appeared essential for the protection and promotion of imperial interests. In return for these positive benefits, the Tory *Standard* believed that the colonist could be required to surrender

> such portion of the right of government as shall make it worth the care of the metropolitan country to protect its dependencies . . . the party by whose fleets and armies he is protected — by whose commerce he is enriched — by whose intelligence he is informed, and who is interested *even more than* he is in the general prosperity of the colony, shall have a voice in its government.'[96]

The selfish interests of colonists had thus to be subordinated to the welfare of the empire at large, and only the imperial authorities could ensure harmony where the two came into conflict. According to Sir James Carnac's understanding of Anglo-Canadian relations, the 'object to be had in view at present was, to uphold the dignity, the honour, and the well-being of the British Crown and the British nation. Canada was undoubtedly entitled to be well governed; but the former consideration should be the first.'[97]

Some extreme Tories further argued that as a conquered colony Lower

---

[94]*Hansard*, 40, 18 Jan. 1838, 169; also *Newcastle Chronicle*, 20 Jan. 1838; *Morning Chronicle*, 14 March 1838.
[95]*Globe*, 25 Dec. 1837 and 2 Jan. 1838; also *Standard*, 4 Jan. 1838; *Devonport Telegraph*, 13 Jan. 1838; *Canadian Controversy*, pp. 47–9.
[96]*Standard*, 28 Dec. 1837; also *A Few Words on the Subject of Canada*, pp. 5, 51.
[97]*Hansard*, 40, 16 Jan. 1838, 58.

Canada possessed no political rights except those guaranteed at the time of its submission or later graciously conceded by the victor. Self-government was not applicable to a colony; its inhabitants were bound to accept the form of constitution bestowed by Britain. Sugden suggested that 'the Canadians should recollect that the British Crown was the superior; that we had by conquest, by treaty, and by possession, the right, which no doubt should ever be exercised for their benefit, of Sovereign dominion over the colony'.[98] In an extremist outburst the *Morning Advertiser* asserted that 'Canada is not an integral part of the British Empire. . . . It is a country subdued and surrendered — its people the *subjects* of Great Britain, but *not participators in the privileges and rights which belong to them*, and Great Britain, according to the recognized law of nations . . . may deal with them as she or her Administrations may please.'[99] Several newspapers, even some of a Tory outlook, protested against the expression of such foolish sentiments. If any attempt was made to govern Canada as a conquered country, it would lead to the loss of the colony. Not only would such a policy preclude a community of interests and willing allegiance, but loyal British settlers expected constitutional government through representative institutions.[100]

Despite the debate over political principles, only radicals persisted in advancing a constitutional interpretation of the rebellions. Whigs and Tories might denounce the activities of agitators and demagogues, but they maintained that the struggle in Lower Canada had its origins in ethnic, cultural, and national antagonisms and was not fundamentally a constitutional dispute. 'It cannot be too much impressed on the British public', emphasised the *Morning Chronicle*, 'that the contest in Lower Canada is really between the men of French and the men of British descent.'[101] The Whig ministry had held this view since the crisis began to intensify during the 1830s, though ministers in their public pronouncements phrased their explanations in more moderate, statesmanlike terms than many of their supporters in parliament and in the press. With a wide franchise and an electoral system that gave due weight to numbers, the basic constitutional clash between assembly and council had been aggravated and embittered by the fact that the French Canadians, who represented more than three-fourths of the provincial population, dominated the lower house, while English settlers found their power base in the upper house and the executive. Despite numerical inferiority, superior commercial

---

[98]*Ibid.*, 23 Jan. 1838, 408; also *Tyne Mercury*, 30 Jan. 1838.
[99]*Morning Advertiser*, 4 Jan. 1838.
[100]For example, the Tory *Liverpool Times*, 30 Jan. 1838, and the radical *Preston Observer*, 6 Jan. 1838.
[101]*Morning Chronicle*, 28 Dec. 1837.

enterprise had given the English an ascendancy which threatened the French hope of preserving their cultural identity in an Anglo-Saxon environment and of constituting one day an independent republic. In the conduct of this fight to retain or achieve supremacy, Whigs and Tories noted a strange paradox: the socially conservative French Canadians, with their attachment to obsolete notions and hostility to improvement, had fought with the weapon of popular institutions, while liberal, enterprising English colonists had sought to defend their interests by employing the powers of the aristocratic part of the constitution.[102]

Confronted with this national antipathy, spokesmen for the Whig ministry considered the British government's role in Lower Canada as that of mediator between the contending parties.[103] Moreover, until the rebellions necessitated positive intervention, ministers had been reluctant to impose on the Canadas constitutional schemes devised in London according to British notions. Contrary to the assimilationist tendencies of imperial administration, Russell claimed that it

> was not now the policy of this country, with its great and extended dominion, to enforce English laws and English customs throughout them all . . . it was desirable carefully to consider the peculiar usages, the peculiar wants, the religious habits, and the peculiar aptitudes of the people over whom they ruled, so as to take such measures as would be best calculated to conciliate their good opinion.

Once the revolts had been crushed, Russell was prepared to uphold the special privileges hitherto enjoyed by the French, and Sir Robert Peel agreed that 'every right which the French Canadians now possess, either by capitulation or by treaty, should be strictly preserved to them'.[104]

Such a generous, conciliatory view as Russell's, apparently free from chauvinistic or assimilationist overtones, may have served the ministry well in the Commons debates, but it hardly reflected past imperial practice, nor did it appear very realistic given the jealous hostility between French and English Canadians. Nevertheless, in the years before the rebellions ministers had believed that there existed in Lower Canada a majority of moderate, reasonable citizens who would support an impartial administration concerned for the common good. Once the demagogues had been exposed as fraudulent and silenced, Russell anticipated that 'the people of Canada will carry on their constitutional government with the freedom and liberty, but likewise, I trust, with the temper and moderation, which

[102]Glenelg, *Hansard*, 40, 18 Jan. 1838, 165–6.
[103]Grey, H.G. Ward, Glenelg, Peel, *ibid.*, 39, 22 Dec. 1837, 1470, 40, 17 Jan. 1838, 101, 18 Jan. 1838, 169, and 26 Jan, 1838, 552; Ellice to Russell, 7 Jan. 1838, Russell Papers, PRO 30/22/3A, f. 43; *Canada. From the Foreign Quarterly Review*, p. 29; *Manchester Guardian*, 6 and 17 Jan. 1838; *Bath and Cheltenham Gazette*, 9 Jan. 1838.
[104]*Hansard*, 40, 23 Jan. 1838, 468–9, and 26 Jan, 1838, 552.

has always distinguished the Parliament of this country'.[105] More important, the forbearance of Whig ministers stemmed not so much from an assumption that national antipathies amongst Canadians were slight and easily dispelled, but from a conviction that British practices and British feelings were bound to predominate in the long run. Ministers continued to think in terms of the gradual but inexorable assimilation of French Canada, and to base their conciliatory policy on this anticipation.

These underlying assumptions and pervasive prejudices were voiced more explicitly by Whig partisans, and even more outspokenly by Tories. Commentators of both parties asserted that the preservation of French customs was undesirable and impossible in a province inhabited by an increasing number of British settlers. It was widely assumed that with continued English immigration, the present French majority would become proportionally smaller each year, and in time the French might find themselves a minority in the province. This fear of being swamped and attempts to forestall it lay behind many of the assembly's recent measures; situated in the midst of Anglo-Saxon communities, the French apparently wanted to preserve their nationality and keep the whole colony for themselves and their descendants. Yet 'every year their chances became smaller of enjoying the monopoly of lawmaking and governing, and being by some successful outbreak another France — *"La grande Nacion Canadienne!"* '[106] If this was indeed their ambition, the French had most unwisely challenged British authority which alone, 'by upholding their *separate* constitution, is their mediator and protector in the presence of millions of the British race'.[107]

While it seemed futile to think of preserving a French cultural identity in an environment increasingly dominated by Anglo-Saxon influences, Whigs and Tories were convinced that the leaders of the assembly had aimed to establish an independent French state. French Canadians enjoyed superior political rights and material benefits under British rule to those experienced as a colony of France, but they resented the proximity of more intelligent, industrious British settlers preoccupied with commercial enterprise.[108] If the French gained complete power, the welfare of the English colonists would therefore be placed in the hands of an implacable enemy. 'Papineau and his gang', reported one alarmist paper, 'recommended that the British inhabitants, lords of a province conquered by the valour of their ancestors, should be hunted down like "wolves".'[109]

---

[105]*Ibid.*, 26 Jan. 1838, 548.
[106]*Morning Advertiser*, 9 Jan. 1838.
[107]*Globe*, 2 Jan. 1838.
[108]Gladstone, *Hansard*, 40, 23 Jan. 1838, 429; *Morning Chronicle*, 25 Dec. 1837; *Manchester Courier*, 30 Dec. 1837; *Cheltenham Journal*, 1 Jan. 1838; *Durham Advertiser*, 5 Jan. 1838; *The Times*, 25 Jan. 1838.
[109]*Newcastle Journal*, 10 Feb. 1838. Also *Newcastle Chronicle*, 30 Dec. 1837; *Bath Post*, 6 Jan. 1838.

If the rebellion had succeeded, Edward Ellice contended 'the English in Canada would have become mere hewers of wood and drawers of water, the very off-scourings of the population'.[110] It was widely held in England that the French Canadians wished to grasp the whole resources of the country into their own hands and drive all British enterprise and capital from the province. If triumphant, the French would strip the English settlers of their lands, impose restrictions on the navigation of the St Lawrence, and prevent further immigration from the British Isles.

Commentators who portrayed these French ambitions were quick to point out, however, that British colonists would not be prepared to succumb to the obscurantist designs of an ignorant French peasantry. Despite a present numerical inferiority, English Canadians comprised by far the most opulent and energetic portion of the people. They would struggle manfully for their rights, and their eventual success would be guaranteed by the support of compatriots in the other British provinces and sympathisers from the United States.[111] British interests and culture seemed bound to prevail; the immediate question of concern was whether this triumph would be accomplished by peaceful means or by civil war. It was confidently predicted that if abandoned by the home government, the English inhabitants would take matters into their own hands, and 'a fierce civil war would be carried on which would probably end in the men of British blood driving their opponents from Canada'.[112] This was not a prospect that appealed to Englishmen; Canadian independence held no attraction for those contemporaries who considered a continued British presence necessary in Lower Canada to keep the colonists from one another's throats.

While frequent reference was made to the government's role as mediator and to the desirability of pursuing impartial justice to all the people of Lower Canada, Whigs and Tories maintained that imperial policy should primarily aim at protecting the interests of loyal British settlers in the province. National honour precluded the government from abandoning fellow Englishmen to inevitable oppression and proscription at the hands of the French. Emigrants had settled in the colony on the faith of living under the rule and protection of Britain.[113] Furthermore, the interests of all the North American provinces were closely interrelated: Lower Canada could not be treated as an isolated entity. It was misleading for

[110]*Hansard,* 40, 25 Jan, 1838, 489; also Ward, *ibid.,* 17 Jan. 1838, 101; *Morning Chronicle,* 30 Dec. 1837; *Berwick and Kelso Warder,* 13 Jan. 1838.
[111]*Manchester Guardian,* 27 Dec. 1837; *Liverpool Mail,* 9 Jan. 1838; *North Devon Journal,* 18 Jan. 1838.
[112]*Morning Chronicle,* 28 Dec. 1837. Also *Kentish Chronicle,* 30 Jan. 1838; Ellice, *Hansard,* 40, 25 Jan. 1838, 489.
[113]Russell, Young, Carnac, *Hansard,* 39, 22 Dec. 1837, 1497, 1480–1, and 40, 16 Jan. 1838, 58; *Globe,* 23 Dec. 1837; *Taunton Courier,* 27 Dec. 1837; *York Chronicle,* 3 Jan. 1838; *Sunderland Herald,* 6 Jan. 1838; *Morning Advertiser,* 4 Jan. 1838; *Dublin Evening Post,* 20 Jan. 1838; *Welshman,* 2 Feb. 1838.

radicals to talk of the wrongs of the Canadian people and prescribe measures for the future government of Canada based on the demands of a malcontent faction in one province.[114] Nothing could be more fatal for the welfare of Upper Canada than the ascendancy of a French party in the neighbouring colony and its possible separation from Britain. The authorities at Quebec effectively commanded the St Lawrence, the Upper Canadians' outlet to the sea, and an independent state on the lower reaches could place restrictive or prohibitory regulations on the river's traffic. The past history of commercial and fiscal relations between the two provinces, as well as French enmity towards everything British, did not augur well for the future of Upper Canada hemmed in by such an independent neighbour. Since Upper Canadians might then consider union with the United States as the only way out of their dilemma, separation of one province from the empire seemed certain to entail the separation of the other.[115] While a few Englishmen mooted the possibility of reuniting the Canadas as a solution to these difficulties, most regarded the aftermath of rebellion as an inopportune time to discuss ambitious, long-term plans.

Faced with the immediate challenge of French-Canadian nationalism, Englishmen reacted to the rebellion in Lower Canada by evincing a hostility to the customs, institutions, and outlook of the French. With varying degrees of explicitness and vehemence, this animosity characterised the views of both Whigs and Tories and was not confined to those who attributed the crisis in the Canadas solely to national and cultural antagonisms. The antipathy to the French displayed by Lord Durham in his Report was fully typical of English opinion before, during, and after the rebellion. Chauvinistic comments reflected the assumed superiority of the British character and intelligence over the backward and lethargic French. The 'mass of French Canadians', declared the *Standard*, 'are far more ignorant, bigotted, and besotted, than the mass of English of Elizabeth's reign'.[116] From personal acquaintance with the state of education in the colony, Ellice disclosed 'that not two Canadians, in a hundred could read and write', and Bulwer noted that 'it often happened that a foreman of a jury could not give in the verdict from the inability to read it'.[117] Such a state of affairs adequately explained why the populace had been exploited by demagogues in the assembly: 'their constituents, though a very amiable and a very virtuous race of men, were yet very ignorant, and little fitted to appreciate the blessings which the constitution bestowed upon them. They were fitted to be deluded by ambitious

---

[114]Peel, Russell, Glenelg, *Hansard*, 40, 16 Jan. 1838, 72–3, 89, and 18 Jan. 1838, 174–5; *The Times*, 27 Jan. 1838.
[115]*Manchester Guardian*, 27 Dec. 1837; *Sunderland Herald*, 6 Jan. 1838; *The Times*, 15 Jan. 1838; *Newcastle Journal*, 20 Jan. 1838.
[116]*Standard*, 28 Dec. 1837.
[117]*Hansard*, 40, 24 Jan. 1838, 489, and 23 Jan. 1838, 398.

and designing men.'[118] It was therefore 'nothing short of burlesque' to dignify as a struggle for independence the uprising of a few French *habitants* who were too stupid to distinguish between freedom and slavery, happiness and misery.[119]

Moreover, the leaders of French Canada were wedded to a culture and a way of life that appeared to Englishmen to be the epitome of backwardness and obsolescence. The French party, Bulwer remarked disapprovingly, was attached, 'Not to the great and wise institutions of the day, but to the worn-out and obsolete customs and feudalisms of four centuries ago'. It was unforgivable that any people in that age of improvement should deliberately turn their back on progress, and even evince 'the most benighted hostility to all the principles of commerce itself'.[120] Glenelg was amazed to find a colonial assembly that was 'unfriendly to commerce, to the spread of intelligence, to the diffusion of education; and therefore not very friendly to the prevailing characteristics of the English race'.[121] The whole policy of the Lower Canadian assembly was condemned as a retrograde attempt to overthrow imperial power in order to establish a Gallican aristocracy with 'absurd feudal laws' and tenures that had been abolished in England in the reign of Charles II.[122] Here was a thoroughly obscurantist movement 'to bind the intellect of Canada with "the fetters of the fifteenth century"', an ambition, incredibly enough, supported by the philosophic radicals.[123] The French preference for seigneurial tenure appeared entirely typical of this backward attitude. It was, the *Morning Advertiser* avowed, 'an attempt to return back to barbarism upon one of the very subjects which is the most connected with freedom, social improvement, and civilization'.[124] The rebellion could be traced to these inveterate, misguided prejudices, but Whigs and Tories agreed that such a community could hardly be left to govern itself. 'Was this a colony fit for independence?', enquired Bulwer. 'Why, if it were a republic tomorrow, it would be a monster in legislation — half jacobinism, half feudalism.'[125]

Staunch Tories and champions of Protestantism also asserted that French-Canadian Catholics could never be considered loyal subjects of Britain, despite their innate docility and record of passive neutrality at the time of the American Revolution and later during the War of 1812. Since English bayonets carried the fortress of Quebec, the French had never been willing supporters of the imperial connection, though superior

[118]Glenelg, *ibid.*, 18 Jan. 1838, 165.
[119]*Liverpool Courier*, 14 Feb. 1838.
[120]*Hansard*, 40, 23 Jan. 1838, 398.
[121]*Ibid.*, 18 Jan. 1838, 165.
[122]Russell, *ibid.*, 23 Jan. 1838, 468.
[123]*Morning Herald*, 22 Apr. 1837.
[124]*Morning Advertiser*, 9 Jan. 1838.
[125]*Hansard*, 40, 23 Jan. 1838, 398.

hatred of the Americans had generally kept them from openly displaying a concealed, dormant enmity towards the British.[126]In addition to the resentments of a conquered people, the French-Canadian papists harboured an implacable, hereditary hatred for Protestant institutions and the rule of a Protestant power. Ardent Tories had no difficulty in discerning the activities of 'Romish priests' behind colonial agitation and in attributing the rebellion in Lower Canada to the spirit of popery.[127] Now was the time to remedy the situation by strengthening Protestant institutions and reinvigorating the Church of England which had been sadly neglected in the past. By such policies the French Canadians might 'be made happy in spite of themselves; and made harmless, if not loyal; but it must be by teaching them that *Lower Canada* is to be a *British* and a *Protestant* state, not a *French* and *Popish* dominion'.[128] Some liberal newspapers protested against these extreme views and attempts to enlist religious bigotry and hatred 'in the plan of summoning Protestant England to arms to extirpate the Canadians, because they are of French extraction and of the Catholic religion'.[129] Nevertheless, closer assimilation of Canadian customs and institutions to those of Britain appeared to Whigs and Tories the most appropriate and effective solution to the situation in Lower Canada. Such a policy reflected the Englishman's confidence in the superiority and universal validity of British institutions and a corresponding disparagement of French-Canadian culture.

When Englishmen came to consider the future policy to be pursued towards Canada, the debate over the respective merits of conciliation and coercion revived. As the advocates of sweeping concessions, the radicals could place no faith in the generosity of a ministry whose repressive measures had created the present discord, and their worst fears were seemingly substantiated when the government unveiled its Bill for suspending the Lower Canadian constitution. Tories continued to urge a resolute, unsparing policy rather than a revival of the vacillation and inactivity that in the past had fostered disloyalty and rebellion. While recent events would leave a legacy of bitter animosity, tensions between the two ethnic groups would only be aggravated if the government adopted a misguidedly

[126]*Cheltenham Journal*, 1 Jan. 1838; *Sunderland Herald*, 6 Jan. 1838.
[127]*Liverpool Mail*, 9 and 19 Dec. 1837; *Newcastle Journal*, 23 Dec. 1837; *Standard*, 28 Dec. 1837; *Leeds Intelligencer*, 30 Dec. 1837; *Wheeler's Manchester Chronicle*, 30 Dec. 1837; *Liverpool Courier*, 3 Jan. 1838; *Nottingham Journal*, 5 and 12 Jan. 1838; *Hull Packet*, 5 Jan. 1838; *Durham Advertiser*, 5 Jan. 1838; *Berwick and Kelso Warder*, 13 Jan. 1838; *Cumberland Pacquet*, 27 March 1838; *Hints on the Government of Canada*, p. 19.
[128]*Standard*, 11 Jan. 1838. Also *Evening Packet*, 9 Jan. 1838; *Leeds Intelligencer*, 20 Jan. 1838; *Liverpool Courier*, 14 Feb. 1838; Inglis, *Hansard* 40, 29 Jan. 1838, 629–30.
[129]*Courier*, 28 Dec. 1837; Also *Bristol Gazette*, 3 Jan. 1838.

liberal approach towards the French Canadians. Only firm, and if necessary severe, measure would be appropriate; they might not assuage mutual hostility, but they would uphold British honour and the supremacy of British interests in North America.[130]

The Whigs' attitude was more ambivalent. Whig newspapers denounced Tory demands for coercion and advocated moderation as the best means of restoring harmony and tranquillity in the aftermath of revolt. They pleaded that the wishes of the colonists should be consulted in the future administration of the province and warned the ministry against attempting to impose a constitution by force.[131] Within the Whig cabinet, however, dissension broke out concerning the appropriate policy. Most ministers were content to adopt the uncompromising expedient of suspending the constitution of Lower Canada and postpone decision on the colony's future government until the present unrest had been effectively quelled. But Lord Howick protested that suppression of the uprisings should be accompanied by measures that would lay the basis for reconciliation and constitutional reform, measures 'calculated to correct the causes of Canadian troubles & not merely to palliate some of the symptoms'.[132] Under Howick's threat of resignation, the cabinet compromised to the extent of agreeing that the governor-general should be given a discretionary power to call a purely advisory convention of delegates from the Canadas to ascertain public opinion and discuss constitutional revision.[133]

A new focus for public comment in England was provided when the government introduced into parliament its Bill to suspend the Lower Canadian constitution. Ministers admitted that it was a harsh measure, but they justified it as a necessary recourse to deal with a temporary emergency and emphasised the value of Lord Durham's mission as a constructive method of settling Anglo-Canadian differences. Since most Whigs were prepared to put their faith in official professions of magnanimity and in Durham's liberal statesmanship, the ministry's plan largely succeeded in reuniting the somewhat disarrayed ranks of its supporters. While some liberal papers criticised the despotic character of the Bill as worse than the disease it was designed to cure, and regretted the conserva-

---

[130]*Birmingham Advertiser*, 28 Dec. 1837; *Berwick and Kelso Warder*, 6 Jan. 1838; *Standard*, 11 and 24 Jan. 1838; *Wheeler's Manchester Chronicle*, 13 Jan. 1838; *Liverpool Courier*, 17 Jan. 1838; *Morning Herald*, 25 Jan. 1838.

[131]*Courier*, 28 Dec. 1837; *North Devon Journal*, 18 Jan. 1838.

[132]Howick to Melbourne, 2 Jan. 1838, Grey Papers/Melbourne; also Howick to Russell, 1 Jan. 1838, Grey Papers/Russell; Howick to Ellice, Jan. 1838, Ellice Papers, E22, fos. 29–32. For details of the plan and cabinet discussion, P. Burroughs, *The Canadian Crisis and British Colonial Policy, 1828–1841* (London, 1972), pp. 96–8.

[133]For criticism of the scheme, see Rice to Howick, 5 Jan. 1838, Grey Papers/ Monteagle; Melbourne to Howick, 2 Jan. 1838, Grey Papers/Melbourne; Melbourne to Victoria, 26 Jan. 1838, Royal Archives, RA Al/92.

tive bias of the government's policy,[134] most Whigs welcomed the scheme as reassuring evidence of generous sympathies. There had been some apprehension lest reliance on Tory support in parliament might lead ministers to resort to oppression in Canada, but they had creditably resisted this temptation and advanced far beyond the sentiment of the British public, which had exhibited on this subject the narrow-mindedness, prejudice, and injustice towards the rights of others for which John Bull had long been notorious. There did exist, after all, Whig supporters felt, a broad distinction between them and the Tories as national rulers.[135] Many Tories, for their part, expressed doubts concerning the competence of the ministry and Durham to handle the situation, but the Tory party was willing to support the Bill at the price of omitting from its preamble all reference to the calling of a convention of delegates to advise the governor-general. The measure was sufficiently rigorous in character to satisfy Tory demands for a forceful assertion of imperial authority; the Whigs had now seen reason and realised that only Tory prescriptions could resolve the crisis.[136]

This confirmation of the prevailing Toryism of the Whigs formed a central theme of the radicals' attack on the latest specimen of Whig despotism. 'Thank Heaven', sighed the *Leeds Times* with relief, 'the cloud has dispersed — the veil is lifted — the embrace of Toryism and Whiggery is revealed.'[137] In a spirit of vengeance, the reform ministry had annihilated a constitution and devised a form of dictatorship that would 'reduce the hitherto self-governed inhabitants of our American province to the abject condition of an Hindoo serf'.[138] Never in a month of Sundays would the Bill restore peace and harmony in Lower Canada; on the contrary, such a bare-faced violation of the colonists' political liberties would gravely exacerbate existing discontent and alienate the sympathies of moderates and loyalists. It could only lead despairing Canadians to 'cherish a lasting detestation of British rule, and a deep-seated aversion to British tyranny', and prove that 'slavery is their lot so long as they are the subjects of Great Britain'.[139] With the proximity and influence of the United States, a dictatorship would not provide a sound or lasting basis for the government of Lower Canada.

[134]*Sun*, 17, 19, and 24 Jan. 1838; *Liverpool Telegraph*, 31 Jan. 1838.

[135]*Durham Chronicle*, 19 Jan. 1838; *Liverpool Chronicle*, 20 Jan. 1838; *Devonport Telegraph*, 20 Jan. 1838; *Carlisle Journal*, 20 Jan. 1838; *Carnarvon and Denbigh Herald*, 20 and 27 Jan. 1838; *Somerset County Gazette*, 27 Jan. 1838; *Berwick Advertiser*, 27 Jan. 1838; *North Devon Journal*, 1 Feb. 1838; *Newcastle Chronicle*, 3 Feb. 1838.

[136]*York Chronicle*, 24 Jan. 1838.

[137]*Leeds Times*, 30 Dec. 1837.

[138]Roebuck, *Hansard*, 40, 5 Feb. 1838, 735; *London Dispatch*, 4 Feb. 1838.

[139]Gillon, *ibid.*, 25 Jan. 1838, 527, and *Canadian Portfolio*, p. 137. Also Grote, Warburton, Williams, *ibid.*, 16 Jan. 1838, 64–5, 17 Jan. 1838, 105, and 23 Jan. 1838, 392–3; *Leeds Mercury*, 20 Jan. 1838; *Liverpool Mercury*, 2 Feb. 1838.

The radicals also turned against the Bill the argument of Whigs and Tories that the uprisings were limited affrays involving only a few agitators and their deluded followers in a couple of isolated localities. If offences were confined to so few inhabitants, the radicals enquired, why should the whole population of the colony be punished? If the vast majority were loyal, was it just or sensible to reward faithful allegiance and patriotic zeal by depriving the entire community of its political rights? Since a rebellion had also occurred in Upper Canada, why was it that only the constitution of the lower province would be suspended?[140] Furthermore, the radicals pointed out that the Lower Canadian assembly had not as a body been involved in illegal activities, even if a few members had joined the insurgents; certainly it did not deserve extinction on the ground of unproven delinquency. Nor did its earlier refusal to vote supplies justify annihilation. There appeared in fact no convincing reason why the provincial assembly should not be reconvened now that the minor outbreak had been put down. But if amendments to the Canadian constitution were required, representative institutions need not be suspended until the new system could be devised and introduced; Roebuck scorned a scheme of constitutional reform based on the 'bright idea of mending the machine by first destroying it'.[141]

Despite the rearguard action and outspoken criticism of the more implacable radicals, the legislation passed through parliament with little dissent and large majorities. By this stage a division of opinion had emerged amongst the parliamentary radicals which led several of them to vote with the ministry and thus isolate what appeared to be a small, disgruntled minority of extremists.[142] Like their prototypes in the French Revolution, observed the *Globe*, they demonstrated a marvellous aptitude for purging their ranks of those suspected of a shade of moderation, and a Tory critic noted that their 'pusillanimity in the House of Commons, last week, was . . . in admirable accordance with their insolent exultation a fortnight ago'.[143] This rift between the ultras and their more moderate colleagues led to mutual recriminations. Edward Baines, the liberal dissenter who edited the *Leeds Mercury* and a critic of the ministry's Canadian policy, advised Leader and Molesworth to be 'less violent & less bitter against the Government, then they were during the late debate in the House of Commons; for I assure you that their tone has considerably prejudiced

---

[140]Lord Brougham was an outspoken champion of the Canadian assemblies, *Hansard*, 40, 18 Jan. 1838, 209–10, and 2 Feb. 1838, 673; also Grote, Gillon, Hume, *ibid.*, 16 Jan. 1838, 64, 17 Jan. 1838, 114, and 29 Jan. 1838, 624–6; *Preston Observer*, 27 Jan. 1838.

[141]*Hansard*, 40, 5 Feb. 1838, 759; also Grote, *ibid.*, 23 Jan. 1838, 401; *Spectator*, 20 and 27 Jan. 1838; *Bristol Mercury*, 27 Jan. 1838.

[142]In minorities ranging from 6 to 39 votes, Leader, Molesworth, Grote, Thompson, Ewart, Hume, and Villiers remained critics, but Buller and Ward went over to the ministry, as did reformers like Bulwer.

[143]*Globe*, 25 Jan. 1838, and *Morning Herald*, 23 Jan. 1838.

the cause they so ably & justly espouse'.[144] On the other side, the *Spectator* denounced the defection of faint-hearted radicals like Charles Buller and H.G. Ward, and those 'so-called Liberals, who disgraced themselves by timeserving speeches, subservient votes, and sneaking absence'.[145] With typical bitterness, Roebuck censured the radicals' incompetence in the House of Commons when 'the peace of the world, the happiness of millions, the fate of great principles was at stake'. The 'courage of the Radicals seemed frozen, their intellect was all in abeyance, and nothing was heard but a puling whimpering that was marvellously like the doleful cries of a whipt school-boy'. Burke or Fox would have torn Russell's 'shallow and miserable sophistries . . . into ten thousand shreds, and gibbetted his reputation for ever. But there is no spirit now-a-days — we are all pigmies — men seem *dwarfed*, and they cannot exalt their under-standings or their sentiments to the height of the great argument before them.' Roebuck was equally critical of O'Connell and the Irish members for deserting the Canadians. Since the radicals had braved obloquy in 1833 to fight the battle of Irish freedom over a Whig coercion Bill, the 'Liberator' and his followers ought now to be attacking despotism in Canada and not skulking in Dublin.[146]

The bitterness among radicals was envenomed by a difference of opinion on tactics. Because fundamental political principles were involved, the Canadian crisis posed in its most acute form the dilemma with which radicals in parliament had wrestled since the passage of the Reform Act: should they cooperate with the Whig ministry to secure reforms in return for votes, or should they create an independent party and work for a realignment of parties that would eventually accomplish the victory of radicalism? The unyielding doctrine of the philosophic radicals seemed to demand the latter alternative and aggressive tactics, but since 1834 realism had drawn them, in company with more moderate reformers, towards a policy of gradualism and cooperation with the Whigs. In November 1837 Russell's declaration on the finality of the Reform Act discredited and destroyed this approach; but just as John Mill and other ultras were planning to form a separate party embracing all shades of

---

[144]Baines to Place, 2 Jan. 1838, Place Papers BM Add. MSS 34, 151, fos. 51–2. Interestingly enough, the *Leeds Mercury*, 10 Feb. 1838, praised Molesworth and Baines for voting against the government. See similarly critical remarks by Joseph Parkes in a letter to Richard Cobden, 17 Jan. 1838, Cobden Papers.

[145]*Spectator*, 3 Feb. 1838; also praise for the ultras in *Leeds Mercury*, 3 Feb. 1838; *Leeds Times*, 10 Feb. 1838; 'Lord Durham and the Canadians', *London and Westminster Review*, xxviii (Jan. 1838). 532–3; *London Dispatch*, 25 Mar. 1838.

[146]*Canadian Portfolio*, pp. 137–9, 140–1. Roebuck was not to know that the ministry had seen the need to instil sense in O'Connell, since amongst the other radicals 'the general feeling is to do nothing that could hurt the Government'. Lord Mulgrave was given the task, and could report before the bill was intro-duced that 'O'Connell has been spoken to and will be all right or at least will do no mischief on the Canada Question'. Mulgrave to Russell, 2 and 6 Jan. 1838, Russell Papers, PRO 30/22/3A, fos, 9–13, 37–8.

radical and moderate reformers, pledged to defeat the Whigs and encourage a political realignment, the Canadian rebellions intervened.[147] The ensuing debates on Canada revealed that implacable opposition to the ministry was confined to a few headstrong philosophic radicals, whose violent views alienated them from the large, amorphous body of reformers in parliament whose support would be needed for the creation of a new reformist party. The moderates still wished to cooperate with the Whigs as a better policy than letting in the Tories, and to this end toned down their language and compromised their principles, or combined hostile rhetoric with supporting votes. Such prominent moderates as E.L. Bulwer and Albany Fonblanque, editor of the *Examiner,* criticised the ultras for futile extremism over the Canadian revolts, and emphasised that the crucial issue was not Canadian policy but the Whigs' continuance in office; a coercion Bill was preferable to a Tory ministry.[148] As Mill sadly recorded, the Canadian crisis 'suspends all united action among Radicals . . . sets one portion of the friends of popular institutions at variance with another, and . . . interrupts for the time all movements and all discussions tending to the great objects of domestic policy'. To his great regret, the 'Canada question in an evil hour crossed the path of radicalism'.[149]

Radicals admitted that the narrow considerations of party politics had determined parliament's handling of the Canadian crisis. Whigs were more intent on preserving the ministry from defeat than examining the dispute on its merits and in a liberal spirit; 'black must be called white, and Members must vote through mud and mire, to keep them in, and "keep out the Tories". In this way, the continuance of Whig rule is corrupting all public morals as well as debasing all public spirit.'[150] The casual passage of a despotic Bill with immense majorities was regrettable, but even more disillusioning for radicals was the conclusion that parliament's views on the Canadian rebellions appeared to reflect public opinion. A hostile Tory newspaper chided 'the malignant kennel of Radicalism, which still ventures to bay forth its stupid yelpings against the universal sense and opinion of the country', and another noted that the radicals' false estimate of popular sentiment over Canada had undermined their

---

[147]Mill to Bulwer, 3 March 1838, *The Earlier Letters of John Stuart Mill 1812–1848,* ed. F.E. Mineka (Toronto, 1963), p. 380. Mill was preparing the article 'Reorganization of the Reform Party' with the intention of publishing it in Jan. 1838, when the rebellions broke out and he substituted the article 'Lord Durham and the Canadians', though reference was made to the formation of a reform party to defeat the Whigs, *London and Westminster Review,* xxviii, (Jan. 1838), 504–10. For the wider question of radicals' relations with the Whigs, see Hamburger, *Intellectuals in Politics,* chs 4–8.

[148]*Examiner,* 14 Jan. and 11 March 1838; also *Weetily Chronicle* (London), 4 Feb. 1838,
[149]'Lord Durham and the Canadians', *loc. cit.,* 504, and Mill to Bulwer, 5 March 1838, *The Earlier Letters of John Stuart Mill,* p. 382.
[150]*Spectator,* 3 Feb. 1838.

strength in parliament and in the country.[151] The truth was that little political support could be generated for abstract principles, idealism, or doctrinaire nostrums. Gradualism and pragmatism remained the prevailing characteristics of British political development to which both Whigs and Tories were glad to cling when their monopoly of power was threatened by outsiders. The Canadian rebellions presented the philosophic radicalism of the 1830s with one of its final challenges; its failure to rise triumphantly to the occasion not only exposed the limitations and dilemmas for doctrinaires working within a political system that proceeded on the basis of pragmatism and compromise, but confirmed the deepening disillusionment of hopes for radical reform generated by the struggle for the act of 1832. In Britain, as in Canada, the future lay with the safe but dull men of compromise.

[151]*Nottingham Journal*, 26 Jan. 1838, and *Albion*, 22 Jan. 1838; also *Weetily Herald* (London) 11 Feb. 1838.

5

JOHN E. FLINT

Britain and the partition of West Africa

'Without the occupation of Egypt', Robinson and Gallagher assert,[1] 'there is no reason to suppose that any international scrambles for Africa, either west or east, would have begun when they did.' Professor John Hargreaves, concerning himself with the beginnings of West African partition, does not differ from this view, at which, substantially, he also arrived by independent research.[2] Concluding their account of the Anglo-French Niger Convention of 1898, which settled all outstanding disputes between France and Britain in West Africa, Robinson and Gallagher comment 'the partition of West Africa was over. As it had begun, so it ended — a disturbance stirred largely by the struggle for Egypt and the Nile.'[3] In line with this thesis the same authors emphasise that British policy in West Africa was essentially subordinated to the greater imperial interests of Egypt, the Nile, and the strategic necessities of protecting East African approaches to that great river:

> Nothing is more striking about the selection of British claims in tropical Africa between 1882 and 1895 than the emphasis on the east and the comparative indifference to the west. . . . The concentration on east Africa shows the preoccupation with supreme strategic interests. The neglect of west African claims on the other hand, show a relative indifference to tropical African commercial gains.[4]

This essay will attempt to show that an almost exactly opposite thesis can provide a more acceptable explanation for Britain's West African role in the partition; that the British occupation of Egypt in 1882 was not a basic consideration of British strategy in West Africa during partition; that far from neglecting her role in West Africa, or conceding claims there in return for Nile security, British decisions in West Africa were based solidly on considerations of commercial advantage; and that the territorial

---

[1]Ronald Robinson and John Gallagher, with Alice Denny, *Africa and the Victorians: The official mind of Imperialism* (London, 1961).
[2]John D. Hargreaves, *Prelude to the Partition of West Africa* (London, 1963), pp. 282–4. In his bibliographical comments Hargreaves notes on p. 366 that *Africa and the Victorians* appeared in time for him to insert references to its thesis, 'which is largely complementary to my own', during the revision of his manuscript.
[3]Robinson and Gallagher, *Africa and the Victorians*, p. 408.
[4]*Ibid.*, p. 408.

expansion of Britain in West Africa may be regarded as a classic case study of commercial imperialism.

The term commercial imperialism needs some elaboration and definition. 'Imperialism', as Sir Keith Hancock once remarked, is no word for historians, yet he with the rest of the profession continues to use it. It is not used here in the sense of an '-ism' of political theory or popular enthusiasm for empire, but in the stricter sense of its Latin root. The formal acquisition of territorial control over a West African region, with the clear realisation that its political destinies would now be determined by decisions and pronouncements of the imperial power, can be described as an act of imperialism. This is an old-fashioned usage, for Marxists and non-Marxists have attempted to blur the distinction between formal and informal empire, particularly by the use of the term 'economic imperialism'.[5] This discussion of partition, however, assumes that the creation of formal colonial territories within an imperial system is of real significance; the histories of Argentina (an area subjected to British informal economic control in the nineteenth century) and of Nigeria (where British formal empire was used to intensify economic penetration and control) developed along greatly different lines because one became subject, while the other did not, to formal British imperial administration.

By commercial imperialism it is meant to imply that decisions to undertake the establishment of formal imperial rule were based primarily on what British politicians and officials considered to be commercial advantage for British traders. The term does not presume a conspiracy theory, in which Hobson's[6] finance capitalists are replaced as actors by commercial groups who manipulate political decisions. There were trading and commercial lobbies which attempted to influence Foreign or Colonial Office decisions, as well as local trading interests in Africa which would press their views on colonial or consular representatives, and these provided a flow of information and prejudice upon which official decisions were often based. These sources of information, and, more important, sometimes of misinformation could determine decisions to take territorial control of an area. Occasionally, as I have tried to show in an earlier study of the Royal Niger Company,[7] the interests and ambitions of a private group of traders appeared to offer the British government ways of achieving their ends without responsibility or expense (though this was an illusion), and

[5] J. Gallagher and R. Robinson, in their seminal and most provocative article 'The Imperialism of Free Trade', *Economic History Review*, 2nd series, VI (1963), defined imperialism as 'a sufficient political function for integrating new regions into the expanding economy'. By this, forms of imperial control could range from mere gunboat diplomacy to Crown Colony rule. It is interesting to note that in *Africa and the Victorians* the same authors do not see partition in Africa as such a 'sufficient political function' for integrating African territories into an expanding British economy, but one undertaken for strategic purposes.

[6] J.A. Hobson, *Imperialism : a study* (London, 1902).

[7] J.E. Flint, *Sir George Goldie and the Making of Nigeria* (London, 1960).

this situation came very close to conspiracy. But in the broad perspective the British government and its officials were not manipulated in West Africa by traders' lobbies or chambers of commerce. The traders were themselves too divided to mount monolithic pressures by the regional differences of their trades in West Africa, and by personal antagonisms between strong-minded characters such as Goldie, A. L. Jones the shipping magnate, John Holt of Liverpool, and numerous lesser figures. Even had this disunity been overcome, British politicians and government officials in the Colonial and Foreign Offices were not of a background or temperament to accept dictation from traders. Their frame of reference was still essentially aristocratic; they regarded themselves as responsible administrators who based their decisions on higher conceptions of British interests than those which could be advocated by any lobby of special interests.

Thus the assertion that the British role in West African partition forms a case study in commercial imperialism implies, not that policy was determined by British traders or commercial interests, but that the 'official mind'[8] made its decisions in the light of what *it* assessed were the needs of British commerce. The development among British officials of an increasingly narrow emphasis upon the protection of commerce, and the corresponding falling away of their concerns with antislavery policies, support for missionary enterprise or encouragement of African attempts at 'modernisation' and 'reform', constitute a kind of intellectual history of the origins of partition. This narrowing of vision had two dimensions: on a plane of realities which will concern this essay the props on which earlier policies had been constructed were collapsing after 1880, but on a different level British politicians and officials were influenced by intellectual currents in Europe to believe in the inevitability of European colonial rule over Africa and the hopelessness of expecting modernisation through African agency.[9]

[8]The term is, of course, culled from *Africa and the Victorians* where it is also used as a subtitle. The authors use the concept in order to stress the final location of decisions, and thus to support their view that broad conceptions of imperial strategy were the determinants. The sources used in the study are also exclusively those created by British official activities, and no reference is paid to missionary, commercial or African materials.

[9]There is not space in this essay to consider this theme. It has been touched on with insight by several writers, including D. Kimble, *A Political History of Ghana: the rise of Gold Coast nationalism, 1850–1928* (Oxford, 1963), J.F.A. Ajayi, *Christian Missions in Nigeria, 1841–1891,* (London, 1965) and E.A. Ayandele, *The Missionary Impact on Modern Nigeria, 1842–1914* (London, 1966). See also H.S. Wilson, ed., *Origins of West African Nationalism* (London, 1969). Such studies refer only to the impact of European disillusionment with Christian and educated Africans on the local African scene. What is still required is a study of the growth of British ideas of the hopelessness of African regeneration without colonial rule. The theme begins to be strongly expressed, and the older views only weakly defended, in the journals such as the *Nineteenth Century, Fortnightly Review, Edinburgh Review* and their like from the mid-1870s. The phenomenon is connected with the reception of Darwin's *Origin of Species,* but may well originate with Egypt's colonisation of the Sudan, and the writings in its justification by Samuel Baker and others.

These attitudes, though it is almost impossible to document them, did affect decisions by accelerating the drift towards solving problems by the establishment of political control.

The literature of partition has tended to emphasise the suddenness of the partition, as revealed in such terms as the 'New Imperialism'[10] and the 'scramble for Africa'. The implication is that partition was something new, breaking the pattern of previous gradual development, somewhat shocking, an aberration, and 'unnatural'. The roots of this historiographical tradition lie in nineteenth-century ideas of history as progress, and are drawn from radical views going back to Adam Smith which maintained that free trade unfettered by colonial shackles was the fairest prospect for human perfectability. When the British government in the 1880s began to indulge again in such antediluvian antics as territorial rivalry, chartering companies, making treaties with 'native princes' and establishing protectorates to foster commerce, it seemed to radicals then, and still seems to many historians, positively and peculiarly reactionary. Such curious goings on seem to call for curious explanations.

But the contrast between the partition period and the earlier nineteenth century may not be so sharp as is commonly supposed. Professor Burroughs begins his essay for this volume with the comment that few historians of the mid-Victorian period any longer suppose that it may be simply categorised an era of anti-imperialism. Gallagher and Robinson's article[11] pointed out the large number of territorial annexations carried out by the British between 1840 and 1880. Admittedly, for West Africa these may appear minor in extent, yet the footholds of territory established by British and French in the first three-quarters of the nineteenth century do show a remarkable continuity with the map of Africa partitioned. The French by the 1860s possessed a real colony in Senegal, and treaty claims, pretensions and commercial *comptoirs* in Guinea, Côte d'Ivoire, Porto Novo and Gabun; the British were committed to Sierra Leone by 1807, gradually the Gold Coast emerged as a formal colony by 1874, the Gambia remained British 'in spite of all temptations to belong to other nations', while the foundations of Nigeria were laid by consul and gunboat in the Oil Rivers from the 1850s and by annexation of Lagos in 1861. The vast inland areas of the savanna might have seemed unpredictably open to competition to an observer of the 1850s, yet even here the outcome revealed few surprises. As early as 1852 the French Ministry of Marine and Colonies was sketching

---

[10]e.g. H.M. Wright ed., *The 'New Imperialism'* (Boston, 1961). Wright's introduction begins: 'During the first two thirds of the nineteenth century the interest of European states in overseas expansion reached its lowest point in several centuries.' After elaborating this point, Wright makes the contrast: 'Suddenly, and almost simultaneously, between 1870 and 1900 the states of Europe began to extend their control over vast areas of the world.' Some such introduction is typically employed by almost all writers on the partition, or analysts of the 'new' imperialism.
[11]'The Imperialism of Free Trade', *Ec. Hist. Rev.*, 2nd series, VI (1963).

plans for an advance from Senegal to Timbuktu, while in the 1860s Faidherbe elaborated schemes for advancing as far as Bussa (thus almost exactly pinpointing the Anglo-French boundary on the Niger agreed in 1898).[12] The British had begun penetrating the lower Niger in the 1830s, the Benue in the 1850s, when Barth was wandering the Sokoto empire sponsored by the Foreign Office; and by 1865 the pioneer firms which Goldie would bring together in 1879 as the prototype for the Royal Niger Company were regularly trading, with the protection of British gunboats, on the lower Niger, in Nupe, and on the Benue. Seen in such a perspective the partition of West Africa looks neither aberrant nor peculiar, but more like the gradual evolution of persistent and consistent tendencies.

Indeed, it may be argued that it was not the partition which was peculiar or unnatural, but the earlier British abstention from territorial acquisition (which, if not total, formed a considered element in policy and did place effective brakes on expansion). The scholar in whose honour this volume is written, in his George Arnold Wood lecture of 1959,[13] firmly applied the words 'Peculiar Interlude', not to the years of partition and imperialism, but to the years of Britain's free trading ascendancy which preceded them. For Gerald Graham it was Britain's early industrial lead and commercial supremacy protected by the Royal Navy's command of the seas which constituted the aberration in history; a peculiar and unique coincidence of circumstances which could allow deliberate abstention from territorial expansion. As such it could neither last nor be repeated. In the West African context the peculiarity which first demands explanation is that strong European powers, already the conquerors of America, south Asia, the East Indies and Australia, possessed of disciplined armies and navies equipped with terrible weapons, should for so long have allowed Africans to keep their independence armed with shields and spears or at best outdated muzzle-loading muskets and cannon.

This abstention from territorial dominion in West Africa can be explained by a mutually reinforcing combination of two broad factors; first so long as Africans were willing and able to satisfy Britain's commercial demands efficiently, they made demands for territorial control appear superfluous and irrational. In these conditions African independence could remain a 'sufficient political function' for integrating Africa's economy into British expansiveness. Thus the effectiveness of African slave-trading middlemen in the seventeenth and eighteenth centuries kept European colonial acquisitiveness down to a few fortresses and castles along the West African coasts. So too the efficiency of the palm oil traders in the Oil Rivers maintained African formal independence until 1884, though the Rivers formed the

---

[12]C.W. Newbury and A.S. Kanya-Forstner, 'French policy and the origins of the scramble for West Africa', *Journal of African History*, x (1969), 254–6.

[13]G.S. Graham, 'Peculiar interlude: the expansion of England in a period of peace 1815–1850' (University of Sydney, 1959).

most lucrative centre of British trade in West Africa, whereas the more costly and inefficient Gold Coast settlements were formally annexed in 1874.

Secondly, however, there were powerful deterrents against formal European administrative rule in West Africa. If the white invader could brush aside African armies with relative ease, he then must face the more formidable mosquito. Mortality rates among Europeans stationed in West Africa in the mid-nineteenth century were sufficient in themselves to make any official pause before counselling administrative expansion, and to convert the prospects of patronage into a macabre joke. Of 111 Gold Coast officials sent out between 1822 and 1825, fifty-five died of disease. In Sierra Leone 1612 European civilian and military personnel arrived in the colony in the five years after 1821; more than half (926) died. The Wesleyan missionaries lost 37 per cent of all European personnel between 1838 and 1850; those fared somewhat better than the 60.5 per cent mortality of Anglican missionaries between 1804 and 1825.[14] For those whites who survived by building up immunities, the tsetse fly made sure they would not penetrate in large numbers far or fast overland by killing off pack animals.

The absence of strong pressures for expansion, and the presence of powerful deterrents, might lead to the conclusion that British attitudes and policies towards West Africa in the nineteenth century were negative in inspiration. But this was not so: 'The general object', wrote Lord John Russell in 1840, 'is to provide for the establishment of Peace, and innocent Commerce, and for the abolition of the Slave Trade.'[15] Even if and when the slave trade were abolished Africa was not to be left alone; it must be 'civilised'. All British observers agreed that it was a savage and barbarous continent, though they differed on the causes of this lamentable state of affairs; for some the innocent humanity of Africa had been scourged and corrupted by the devil's work of the slave trade, others maintained a scepticism about the capabilities of Africans. 'Civilisation' was easy to define; self-evidently it was that which had made Great Britain what she was — free commerce and protestant Christianity. The development of legitimate commerce would, by its own competitive superiority, in the long run eliminate the slave trade more surely than any naval blockade. Production for the market prepared the soil for more than cash crops by inculcating in a practical discipline the virtues on which Christianity and civilisation could flourish — thrift, foresight, hard work, individual initiative, disciplined hours, capital accumulation.[16]

---

[14]Figures from P. Curtin, *The Image of Africa : British ideas and action, 1780–1850* (London, 1965), pp. 484–6.

[15]Russell to Doherty, 30 September, 1840. CO268/35.

[16]Most writing on West Africa from 1830 to 1870 is suffused with these sentiments. The classic example usually cited is T.F. Buxton's *The African Slave Trade and the Remedy* (London, 1839), as a statement of humanitarian anti-slavery ideas. Almost all the explorers of West Africa including the Landers, Oldfield, Baikie and many others made the same points with a more commercial emphasis.

Within such a frame of thought there was a constant temptation to speed the process of cultural change by direct colonial methods. The humanitarians were far from doctrinaire believers in anti-imperialism. Fowell Buxton and Dr Lushington, the 'Negroes' Friend', who urged Lord John Russell to establish a model agricultural experiment on the Niger in 1840 and enumerated the benefits which would radiate across Africa by its example, concluded with a classic statement of an imperialist philosophy to which little could be added by the enthusiasts of the 1890s:

All that is known of Africa, whether from British officers or missionaries, or scientific travellers, seem to concur in proving the settlements of this description must be kept apart from the contamination of prevailing native practices, and that their internal prosperity, not less than their external security, can be maintained in no other way than by placing them under the protection of the British Crown.

It is clear that in the districts where the experiment is made, the sovereign power must be held by the British government, and the natives obey our laws. . . . Our rule and institutions would be a pure gain to Africans. . . .

It is not too much to say, that wherever British sovereignty shall be firmly established, there religious and civil liberty would instantly prevail, intestine wars and anarchy would cease, the aborigines would be protected, equal rights be enjoyed by all, and every motive, aid, and opportunity which public and private benevolence or enterprise might contribute towards the civilisation of Africa would be most successfully brought into operation.[17]

Other interests besides the missionaries and humanitarians, however, were not so enthusiastic for territorial dominion. The traders looked to the protection of consul and gunboat, but had no wish to pay for it by the regular taxes of a colonial regime, and often resisted the tendencies of local officials who wished to extend the coastal jurisdiction of a colony to gather more ports of entry into the net of customs duties.

Until the 1880s it was the British government which checked tendencies towards territorial acquisition, whether from humanitarian interests or from its own officials. After the disastrous failure of Buxton's Niger Expedition of 1841–42, in which 55 of 149 Europeans died, no further backing was given for wouldbe martyrs to commerce and Christianity. On the other hand no withdrawals took place, despite the famous recommendations of the 1865 Parliamentary Select Committee.[18] Governors

[17] *Parliamentary Papers*, 1843, xlviii (472), Buxton and Lushington to Russell, 7 Aug. 1840, p. 17.
[18] *Parliamentary Papers*, 1865, v (412). C.W. Newbury, *British Policy towards West Africa: Select Documents 1786–1874* (Oxford, 1965), quotes the resolutions pp. 529–60. The committee was very guarded in its advocacy of withdrawal, which it advocated as long term policy for all 'except, probably' Sierra Leone. It forbade new settlements, but added that extension of existing settlements might be necessary 'in peculiar cases' for improving efficiency and economy.

and officials in the colonies were allowed, especially where their arguments seemed to offer the prospect of increasing revenue for little additional expenditure, to make minor extensions of frontiers. With the declaration of the Gold Coast Colony in 1874 it became clear that Britain would not retire from West Africa. Nor did there seem much prospect of large-scale partition; the desperate losses through sickness in campaigns against Ashanti ruled out any desire to administer that nation, a governor of Lagos was recalled for fear of entanglement in troubled Yorubaland,[19] and Britain firmly resisted the temptation to annex the profitable Oil Rivers or Niger markets.

These comfortable policies rested, in the last resort, upon the special European commercial and international situation of Gerald Graham's 'Peculiar Interlude'. First in the industrial revolution, Britain was able to outsell her rivals without recourse to protective tariffs in colonial markets. Trade flourished without the flag. Normally less favoured powers could be expected to offset commercial disadvantage by carving out spheres of tariff-protected colonial territories for themselves, as England and France had done against the Dutch in the seventeenth century. But before the late-1870s none of the industrialising nations was in a position to challenge British overseas commercial supremacy with imperialism, and West Africa was hardly a tempting area. Germany and Italy were not unified until 1870, the Austro-Hungarian empire faced far too formidable internal problems. The United States was preoccupied by the long crisis which culminated in its civil war, and was fully engaged with colonisation in the western lands, as was Russia in Asia. France, Britain's traditional colonial rival since the late-seventeenth century, did present minor challenges in West Africa, and there were little local scrambles for territory after 1850 on the frontiers of Sierra Leone and around Lagos after the British annexation. But the French colonial tariffs were mild after the 1830s,[20] and above all France's internal situation, with revolutions in 1830 and 1848, Louis Napoleon's *coup* of 1852, and Prussian invasion and civil war in 1870–71, worked to undermine any consistency in her West African policies.

The feasibility of the policy of carefully restraining British territorial expansion in West Africa thus rested on three main props: the ability of West African states and societies to supply the needs of British commerce (and to respond to the cultural impact of missionaries[21]); the problem of the

[19]Glover of Lagos, recalled by the Colonial Office in 1872.

[20]B. Schnapper, 'La Fin du régime de l'exclusif; le commerce étranger dans les possessions françaises d'Afrique tropicale (1817–1870),' *Annales Africaines* (1959), pp. 149 ff.

[21]The assumption made by the British, which was not altogether incorrect, was that African societies which welcomed missionaries would also welcome legitimate trade and discourage the slave trade. Dissident groups, or claimants to kingship within African states could thus espouse these causes in order to secure British

mosquito and tsetse fly in impeding white residence and animal transport inland; and the absence of any serious foreign challenge to Britain's informal commercial predominance in such trading centres as the Oil Rivers, lower Niger, or the producing regions behind her colonial nuclei in Sierra Leone, Gambia, Gold Coast and Lagos.

By the late-1870s one of these props was knocked away, another was cracking, and the third was about to break. By 1870 the local deterrents to penetration were no longer serious in reality, though they remained so in imagination. Quinine, first used systematically by Baikie, the surgeon in command of the Niger expeditions of the late 1850s, proved its effectiveness as a prophylactic against malaria. The steamship was immune to tsetse fly, and the explorers had mapped the main navigable waterways by 1860. Railways with steam locomotives could be built where no navigable rivers would serve. The 1870s also witnessed the growth of an almost total disbelief, among traders and missionaries alike, in the older view that Christianity and commerce might 'civilise' Africa through the agency of existing African states or through a new Christian-influenced class of Africans; in British eyes the West African states and societies were ceasing to be 'a sufficient political function'.

The background to this disillusionment was complex, and not in fact the result of any lessening of African responses to British commercial stimulus. The British traders, spurred by the success of Niger penetration, became increasingly irritated by the resistance of coastal African middlemen to any direct trade with their interior producers. These dreams of forcing a way into the interior were intensified as palm oil prices slumped after 1873, and well organised African middlemen tried to maintain traditional buying prices and slice the British firms' profits, encouraging the competition of new firms from Glasgow or London into the traditional preserves of Liverpool. At the same time British traders resented the competition of mission-influenced Lagosians or Sierra Leoneans trading on small margins, often after having learned the techniques of trade through clerkships with British firms. A number of scandals in the all-African Niger mission added to the gathering image, popularised by 'scientific' ideas of the biological inferiority of the Negro, of the mission-influenced West African as an untrustworthy, untruthful cheat. The missionaries on their side began to divide along racial lines on such issues,[22] while generally becoming disillusioned with the 'civilising' effects of a commerce in which gunpowder and alcoholic liquors figured

backing. Docemu of Lagos built up his image for the British into that of an anti-slavery pro-Christian claimant who would stimulate legitimate trade, and was supported in his successful bid to depose the 'wicked' Kosoko. See J.F.A. Ajayi, 'The British occupation of Lagos, 1851–61', *Nigeria Magazine*, no. 69 (Aug. 1961).

[22] Ajayi, *Christian Missions*, explores these themes with great skill.

among the major imports used to purchase African produce. Commerce and Christianity ceased to march hand in hand, and when the atheist Goldie united the Niger traders into the United African Company in 1879 the Church Missionary Society sold its shares. By this time both Goldie and his competitors in the Oil Rivers were contemplating the idea that amalgamated companies with armed steamers might acquire political rights from African rulers by treaty, and use these to exclude competitors from their markets.[23]

Neither improvements in European health conditions nor the dissatisfaction of traders, however, were powerful enough to prompt the British government to begin a policy of territorial expansion. Quinine and the steam engine made expansion possible, but not necessarily desirable, while it was not the duty of the British government to ensure that British traders overseas made profits.[24] The catalyst which transformed British policy from one of consolidation and economy in the 1870s into coastal partition in the 1880s and interior expansion in the 1890s was the challenge of French imperialism. Even this might not have sufficed had the French not adopted protectionist policies designed to exclude British traders from her old and new West African colonies.

These crucial changes in French policy towards West Africa occurred between 1877 and 1879.[25] They were totally unrelated to the Egyptian question, for France and Britain were in close cooperation in Egypt during these years. A number of factors came together to determine this revolutionary departure in French policy, and significantly West African conditions were only peripherally concerned. The roots of the new departure lay in France's domestic situation and her European and international

---

[23]The Niger traders used armed steamers even before amalgamation under Goldie in 1879. The UAC undertook 'punishments' of some towns on the Niger as early as 1879, and made a monopoly treaty with Nupe (broken by its Emir the next year) in 1880. For details see Flint, *Goldie*, Chapter 3.

[24]Unless it could be shown that 'native rulers' and 'uncivilised states' had placed artificial barriers upon free commerce, in which case Britain might remove these by force. It is possible that British traders might have secured such support to break the monopolies of African middlemen, or have organised themselves into chartered companies with official blessing to do so, even without the development of a 'scramble'.

[25]The analysis of French intervention which follows is based heavily upon the brilliant article by Newbury and Kanya-Forstner, 'French policy and the origins of the scramble for West Africa', *Journal of African History*, x, (1969) 253–76 which is heavily documented from primary sources, and to this author, conclusive and definitive. Their treatment of the chronology of partition may be compared with earlier arguments which placed the emphasis on the Egyptian occupation of 1882 such as Robinson and Gallagher, *Africa and the Victorians*, pp. 167–75, Hargreaves, *Prelude*, pp. 278–315, or those which have stressed French rivalry with Leopold of the Belgians in the Congo as touching off the scramble, such as J. Stengers, 'L'impérialisme colonial de la fin du XIXe siécle: myth ou réalité?', *Journal of African History*, III (1962), pp. 469–91 and H. Brunschwig, 'Les origines du partage de l'Afrique', *Journal of African History*, v (1964), pp. 121–5.

position. These were the years in which the Republicans at last took control of the Third Republic. 1879 also marked the beginning of Bismarck's alliance system with the signing of the Austro-German alliance, but well before this Bismarck had made it very plain to the French that their imperial ambitions would be given solid German support.[26] In her isolated condition, humiliated by the defeat of 1870, France was thus offered a colonial field upon which to play a role in international affairs. French ambassadors in all the major European capitals pressed their government to make such spectacular yet harmless moves, to take some initiatives seemingly worthy of a great power.[27] These views were echoed publicly by a growing group of colonial enthusiasts, composed of explorers, geographers, railway engineers and some deputies, who demanded the creation of a vast French empire from Algeria to Senegal and the western Sudan as the sole means of national revival and future great power status.[28]

Meanwhile Brière de l'Isle, the energetic new governor of Senegal appointed in 1876, had set about transforming the tariff structure of the colony into a protective system with differential duties on foreign shipping, extension of customs posts southwards towards Sierra Leone, and plans for a comprehensive differential tariff system.[29] At the same time Brière mounted military campaigns in 1877 and 1878 not only to secure the eastern districts of Senegal but to open up routes for an advance to the upper Niger. He revived Faidherbe's grand schemes, now to be achieved by the construction of a Senegal-Niger railway, and warned Paris that if France did not at once begin the advance into the Sudan, the British would eventually acquire the commerce of those supposedly fabulous markets.[30]

Colonial enthusiasts in France might support the local initiatives of a

---

[26]The role of Bismarck in provoking the partition of Africa and the general movement of imperialism has been seen by most historians essentially as the problem of explaining the German colonial interventions of 1884–85. To do this, however, is to examine a secondary phenomenon. Bismarck was a prime influence in beginning the partition in the 1870s. His policy was designed to prevent any possibility of a future cooperative system between France, Britain, and perhaps Italy, by encouraging all three to embark on colonial acquisitions in Africa. With the collapse of Turkish, Egyptian and Tunisian finances after 1875 Bismarck constantly pressed France to take Tunis, Britain Egypt, and Italy Tripoli, knowing that this would provoke disputes between all three.

[27]This statement rests on a general reading of the despatches of French ambassadors from Berlin, Rome, Constantinople and Petersburg from 1876 to 1880 as published in the *Documents Diplomatiques Françaises*, vols II and III.

[28]See A. Murphy, *The Ideology of French Imperialism* (Washington, 1948). A. Duponchel's *Le Chemin de fer Trans-Saharien* (Montpellier, 1878), was a minor sensation, its author was granted 4000 frs by the Ministry of Public Works, and a commission was established to report on the ideas.

[29]Newbury and Kanya-Forstner, 'French policy,' pp. 257–8.

[30]The western Sudan early acquired a reputation of a romantic kind as a potentially vast market for cotton cloth. All the European explorers were struck by the voluminous robes, of local manufacture, worn by the population.

Brière de l'Isle to carry through frontier expansions, but the grandiose imperial plans for a railway empire in northwest Africa needed the support of the French government. That this could be forthcoming was revealed by the enthusiasm with which the French Chamber voted credits for the Senegal-Niger railway survey in May 1879. In December 1879 Freycinet became prime minister of France. He shared the view of the diplomatic corps that France must regain her status by colonial expansion, but more than this, he was a railway enthusiast, and convinced that the partition of Africa was at hand. 'C'est en effet par les voies de communication que la civilisation s'étend et se fixe le plus sûrement. Il faut essayer de rattacher les vastes territoires que baignent le Niger et le Congo,' he declared on assuming office.[31] Assisted by Admiral Jauréguiberry, the former governor of Senegal and enthusiastic advocate of Sudanese expansion who now held the Ministry of Marine and Colonies, Freycinet launched his government on a course of West African expansion.

The detailed story of French advance from Senegal to the Niger and on into the West African savanna need not concern us here.[32] The military advance from Senegal eastwards became henceforward a constant French activity until the 1900s. For the British in the 1880s it threatened to limit the prospects of Sierra Leone, and might result ultimately in a challenge on the lower Niger and in the Sokoto empire, regarded by Goldie's company as a commercial preserve. The increasingly protectionist clauses of the French treaties negotiated with African rulers in the western savanna were regarded by the British as unfortunate and mistaken, but there were no vested British interests there to be excluded by them.[33]

On the West African coasts, however, the British government could not but be alarmed at French moves close to traditional areas of British predominance. The fall in palm oil prices, and thus of revenues, had induced the various British colonial governments to try to increase their falling incomes by minor annexations along the coastlines from Lagos, the Gold Coast, and Sierra Leone. A British naval blockade of Dahomey's coastline in 1876 first stimulated French merchants to press for a revival of French claims and the declaration of a protectorate, on the mistaken assumption that Britain might annex the country. In April 1878 the French obtained a treaty ceding them the town of Cotonou. In September 1879 Governor Ussher of the Gold Coast annexed nearby Katenu. By this

---

[31]Quoted in Newbury and Kanya-Forstner, 'French policy', p. 262.
[32]The story is well told in S. Kanya-Forstner, *The French Conquest of the Western Sudan* (London, 1969).
[33]See undated minute by Lord Kimberley on the French treaty with Segu, published in May 1881, CO 96/136 n.d. Kimberley had sanctioned Gouldsbury's expedition to Futa Jalon (Jan.–April 1881) to make treaties of friendship designed to pull the interior commerce to Sierra Leone. This only convinced the French that the British had designs on the area and hastened their military conquest of Futa. Hargreaves, *Prelude*, pp. 265–71.

time bitter local disputes were under way to the north of Sierra Leone, where the French had responded to the British governor's attempts to extend the collection of customs dues by military occupations culminating in March 1879 with the occupation of Matacong island, which Sierra Leone had annexed in 1877. At the end of 1879 disputes erupted in the coastline of what was to become the Ivory Coast.[34]

Most of this rivalry was trivial in its implications, and undertaken by local officials with little or no encouragement from their home governments. Lord Salisbury, Disraeli's foreign minister, was particularly anxious to curb local proconsuls, and insisted that proposed annexations should first go to Cabinet; Ussher's annexation of Katenu defied this procedure. He was censured but the annexation was not reversed.[35] Salisbury believed that if the rivalry were damped down, France and Britain could come to an amicable arrangement in which they would limit their activities to specific areas of the West African coast. Thus Britain would have no need of empire building and could continue to preserve a free trade area of informal influence, and for this Salisbury was even willing to transfer the Gambia colony to France. But though the French ambassador showed interest, the Colonial Office strongly opposed a formal offer of the Gambia, and nothing had been achieved when the Tory government fell in April 1880.[36]

Gladstone's new Liberal government was more doctrinally and temperamentally committed to policies of non-expansion in West Africa than its predecessor. Gladstone had already publicly written in some detail of his hostility towards a British role in the partition of Africa, should it come.[37] Neither Granville at the Foreign Office, nor Kimberley until

---

[34]The details of these moves are elaborated in Hargreaves, *Prelude*, pp. 201–40.

[35]Ussher to Hicks Beach, 29 Sept. 1879, and minute by Hemming, 10 Nov. 1879. CO 147/38. As a result Salisbury in January minuted, 'I must decline except under specific instructions in each case from the Cabinet to assent on the part of this dept. [i.e. the FO] to any further annexations in West Africa.' Minute by Salisbury, 29 Jan. 1880. FO 84/1581.

[36]Hargreaves, *Prelude*, pp. 234–7. The Gambia cession idea was an old one, which had earlier been frustrated by merchant and African opposition. The object of surrendering it to France was to allow the French to concentrate on a solid block of territory, into which the long narrow Gambia intruded, in the hope that Britain could be left all the coast to the south for informal control and free trade.

[37]W.E. Gladstone, 'Aggression on Egypt and freedom in the East', *Nineteenth Century*, Aug.–Dec. 1877, pp. 149–66. In this brilliantly written article Gladstone almost exactly anticipated the thesis of *Africa and the Victorians* in so far as it applies to East and southern Africa (and Robinson and Gallagher have proved least vulnerable to critics in their analysis of those areas). Gladstone argued that 'our first site in Egypt, be it by larceny or be it by emption, will be the almost certain egg of a North African Empire, that will grow and grow until another Victoria and another Albert, titles of the Lake-sources of the White Nile, come within our borders; and till we finally join hands across the Equator with Natal and Cape Town, to say nothing of the Transvaal and the Orange River on the south, or of Abyssinia or Zanzibar, to be swallowed by way of *viaticum* on our journey'.

1882 nor Derby who took the Colonial Office from him in that year were as prepared as the Conservative Hicks Beach had been to sanction annexations. As in Egypt and South Africa, so in West Africa Gladstone's band of anti-imperialists was dragged into formal defence of British interests by the pressure of events.

Granville's and Kimberley's instincts, therefore, were to follow Salisbury's scheme for settling local disputes by agreements in London or Paris. The Liberals were even naïve enough to think that France might then revert to informal influence in her spheres, and agree not to practice discriminatory tariff policies. But the French were adamant on the tariff issue, revealing clearly what the objects of French expansion would mean for British traders; the British, anxious to end frontier rivalries in Sierra Leone and the Gold Coast, backed down. A joint demarcation commission established a northern frontier for Sierra Leone, and Britain agreed not to interfere between it and the Gambia boundary; France accepted that she would not interfere south of Sierra Leone to the Liberian border.[38] The arrangement settled only local issues; it was far less than the overall settlement to create recognised informal spheres which the British would have liked, but even so it produced bitter opposition in France from French commercial interests.

The real significance of the Convention was its revelation to the British that French expansion was directed towards the creation of tariff-protected havens for French trade and shipping. The 'Peculiar Interlude' was coming to an end. Even so, this did not immediately produce a British determination to react defensively to preserve her spheres of informal control. For this to happen needed a credible French threat to the major centre of British West African commerce on the Niger and Oil Rivers, whose combined palm oil and other trades were worth more than that of all the other British West African trade *in toto*,[39] and where (except for Lagos island) Britain had no formal control.

It was exactly this threat which materialised steadily from 1880 to 1883 in a series of French moves which gave the appearance of a deliberate

---

[38]For these negotiations see Hargreaves, *Prelude*, pp. 247–52; the Anglo-French Convention of 28 June 1882 is printed in Newbury, *Documents 1875–1900*, pp. 175–8. It was never ratified because of opposition in the French Chamber, but was adhered to as a working arrangement.

[39]Precise statistics are difficult to assess, for they were not collected in forms which could substantiate this point exactly. The best published figures are in Newbury, *Documents, 1876–1914*, tables III and IV, pp. 599–617. In arguing the primacy of the southern Nigeria coast the Lagos trade figures should be set with the estimates for the Niger and Oil Rivers. The total in the 1880s may be estimated as from £1–1·5 million imports to the area, and £1·5–2 million exports to Britain. In terms of total British trade, of course, this was an insignificant amount. But there is no evidence that British officials regarded it in such relative terms, for them it was not a negligible commerce, and deserved suitable protection. The fact that it was of no consequence in comparison with the trade of South Africa or India thus has no bearing on the question of its protection.

policy of challenging Britain's informal predominance in the lower Niger region, and when connected with the advance from Senegal into the savanna, could be seen as a grand design to secure complete control of the Niger from its sources to the Delta. Scarcely had Goldie formed his monopoly by amalgamation in 1879 than it was broken into by French competition after 1880. In 1881 the French trading agent Mattei was appointed French consul for the Niger, his ships intervened with Goldie's in the civil war in Nupe in 1881, and by 1882 two French firms were as strong as Goldie's group in the lower Niger trade. It was these developments which prompted Goldie to form the National African Company in 1882 with the object of securing administrative control of the Niger territories to enforce his monopoly.[40]

Meanwhile a similar threat seemed to be developing southeast of the Oil Rivers. Since 1880 Savorgnan de Brazza, authorised by the French government to make treaties at Stanley Pool, and financed partly by the French committee of the International African Association with subsidies from Jules Ferry's Ministry of Education and the French Colonial Office, was laying the foundations for a French colony north of the Congo mouth.[41] James Hutton, the Manchester merchant and member of parliament who was also on Goldie's board of directors, reported to the Colonial Office that de Brazza had originally been instructed to make treaties on the Niger.[42] Edward Hewett, British Consul in the Oil Rivers, feared that de Brazza would move northwestwards, behind the coastal city states of the Oil Rivers, and seize the Ibo palm oil producing lands for France, thus forestalling the British merchants' ambitions of direct penetration to the markets. He demanded action to forestall this, either a protectorate, a Crown Colony, or a 'chartered company of British merchants'.[43]

Elsewhere[44] I have argued that it was this alarmed request from the Oil Rivers Consul, supported by the Chambers of Commerce and Goldie's company directors, which initiated discussions between Foreign Office, Colonial Office and Treasury. These would eventually result, for lack of Colonial Office willingness to annex and face the problems of implementing mandatory legislation such as the Anti-slavery Act of 1833, and for lack of Treasury support, in the creation of the Oil Rivers Protectorate of 1884 and the chartering of the Royal Niger Company in 1886. The threat from France was thus realised, and discussion on countermeasures

---

[40]Flint, *Goldie*, pp. 35–46. The Nupe situation, and the activities of the French, hare been considerably expanded upon by Michael Mason, 'The Nupe kingdoms in the nineteenth century: a political history', Ph.D. thesis, University of Birmingham, 1970, chapters 7 and 8.

[41]H. Brunschwig, *L'Avénement de L'Afrique noire* (Paris, 1963), pp. 133–68, is the fullest account of these events.

[42]FO Conf. Print 4825, no. 2, p. 2 enc. in CO to FO 6 Jan. 1883.

[43]Hewett to Granville, 14 Jan. 1882, FO Conf. Print 4824, no. 9, p. 20.

[44]Flint, *Goldie*, pp. 48 ff.

initiated, before the occupation of Egypt, and certainly well before it could be argued that Britain's failure to withdraw rapidly from Egypt had alienated the French.[45]

Nevertheless it must be admitted that these discussions took place against a background of intensifying French pressure, which came to a climax in the years 1883–84, by which time the effects of the Egyptian occupation had time to be felt. In November 1882 de Brazza's treaty was unanimously ratified in the French Chamber, and he returned in February 1883 to the Congo with the formal title of Commissioner to organise the new colony. Mattei began making treaties on the Benue river in September 1882, and in January 1883 Jauréguiberry (back at the Ministry of Marine since the previous year) ordered an assault on the lower Niger; the French navy was to make treaties with the city states of Bonny and Calabar, and Mattei to do the same on the lower Niger at Brass, the centre of African middleman opposition to Goldie. From May to August 1883 these attempts were made, failing largely through the efforts of pro-British African Christians.[46] Jauréguiberry also pushed through a new challenge to the British position west of the Niger delta; in April 1883 the French ran up their flag at Porto Novo and a number of other coastal towns, establishing the base for the future colony of Dahomey.[47]

The British position now stiffened considerably. Sir Percy Anderson, senior clerk in the Foreign Office, composed a definitive memorandum in June 1883, in which he made it clear that a partition of West Africa had begun, and that Britain must reply with a policy of protectorates designed to secure British trading interests, especially in the Oil Rivers and Niger. 'If there is one thing clearer than another', he commented, 'it seems to be that the French have a settled policy in Africa.'

> If we remain passive, we shall see our trade stifled, we shall find our traders furious, and we shall hardly escape grave complications with the French as successive protectorates produce fresh irritation till, *when the field is finally closed against us,* we shall have to deal with chronic grievances and complaints. . .
>
> Protectorates are unwelcome burdens, but in this case it is, if my view is correct, a question between British Protectorates, which would be unwelcome, and French Protectorates, which would be fatal.[48]

---

[45]The French, of course, had been invited to join in the occupation of Egypt, but withdrew. They could thus have no reason immediately to become angry at the event. Robinson and Gallagher, *Africa and the Victorians*, p. 166, stress that it was not until the *end* of 1882 that France became embittered with the realisation that Britain was not about to withdraw rapidly and was establishing a régime in Egypt.

[46]Flint, *Goldie*, pp. 51–2; Newbury and Kanya-Forstner, 'French policy', p. 269.

[47]Hargreaves, *Prelude*, pp. 294–300.

[48]Memorandum by Anderson, 11 June 1883, FO Conf. Print 4819. My italics, not in original.

By November 1883 the policy of establishing protectorates for the Niger and Oil Rivers was endorsed by the Cabinet, 'with a view to the maintenance of an unfettered trade, which unhappily is not favoured by the arrangements of the French in those latitudes'.[49]

The story of how this decision was substantially[50] implemented is too well known to elaborate in detail.[51] The achievement was vastly complicated by Bismarck's decision to establish German colonies in Togo, South-West Africa and Kameroon in May 1884, just as Consul Hewett received his instructions to make treaties on the Niger and in the Oil Rivers. Bismarck's decision was part of a broader aim of embittering Anglo-French relations by joining with France in calling the Berlin Conference of 1884–85 whose object was initially to destroy British informal control of the Congo and lower Niger rivers. By this stage the British government was determined to save the Niger for exclusive British control,[52] and in this objective they succeeded thanks to a cooling of German–French cooperation and Goldie's timely purchase of his French competitors. The Conference concluded by recognising British control of the lower Niger, and the way was clear for chartering the Royal Niger Company in 1886.

In the unfolding of these events it should now be clear that the occupation of Egypt and its repercussions neither originated the partition of West Africa, nor even significantly affected its course. The British decision to move from informal control to formal protectorates to defend their interests represented a reaction to a revived French imperialism which occurred in 1878–79, and was irrelevant to the Egyptian question. The peculiar conditions of 1815–70 had come to an end, and the more natural Anglo-French rivalry for empire once again reasserted itself. Reluctantly, British governments searched about for the cheapest forms of imperial control, and found them in the chartered company and the lightly administered Foreign Office protectorate, which would later be adopted even by the Colonial Office. The Egyptian question may have exacerbated French hostility after the end of 1882, but there is no evidence that French activity in the Oil Rivers, lower Niger, Dahomey, Gabun and Congo was designed to produce British concessions in Egypt. Like the advance from Senegal, these moves originated from France's contemplation of her position in West Africa, her interests there, and her fears of Britain's West African policies. The British neither imagined that they must make Egyptian concessions to calm the West African situation, nor wished to do so. For Britain too the problem was seen in the context of West Africa

[49]Cabinet Papers 41/17, Cabinet Minute 22 Nov. 1883.
[50]The plan envisaged a British protectorate over the Cameroons, where there was substantial British trade, Baptist missionaries, and the prospects of a hill station for the Consul. Hewett was forestalled by the German intervention in July 1884.
[51]See Hargreaves, *Prelude*, pp. 314–38; Flint, *Goldie*, pp. 55–85.
[52]Three days before the Berlin Conference began Goldie's company was authorised to hoist the Union Jack over its stations. For details see Flint, *Goldie*, p. 68.

and her commercial interests there emerged as the crux of all considerations.

Bismarck's decision to found a German colonial empire may have been influenced by a desire to demonstrate to Britain how dependent she now was on Germany's vote if the International Debt Commission was to allow reform of Egypt's finances. But the intervention had much deeper roots than the opportunity created by Egypt; since 1876 Bismarck had consistently encouraged French and British expansion in Africa in the hopes of intensifying their colonial rivalries, and the German annexations of 1884–85 were intended to add further stimulus to the excitements and uncertainties of the scramble for territories. For the British, protectionist France remained the real rival; German colonies might be awkward diplomatically, but they were not protectionist, and British trade continued to develop in them, as did German trade in British West Africa.

British commercial imperialism remained consistent during the subsequent partitioning of West African territories from 1884–98. During the 1880s it was primarily defensive, seeking to preserve existing and real commercial areas of predominance. There was thus no grand design like the French, so that Gambia, Sierra Leone, Gold Coast and southern Nigeria became separated, and the earlier aspirations of educated anglophile Africans for a British West African federal dominion foundered. By the 1890s the reluctance to expand largely fell away, and even before Chamberlain took the Colonial Office in 1895 British commercial imperialism was looking to the assertion of control over interior producing regions in Ashanti and the northern regions of Gold Coast, but above all to the preservation of a future British dominion in the Sokoto and Bornu empires, bringing their as yet unassessed but surely lucrative commerce down to the sea by railways yet to be built.

When the French challenged the effectiveness of Goldie's Niger Company frontiers, Chamberlain was ready to organise military resistance through the West African Frontier Force and if need be, to go to war to protect British dominance of northern Nigerian markets. Neither in the 1880s nor in the 1890s did Britain make any West African concessions to France to relieve the pressure on Egypt or the Nile valley. Those pressures could be, and were, met eventually by Kitchener's conquest of the Sudan; in the meantime the present and future commerce of British West African coasts and hinterlands would be assured by expansion as and when it seemed necessary. By their fruits are they known; and although French acquisitions in West Africa after 1879 appeared enormous on the maps, they were to a considerable extent what Lord Salisbury once injudiciously referred to as 'light land'.[53] The four British territories,

[53]Lady Gwendolen Cecil, *Life of Robert, Marquis of Salisbury* (London, 1921 etc.) v, pp. 323–4.

expanded from their earlier coastal nuclei, between them controlled the denser African populations, the larger productive capacities, and the preponderance of trade.

6

E.A. AYANDELE

The Phenomenon of Visionary Nationalists in Precolonial Nigeria[1]

For a long time, until the different parts of the British Empire began to assert independence, the focus and context of imperial studies were basically metropolis-oriented. This orientation was in perfect consonance and harmony with the concept of the empire which saw Britain as the parent and the other parts as offspring; which saw British laws, norms, cultural heritage, and thought patterns as the models which her offspring should seek to copy. In such an empire it would be heretical to contemplate a different or separatist identity, much less preach a new-fangled credo of nationalism.

This concept of the British Empire which unified under one crown diverse peoples and cultures scattered all over the terrestrial globe, disregarded race and colour. Hence in nineteenth-century West Africa the subjects of the crown were encouraged by their British political and social mentors to know and imitate the British model in matters of religion, laws, constitution, government and ways of life. This is the explanation for the picture of the educated elite of the pre-scramble era which has emerged from the studies done so far[2] — a picture that reveals the hybridised elite as protégés of the British, as veritable agents and instruments of British cultural, religious, intellectual, political and economic manifestations. Quite rightly, too, this picture also exposes the political, cultural, social and religious differences between the educated elite and the unlett red indigenous Africans.

And yet, as scholars who have examined the reaction of subject peoples to the imperial metropolis have discovered, there never was a time when subject peoples did not manifest the spirit of self-identity. Paradoxical though it may seem, this spirit of self-identity was not in fact incompatible with loyalty to the British Empire.

To return to the tiny pre-scramble educated elite in Nigeria, much as

[1]The term 'Nigeria' is used rather loosely to refer to the area that became a single political unit under the British.
[2]See in particular J. Herskovits Kopytoff, *A Preface to Modern Nigeria: the 'Sierra Leonians' in Yoruba 1830–1890* (Madison, Wisconsin, 1965); Robert W. July, *The Origins of Modern African Thought* (London, 1968).

112

the picture of them wearing the toga of British imperialism is substantially authentic, it ignores the fact that they were also purveyors of the concept of Nigeria for the Nigerians. This peculiar set of semi-Nigerians would have been less than human if they had completely transformed themselves into Britishers or become totally unconscious of, or unaffected by, their Nigerian origins. They were not unaware that in the Nigerian territory they were a separate and new class with a distinct identity and with stakes, hopes and visions different from those being nurtured by their British mentors.

The truth of the matter is that from the early days, though they were not organised into a collective movement, they were individually conscious that they were a group different from their British mentors, no less than they were aware of their differences with their unlettered countrymen who would not follow these *Saro* (as the emigrants from Sierra Leone and their descendants were called) to spiritual or mental or cultural exile. Thus while they had received Christianity from the white man they saw no reason why he should not begin to relinquish to them leadership of the Church within a generation. The elite began to clamour that it was their duty to propagate Christianity in their own country. Thus while they expected the British to launch the Westminster style of parliamentary government, they did not wish that Nigerian participation should be of a nominal or advisory capacity, or that the legislative chamber should be numerically or effectively dominated by representatives of British interests in Nigeria.[3] While they were delighted at the establishment of a British form of civil service in Nigeria the educated elite believed that this institution should be more Nigerian than British.[4] While they approved of increased trade between Nigeria and the wider world, particularly Europe, the elite leadership hoped that Nigerian participation would be primary and greater than that of the Europeans.[5]

The instincts of independence and self-preservation exhibited by the educated elite before the British imposed colonial rule on Nigeria were real, and constituted an embarrassment to their mentors. In Church and State British representatives were literally stupefied by the extraordinary phenomenon of a first generation elite, barely 'civilised', assuming that they were already 'civilised' and irritatingly impatient to run before they could walk. As early as 1863 Governor Freeman had quoted for the British government the 'Africa for the Africans' motto of the elite leaders in Nigeria, leaders 'who would rejoice to see their benefactors and supporters, the English, either swept from the coast or subjected to the dominion of the blacks'.[6] By 1885 the white man's informal but imperial

[3] *Lagos Times*, 9 March 1881; *Lagos Observer*, 3 July 1886.
[4] *Lagos Times*, 23 May 1883; *Lagos Standard*, 26 Nov. 1902.
[5] James Johnson to Fox Bourne, 17 June 1893. Rhodes House, Oxford, APS. *Liverpool Courier*, 23 Sept. 1897.
[6] H.S. Freeman to Duke of Newcastle, 31 Dec. 1863. CO 147/4.

presence in Church and State was to the educated elite a 'yoke'[7] of which many wished Nigeria to be relieved. In the language of an anguished CMS white missionary:

> There is amongst some of the most prominent and influential natives of this Coast a strong and frequently expressed feeling that Africa should be for the Africans. They desire that Africa should rise: in which desire they will have the sympathy and best wishes of every right thinking person. They would go farther and say, Give us the means of raising her and leave the rest with us. With such persons the presence of the white man in the country is only partially welcome. They think there is little, if any need of his assistance in Christianising and Civilising Africa.[8]

How did these double-faced semi-Nigerians, in a sense a part and agents of European imperialism in Nigeria, come to have a vision of, and demand, independence for Nigeria? It was natural that such a distinct class should desire a distinct identity. In a way that the creoles of Sierra Leone Colony were never to claim, the Nigerian elite were imbued with the conviction that Nigeria was their country, the fatherland of their *Saro* parents or of themselves, where they were among, or in close proximity to, their kith and kin. With this conviction they were not absolutely alienated from their unlettered countrymen. But they assumed that the latter, the vast majority, required their leadership on issues concerning the transformation which the future Nigeria needed; they felt as well that their unlettered countrymen should be guided by them, the educated elite, against the imperial ambitions of the British. Their envisioned Nigeria was one in which Christianity would flourish to the point of displacing African traditional religion and Islam, in which literary education would leaven society, and government be administered in the light of ideas and concepts borrowed from the white man's world. In its economic aspect their ideal state would emphasise intensified international trade and encourage cash crops, adopt European technology and make the English language the *lingua franca*.

How did the educated elite acquire the conviction and confidence that they were qualified to be leaders in precolonial Nigeria? By far the biggest fountain of their ideas, aspirations and vision was Christianity. The ideological potential and the baiting capacity of Christianity were to the educated elite beyond dispute. As conceived by the semi-Nigerians, this religion was to bring salvation, greatness, prosperity, stability and happiness to Nigerians; it was the prime mover of the economic, technological and scientific revolution that should occur in Nigeria. Christianity

[7]A. Mann to Secretaries, 16 June 1882. Church Missionary Society Archives, London (hereafter cited as CMS), CA2/01.
[8]J.B. Wood to Secretaries, 27 Sept. 1881. CMS, G3/CA2/01.

114

was the ultimate and final religion of humanity, the lever which lifted mankind to the peak of material, social, moral and political achievement.[9] The nationalist message in, and ethical laws prescribed by, the Bible could not but shape the pattern of thinking and attitude of the elite to their white mentors. For taking their weapons from the arsenal of utopianism, proclaiming the racial and cultural neutralism of Christianity, the equality of peoples and Providence's countenance of the observance of moral and social virtues, the educated elite demanded application of these prescriptions to the relations between themselves and the British. In this respect the tension unleashed by the contradiction between the behaviour of missionaries and scriptural instructions is to be understood. But Christianity inculcates other notions as well — concepts of the nation-state, of the status of the individual in society, of government, and of the source and use of power and authority, of obedience, citizenship and the rights of the individual. Little wonder that a Nigerian disseminator of Christianity declared on 20 September 1891: 'Christianity in itself was in its origin and entirety the grandest and greatest revolution that has ever affected humanity.'[10]

Another source of inspiration to the elite, particularly in the third quarter of the nineteenth century, was the Englishman Henry Venn, Secretary of the Church Missionary Society from 1842 to 1872, who, far away in Britain, perceived the nationalist message of Christianity and the sense of national or racial identity which the planting of the Church in Africa was bound to have. His scheme for the 'euthanasia' of missions certainly went a long way to instil in the elite leadership in Nigeria the hope that religious and ecclesiastical independence for Africans was only a matter of time, a time that was expected to be short and which many interpreted in the apostolic Pauline sense, according to which Paul merely sowed the seeds and left their germination and nurture to the 'God of missions', refusing to be the director and controller of the churches he founded. Moreover Henry Venn went a long way to give many of the Nigerian elite the sense that the destiny of Nigeria would be in their hands once they surrendered themselves to be groomed as church leaders, teachers, clerks, cotton-ginners, traders and artisans. Hence the reverence with which men like Bishop Ajayi Crowther, James Johnson, Henry Robbin, J. A. Otunba Payne, Captain J.P.L. Davies and Dr J. B. Horton regarded this uncommonly clairvoyant and unstintedly benevolent patron of Africans.

One other source of nationalist inspiration was the political message conveyed by western literature. No one familiar with the liberal education which the leaders of thought in nineteenth-century Nigeria acquired, largely through avid reading, can fail to perceive the impact on them of

[9]*Lagos Times*, 9 Nov. 1881, 28 Dec. 1881.
[10]*Sierra Leone Weekly News*, 5 March 1892.

examples of other patriotic and nationalist movements in history. The Protestant Reformation, the War of American Independence, the French Revolution and the forcible unification of Italy and Germany in the nineteenth century were events which influenced many, before the end of the century, to expect pentecostally a 'revolution' that would usher in the Nigeria of their dreams. A streak of millenarism was to be found among a few ardent Christians who gave a totally subjective interpretation to 'Ethiopia stretching forth her hands unto God'.[11]

The elite who dreamed of a utopian Nigeria under their control were for a while oblivious of the major and fundamental differences between themselves and their white mentors on the one hand, and between themselves and their unlettered countrymen on the other. In their view by the eve of British colonial rule they had much to be proud of in empirical data which seemed to confirm their illusions and buoy up their hopes about the realism of their vision. Although numbering no more than a few thousands in the last quarter of the nineteenth century, they had produced leaders in various walks of life, who would do credit to Africa. In medical science Dr Nathaniel King, an Egba, was to serve the Lagos community until his death in 1885. By 1900 Drs Obadiah Johnson, J. Lumpkins, Oguntola Sapara, J. K. Randle and Obasa had been for years practising in Lagos or serving in government hospitals. Many of their clients were non-Africans and three of them served as consultants to European firms. There were no less than a dozen university graduates at the end of the century. As early as 1878 Isaac Oluwole, later assistant bishop, had graduated from Fourah Bay College, and in 1885 Henry Rawlinson Carr, also a Fourah Bay graduate and a distinguished educationalist, began to tutor in the CMS Grammar School, Lagos. For the greater part of the last quarter of the nineteenth century, the CMS Grammar School and Methodist Boys' High School were headed by Nigerians. In the legal and engineering professions men like Sapara Williams and Herbert Macaulay (respectively) were professionally qualified, while in the civil service J. A. Otunba Payne, Nash H. Williams and the Willoughbies were respectable high calibre people. Even in commerce a number of educated Africans held their own. Henry Robbin of Abeokuta was nicknamed 'Olowo Ake' (the rich man of Ake), while Richard Beales Blaize was one of the wealthiest men in West Africa.

Not that the educated elite believed that they were already ripe for political independence in the 1880s. They knew quite well that the number of Nigerian experts in the various walks of life was still very small and that the Nigeria of their dream was a remote possibility. As one newspaper put it:

[11]For a full discussion of Ethiopianism see E.A. Ayandele, *The Missionary Impact on Modern Nigeria 1842–1914: a political and social analysis* (London, 1966), ch. 6.

We are not clamouring for immediate independence, for the sufficient reason that we are *not* prepared for it; but it should always be borne in mind that the present order of things *will not* last for ever. A time will come when the British colonies on the West Coast of Africa, Lagos included, will be left to regulate their own internal and external affairs.[12]

However, the essential point is that they had a vision of political independence for West Africa in general; Thomas Paine's principles of 'the Rights of Man' had been appreciated as early as 1882, and the American Revolution had acquired special meaning for them. As a newspaper editorialised: 'The principles which led, for example to the declaration of American independence are eternal. They lie at the very root of human nature, and are as powerful in the Negro as in any of the other great families of man.'[13] Indeed by the early 'eighties demand was made for 'Native Houses of Assembly', with members elected by universal suffrage.[14]

In the Church the elite had the greatest talent, and recorded achievements which made them ask for religious independence in the 'eighties. For nearly a quarter of a century Bishop Samuel Ajayi Crowther was the overseer of a mission which had the greatest thrust of any into the interior of West Africa, and numbered among its adherents martyrs for the Christian cause. In the Anglican Church no white bishop with his seat in Nigeria was to be appointed before 1894. And though Henry Johnson and Dandeson Coates Crowther were made archdeacons in 1878, there was no white archdeacon ppointed for Nigeria until 1885. Indeed for the rest of the century other Nigerians in the Anglican Church — 'half' (assistant) bishops Isaac Oluwole, Charles Phillips and James Johnson — were to hold positions which made them ecclesiastical superiors of whites. In a less spectacular way, educated Africans in other missions throughout southern Nigeria were gaining leadership in the Church. In Lagos and the interior Africans were appointed district superintendents by the Methodists, and the rules of the congregationalist Baptists made participation in government by the members obligatory.

The belief that independence in Church affairs must prepare the way for secular independence was held by several educated Africans in nineteenth-century West Africa. Independence in religious affairs, it was felt, must be around the corner. In the belief that by 1900 enough personnel had been produced, British tutelage in Church affairs came to be regarded more as a liability than as an asset. The elite eagerly looked forward to the period when the Church 'would become thoroughly African — purely Native without foreign admixture or control — supporting itself and with

[12]*Lagos Times*, 9 March 1881.
[13]*Ibid.*, 10 May 1882.
[14]*Ibid.*, 14 June 1882.

a purely Native ministry, directing its own affairs'.[15] They believed that demonstration of ability to rule themselves in the Church was a *sine qua non* to the path to political independence: 'The people who are incompetent to sit as rulers in their own spiritual affairs can scarcely be said to be qualified to sit as Civil Legislators.'[16]

The vision of complete independence in the Church and a great measure of independence in the state entertained by the leaders of the educated elite in Nigeria before the partition was wild, fantastic and blatantly quixotic. There was nothing in the Nigerian milieu to encourage their vision. They were a myopic people who though they had eyes could not perceive. For had they descended on the earth from their dreamland they would have seen that their demand for independence in the Church never received the blessing of their white mentors; that their hopes for unimpeded advancement in the civil service and for leadership of the unlettered majority were entirely lacking in validity or legitimacy. Certainly the patterns of thinking of white missionaries and those of the unlettered masses were totally different from the pattern of thinking of the presumptuous elite.

The white missionaries in nineteenth-century Nigeria were much less imaginative than their Nigerian wards, who judged their masters by what the Bible said and by what Christianity was believed to prescribe. Whereas people like Henry Venn and Afrophile philanthropists in Britain laid much store by the educated elite and the crucial significance they should have for Africa in general, the missionaries in West Africa conceived of no day when the educated elite would be absolutely on their own without the guidance of the white man. These missionaries could not see how 'Christianity, commerce and civilisation' could be firmly or widely established in West Africa except in the remote future. And with the qualities being evinced by Africans they were not convinced that the educated elite would be the people to establish this trinity of the C's. For they failed to see in their wards genuine Christians who could safely be left alone, and much less be the exclusive agency for the spread of Christianity. Hence the low view in which the *Saro* were held by white traders, secular officers and missionaries; hence the amazement, if not shock, of the local missionaries when the educated elite began to take initiatives in educational and evangelistic affairs, without first obtaining clearance and guidance from their white mentors;[17] hence the opposition of the missionaries to the policies initiated by headquarters to devolve power and authority on the Nigerian converts.[18]

---

[15]*Ibid.*
[16]*Ibid.*
[17]See E.A. Ayandele, *Holy Johnson: Pioneer of African nationalism, 1836–1917* (London, 1970), pp. 88–91.
[18]Ayandele, *The Missionary Impact*, pp. 189–91.

The views of white missionaries concerning the educated elite were closer to those of pseudo-anthropologists like R. F. Burton, T. J. Hutchinson and Winwood Reade than to those of the mission headquarters and Exeter Hall. As the head of the CMS in Lagos felt compelled to protest to headquarters in 1885:

> The African has been petted and spoiled and told that he is so good, that he greatly believes it even when he is living in gross immorality. There are many sad cases here in Lagos, such as would startle the friends of Missions. Don't increase our difficulties by proclaiming the goodness of this wicked place.[19]

Thus, forty-six years after the Wesleyan Mission had been established in Yorubaland and an impressive number of native clergy had been raised up, the Reverend T. J. Halligey, Superintendent of the Mission, could write of the clergy in 1888:

> To them [Africans] the ministry is a respectable profession — not a Divine call. This new Yoruba Mission will not be worth much until Europeans can labour there. After all my experience on this coast my deliberate conviction is that if Africa's evangelisation is to wait for Africa's sons — I refer only to the West Coast — the millenuium will have to be indefinitely postponed. Alas! that it should be so, but so it is. West Africa has not yet produced her Apostle.[20]

Or, as another missionary wrote of the African agents of the Church Missionary Society on the Niger:

> One cannot help feeling . . . whether, with the majority of the agents, conversion of heart has ever taken place; and whether they are not actuated by the lowest motives . . . a Christianity which lives only on the lips, and has no place in the life is only a mockery, and not that which can be propagated for the good of men.[21]

The missionaries did not look on themselves as did the Apostle Paul. By 1902 only one of them — the Reverend S. G. Pinnock of the Southern American Baptist Mission, rejoiced 'at the independence manifested by the Churches, when Episcopal authority, Methodist Prerogative, or Baptist lordship seeks to deprive them [Nigerians] of their right to independence'.[22] Rather, by far the majority of missionaries believed in lording it over God's heritage. The visionary nationalists seemed to the missionaries as nothing more than 'adult children', who could not be

---

[19]J.H. Hamilton to R. Lang, 4 June 1885. CMS, G3/A2/03.
[20]T. J. Halligey to Osborne, 26 Feb. 1888. Methodist Mission Archives, London.
[21]T. Phillips to Lang, 11 Jan. 1883. CMS, G3/A3/02.
[22]S.G. Pinnock to Editor, *Lagos Standard*, 9 January in the issue of that paper 22 Jan. 1902.

expected to mature for a long time to come. A woman missionary writing of the Christian leaders in Lagos commented:

> The present generation will remain so, like some children who are pampered and spoilt and put forward before they have begun to learn control of self-discipline or self-denial or so remaining weak creatures all their lives. I get almost angry with the *men* here sometimes they are so *babyish*, there is nothing manly about them.[23]

Missionaries who regarded the Nigerian Christian leaders as 'babyish' could not be persuaded that they had any valid claim to lead the unlettered masses, nor did they recognise the nationalist message of the Christian religion. They consciously transplanted metropolitan versions of Christianity to Nigeria and were disinclined to recognise that there could be a Nigerian brand of Christianity or Church as valid as that of Europe or America. And whilst the missionaries knew that nation-states were being created in Europe and regarded forces such as liberalism and democracy as essentials in the march of contemporary European countries to 'progress', they saw no reason why, or how, these forces should apply in the milieu of contemporary Nigeria. The vision of most missionaries was inhibited by localism; they could not have nursed, nor have been expected to nurse, pan-Nigerian ideas. Many were prejudiced in favour of the subethnic groups among whom they worked in the latter's claims against rival neighbours. On the Niger the CMS consciously, though rightly, emphasised the conflict of interest of the *Saro* leaders and the unlettered masses.

Just as the whites rejected their claims, so too did the unlettered mass of Nigerians refuse to recognise the vision and pretensions of the educated elite. Though the masses recognised that the colour of the skin tied them and the educated elite together, the illiterate developed different and uncomplimentary views of the semi-Nigerians. The unlettered masses regarded the educated elite as black people with white minds displayed in their devotion to the white man's religion, the white man's clothes, the white man's language, the white man's mentality, and the white man's marriage and burial customs. It was for this reason that in the interior the educated elite dared not assert leadership in the precolonial era; in Lagos and other coastal areas the educated elite would have been thrown out by the indigenous leaders as a danger to society and national interest, but for the naval presence of Britain. In some parts of southern Nigeria the educated elite were regarded as being as bad as the white man; hence the refusal of the Ijebu and the Edo, for instance, to receive back liberated Ijebu and Edo from Sierra Leone and the New World. The Egba, the only people in the interior of Nigeria who were generous in welcoming returned ex-slaves or their offspring, had by 1891 regretted their acceptance

[23]Miss Goodall to Lang, 6 Aug. 1890. CMS, G3/A3/02.

of *Saro* leadership, seeing them as tools of British imperial intrusion into their fatherland.

The leaders of the educated elite were not only visionary patriots but also bundles of contradiction. Thus while they professed adherence to the Christian religion and were ready to exert themselves on its behalf, many of them could not conquer the sentiments of subethnocentrism. For example, although Mojola Agbebi recognised that Christianity ignores political frontiers and the ethnic label, and actually spread the gospel among several non-Yoruba peoples, yet he was a member of the Ekiti-parapo, one of the clannish Yoruba groups which intensified and prolonged the Kiriji War of 1877 to 1893. Many of the 'nationalists' were anything but pan-Nigerian or even pan-Yoruba in their activities. In Lagos, which was the chief base of their operation, the educated elite were divided into subtribal groups which stood for sectional, rather than pan-Yoruba identity, and they never hesitated to work against one another. The Egba and Ijebu 'National Associations' were dismayed by the activities of the 'Yoruba National Association', an organisation of the Oyo Yoruba, which consciously encouraged Governor J. H. Glover to seek a new route via Ondo into the interior at the expense of the economic and political interests of the Egba and Ijebu. J. A. Otunba Payne was a disciple of James Johnson in the latter's crusade for pan-African independence in religious affairs and was keenly interested in chronicling the chief events of Yorubaland, but he had greater veneration for Queen Victoria than for any ruler in Nigeria. Richard Beale Blaize was the owner-founder of *Lagos Times* in 1880, which in its early issues spoke of the virtues of self-government, and he refused to be a nominated member of the Legislative Council on the ground that he would prefer to be elected by the masses, but he had little in common with the unlettered people in Lagos and in the interior whose support he would have needed for election. Moreover, though a few of the educated elite appreciated the mystic significance and purposefulness of the traditional Ogboni freemasonry, most of them — J. A. Otunba Payne, C. A. Sapara Williams, J. B. Benjamin, Kitoyi Ajasa, C. J. George, Herbert Macaulay, to name examples — were British freemasons.

Perhaps the best illustration of the dilemma in which the visionary patriots found themselves may be seen in the way in which George William Johnson attempted intermittently between 1866 and 1893 to give the Egba a constitution that would create centralised monarchical government. Like many of his co-visionaries he envisaged his kind leading Africans with alien ideas, and G. W. Johnson was a bumptious and presumptuous *Saro*. Born in 1828 in Sierra Leone he was a tailor, a profession he later abandoned for flute-playing with the West African Squadron. In 1865 he settled himself in Abeokuta, where he began to dream of a centralised Egba state with the Alake as the monarch to whom all other chiefs should be subordinate, and with the educated elite setting up a civil service. His grand vision was to create an 'enlightened and Christian' government which would receive the recognition of European powers, an administration in a sense similar to J. B. Horton's for the Fanti, in which harmonious and effective partnership would be achieved by the 'natural' rulers and the educated elite. With greater foolhardiness than discretion the incorrigible 'Reversible Johnson' — who had to reverse ineffective proclamations almost as soon as he made them — consistently put before apathetic, irritated and unconcerned Egba rulers and their people his model constitution prescribing an Alake holding a position similar to that of Queen Victoria. To this end in 1880, 1881, 1883, 1886 and 1892 he made proposals which altered the details but never the principles of his 1866 proposals. In 1881, for instance, he proposed a revised Board of Management on which the three religious groups — Christians, Muslims and 'pagans' would be represented.[24] In 1883 he discarded this idea in favour of one in which revenue would be guaranteed to the Alake through the taxing of wealth — export duties on cotton and palm products. In 1892, when it was rather too late, he attempted to plead for greater recognition of the Oshiele, the Agura and the Olowu — the three other *Obas* in Abeokuta. However, in all his proposals the Alake remained the centre and the focus of power and authority, at the expense of the other *Obas* and chiefs.

Reversible Johnson's vision and pretensions were entirely lacking in reality and clearly unrelated to the facts of the situation in Egbaland. The Alake in the circumstances of nineteenth-century Abeokuta was a nonentity whose authority hardly went beyond the Ake quarters. Apart from the hundreds of chiefs who were masters in their own quarters and townships, there were the *Olorogun* (the warriors) and the *Ogboni* (civilian rulers) who arrogated importance to themselves and rivalled one another in the bid for supremacy. Largely because of this rivalry there was no Alake from 1869 to 1877 nor from 1881 to 1885. None of the Alakes from Okukenu to Oluwaji was respected by these powerful rivals. In 1863 Ogundipe, the uncrowned ruler of Abeokuta until his death in 1887, scolded Alake Okukenu in the presence of British visitors. Ademola, who reigned from 1877 to 1879, was no more than a protégé of Henry Robbin, a *Saro*. Oyekan, who succeeded Ademola in 1879 was a penurious man with very little influence even in Ake quarters. Oluwaji, who ascended the throne in 1885, was never visited by the chiefs throughout his reign.

The non-recognition, or relegation to a subordinate position, of the *Obas* — the Oshiele, the Agura and the Olowu — by Reversible Johnson was a great blunder for which this visionary paid dearly. In 1881 his fellow Owu stripped him, flogged him, and put him in chains.[25] The *Obas* and chiefs did not fail to see that Johnson would run the government with

---

[24]See 'Egba Documents 1865–1934' (University of Ibadan Library photostat), document dated 12 Oct. 1881.
[25]*Lagos Times*, 24 Aug. 1881.

Saro ex-slaves and outcasts, among whom he actually distributed the posts of secretary, chairman, treasurer, master of trade, inspector of nuisances and court physician, retaining for himself the title *Amona Oba*, 'king's guide', a position that would make him, son of a slave, head of government.

But there were other reasons why Johnson's vision and pan-Egba patriotism could scarcely have been put into practical effect. There was the hostility of white missionaries which he had incurred since 1867 when the missionaries believed that he was the brain behind the *Ifole* of that year, in which the white missionaries were expelled from Abeokuta and their property was destroyed. By 1884 he had in the Reverend J. B. Wood, a 'political' missionary, more than a rival for the attention and hearing of Egba rulers. Little wonder that Reversible Johnson was for Wood no more than 'an upstart and a meddler'.[26] Moreover Johnson did not obtain the support of the majority of the educated elite in Abeokuta in his constitution-making effort. In fact the Christians regarded him as an enemy because it was they (as traders in cotton and palm products) whom he sought to tax with his revenue measures. To the chiefs Johnson was not a full-blooded Egba but a jester and semi-crazy meddler with extravagant pretensions. From 1880 onwards, when he sought to introduce an Egba national flag with the portrait of Queen Victoria on it, the chiefs saw Johnson as a tool of British imperialism in Egbaland.[27]

Realising that he had been quixotically charging at windmills, Johnson exiled himself to Lagos, where he died a disillusioned man. But by 1899 when Johnson had witnessed a reversal of his hopes, all the educated leaders of thought and dreamers like him had been shocked out of their illusions. People like J. A. O. Otunba Payne, James Johnson, R. B. Blaize, J. B. Benjamin, G. A. Williams, J. H. Samuel and Herbert Macaulay, all of whom at one time or the other had expected that independence in Church and state would be progressively and consciously given by their white mentors, and that the civil service would be Africanised, had begun to be disappointed as the 'scramble' acquired accelerated momentum. In commercial life the white man's competition was so ruinous that men like R. B. Blaize, J. J. Thomas, J. S. Leigh, J. P. Haastrup and the Crowther brothers cried out against what they considered the unfair measures of white traders and companies, particularly the strangling monopoly of the Royal Niger Company.[28] From 1887 onwards the big firms such as John Holt, G. L. Gaiser, Lagos Stores, McIvers, Witt and Busch began

[26] J.B. Wood to Lang, 12 Nov. 1885. CMS, CA2/04.
[27] M. Holley, *Voyage à Abeokuta* (Lyons, 1881), pp. 23–31.
[28] For a detailed discussion of the relations of the elite with the Royal Niger Company, see E.A. Ayandele, 'Background to the "Duel" between Crowther and Goldie on the Lower Niger, 1857–1885', *Journal of the Historial Society of Nigeria*, IV (1967), 45–63.

to assume a gargantuan prominence in southern Nigeria at the expense of African entrepreneurs. In the Church practically all the missions reversed the policy of Nigerianisation of the leadership that had existed for about a decade. Thus from 1877 onwards Bishop Samuel Ajayi Crowther was virtually superseded by white people until 1891, when he was hastened to the grave partly by the cumulative hostility that had been built up against the colour of his skin. After his death no Nigerian was appointed Anglican Bishop until 1953. The Wesleyans were even less ceremonious in brushing aside their few African leaders, men like J. H. Samuel and J. B. Thomas. The Baptists, who had never pretended that there should be Nigerian leaders of the Church, began to dismiss most of their African agents. As the American who conducted the purge recorded, without regret, in 1894:

> Any inquiry in regard to native workers in Africa is most uninteresting to me for I don't take much stock in them. . . . You know it has been my lot to dismiss more of them than all of the other missionaries on the field during the last five years and to appoint fewer of them to work for I have never appointed but one. I have very little hope of saving Africa with employed natives. . . . You know that Europeans do not understand the Negro as we do.[29]

In the civil service not only were the hopes that educated Nigerians would be made heads of departments dashed to the ground in the 'eighties but the few such appointments that had been held earlier by Africans were filled by white successors with increased salaries. Although Dr Nathaniel King had once acted as colonial surgeon, Africans who qualified in medicine before 1888 were not even employed by the government. Gone were the days when Nash H. Williams acted as the crown prosecutor, when I. H. Willoughby was superintendent of police, when William Emmanuel Cole (one of the founders of the UNA Church) was the postmaster, and Henry Carr was an independent inspector of schools. By 1893 educated Africans who held positions of responsibility were either humiliated by having white masters put above them while they, Africans, went on doing the job, or they were relieved of their posts entirely. Thus Henry Carr who was chief clerk, the last African to hold the post, was in 1893 relieved of this post and given another assignment. E.H. Oke, head of the Prison Department, a man of considerable experience who had been sent abroad for training, continued to be paid a salary of £72 per year, while a white man described as 'Gaoler' was appointed at a salary of £250 per annum. Herbert Macaulay, sent abroad to qualify as a civil engineer, was given the grand title of surveyor of crown lands in the public works department on a salary of £90 a year, raised with difficulty to £120 per annum, whilst unqualified European 'foremen' were being paid much higher salaries.[30]

[29]C.C. Newton to Tupper, 15 June 1894. Robertson Collections.
[30]*Lagos Weekly Record*, 21 Oct. 1893.

Seen in the context of these experiences, it is clear that by the 1890s it was foolhardy for educated leaders to continue to entertain any vision of self-government. In both Church and state the imperialist forces of European powers had been unleashed by the partition; and they were forces against which it was absolutely useless to contend. The writing on the wall was clear: the independence of the myriads of states and kingdoms, which were to be welded into Nigeria, were to be crushed by the British imperial Juggernaut.

Indeed by 1890 the 'scramble' had more or less been accepted by the visionaries as an inevitable event. In relation to this event their double loyalties were clearly exposed. Wedded to British thought patterns, literary educational system, styles of dress, language, marriage customs and so on, they believed that should the choice of a colonial master be necessary the British were infinitely preferable to any other. To this end the elite consciously worked for the establishment of British imperial interests rather than those of any other European power. Thus when in 1888 the danger of a French protectorate treaty was held out to the Egba elite in Lagos, they forgot their grievances against the British and sent deputations to Abeokuta to persuade the rulers to reject France in favour of Britain,[31] in a way reminiscent of the reaction of the Efiks of Calabar to the French a few years before. Not that the elite thought that the ideal situation was that the British should establish a colonial administration in Nigeria. What very many of them wanted was a British presence, which would give strength and support to the ambitions of the elite.

Thus very few educated Africans were happy at the way in which the British 'pacified' Nigeria, with military expeditions brushing aside the traditional rulers. But there were great inconsistencies in their attitudes. Ideally they hoped that the British would effect the creation of the national state, yet the educated elements had no precise criteria for defining the revolution. How many African officials, how many technicians, how many African traders, industrialists, teachers, or doctors could be deemed sufficient to create a self-sustaining, independent movement of modernisation was a question which none seriously discussed. Few addressed themselves to the moral dilemma that the vision of the united Nigeria taking its place as a recognised entity in the 'modern' world could only be carried out at the expense of the unlettered majority; nor faced up to the fact that the traditional religion, the hundreds of political units, the 'natural' rulers like Jaja, Overami and the Emirs, must needs be crushed. Only the British and a colonial situation could have begun the partial implementation of the social and economic revolution the visionary nationalists envisaged for Nigeria. In this respect the observation made by a Nigerian lady debater on the 'scramble', in Lagos in 1885, was apposite:

[31]Wood to Lang, 15 May 1888. CMS, CA2/05.

I maintain that the present efforts of European countries to acquire and increase their possessions and protectorates in Africa, and to develop their commercial interests therein, are calculated to be an advantage to Africa and the Negro Race generally. Firstly, because it is a civilising agent; secondly, because it enriches the country; and lastly, but not the least, because it aids the propagation of Christianity . . . until such time [when Africans would be able to govern themselves], it is best to have foreign government and strangers to bring order and their improvements. [32]

The visionary nationalists were so undiscerning that they were taken by surprise that the leadership of an emerging Nigeria was assumed by the British missionaries, merchants and secular officers — at the expense of themselves. By the last decade of the nineteenth century the whites were convinced that the educated elite were unqualified and unworthy to be leaders of the emerging Nigeria. Contempt for this set of semi-Nigerians was very great indeed. The idea that gained ground, and which was translated into policy, was that the elite were useful only as low calibre cadres in the literary and technical fields. Hence the horror of Governor Henry McCallum, that Nigerians were ever allowed to believe that they could become medical doctors. Africans in his view were gifted with 'insufficient mental development' for medicine, and should never be expected to be trained beyond the status of apothecaries. [33] The visionary nationalists were nothing more than 'the trousered Africans with European veneer', 'half-educated mischief mongers and wretched clerks'. [34] Even in the Egba capital where the educated elite rallied round the chiefs and believed that they were offering leadership, the whites were unimpressed by their activities and pretensions. As McCallum described them, they were 'a set of partially educated English-speaking native loafers who pose as advisors to the chiefs and fatten on the misrule of their employers'. [35]

White controllers in Church and state were convinced that the visionary nationalists had no true sparks of patriotism, and could not really be described as 'nationalists'. This often repeated view stemmed from the sociological differences between the educated elite and the illiterate masses. The only way to begin to remove these differences, so it seemed to the British, was for the elite to be prepared to strain themselves financially by sponsoring projects and measures that would confer benefits on all sections of society. Thus in 1889 the white rulers in Lagos Colony were prepared to introduce a Municipal Council in Lagos, a measure which would have given the visionary nationalists an opportunity to begin to have some say in the administration of the island. But to the surprise of

[32]*African Times*, 1 Aug. 1885.
[33]Henry McCallum to Chamberlain, 12 May 1897. CO 147/113.
[34]*Lagos Standard*, 16 Feb. 1898.
[35]McCallum to Chamberlain, 5 May 1898. CO 147/132.

the British the scheme was opposed by nearly all the elite because it would involve payment of tax.[36] In the same manner the educated elite in Lagos opposed measures suggested in 1895 to install street lights, and in 1897 to effect sanitation. As an irate Governor Carter observed with some justification:

> There is almost a total absence of public spirit amongst the wealthier natives of Lagos. Selfishness reigns supreme and nobody cares to benefit his neighbour. . . . I have never disguised my opinion that it would be futile to grant a municipality to Lagos. I do not know a single native who would be likely to give his time or energy to the necessary work of such a scheme — as they knew it meant taxing themselves.[37]

The visionaries knew only too well that there would be a high financial cost for Nigeria to undergo the social, political and economic revolution they envisaged. But not only would they not initiate the measures that would make a start for the revolution they advocated but they would support nothing that would make them, beneficiaries of 'western civilisation', bear the burden of taxation. In this respect there was an element of truth in Bishop Tugwell's denunciation of the educated elite as unpatriotic, in a confrontation with them in 1901.

> It is the spirit of the Patriot that we need. That is the spirit, the one great quality, which is wanted in Lagos. . . . If it be asked where are we to look for the manifestation of this spirit? My answer is, to the Educated classes. . . . Let it be clearly stated that it is the duty of the People and not of the Government to effect those Reforms. . . . Direct Taxation is a product of civilisation based upon a spirit of Christian Patriotism.[38]

Nevertheless despite their serious shortcomings the visionary nationalists achieved some measure of success. They continued to see themselves as Nigerian patriots and worthy leaders of the unlettered masses. They did not approve of the leadership of the country being seized by their white mentors. They believed that they should exert themselves financially and otherwise only in respect of institutions which they could own, control and direct. In the circumstances they found the Church the only institution in which they could assert their claims to leadership. Consequently between 1888 and 1902 not less than eight independent African churches were founded in southern Nigeria.[39]

[36]See Ayandele, *Holy Johnson*, pp. 183–6.
[37]Minute by G.T. Carter on Denton to Chamberlain, 10 Aug. 1895. CO 147/100.
[38]Address to the Lagos Institute by Herbert Tugwell, enclosed in Macgregor to Chamberlain, 21 Sept. 1901. CO 147/157.
[39]The Native Baptist Church, April 1888
The Providence Christian Church (Baptist) formed Jan. 1891
The United Native African Church, Sept. 1891
The Delta Pastorate, April 1892

Though, as has been pointed out by scholars, these African churches were not Africanised wholesale in matters of theology, liturgy and the 'non-essentials' of Christianity, their nationalist significance in the early days should be appropriately recognised. The educated elite used these churches for psychological, political, cultural and ideological purposes. Politically the independent Church became the only institution in which the elite leadership felt they could demonstrate their capacity for self-government. Practically all leaders of thought subscribed to the ideology of independent African churches or a single African Church. Thus James Johnson was the ideological father of the African Church movement, just as J.A. Otunba Payne, Dr Obadiah Johnson and others like them who stayed on in western established churches, subscribed financially towards the establishment of some of the eight 'African' churches listed above. Dr Mojola Agbebi was a leader of the African Church movement, G. A. Williams, editor of the *Lagos Standard* for a number of years, was an ardent lay leader of the UNA. Indeed, ideologically, Mojola Agbebi came to the conclusion that true political independence must be preceded by true religious independence. 'The start is rightly made when it commences with matters relating to the soul', he proclaimed in 1892.

> When the soul is free, the intellect will be untrammelled . . . and the body fully emancipated . . . when no bench of foreign Bishops, no conclave of cardinals, lord over Christian Africa, when the Captain of Salvation, Jesus Christ himself leads the Ethiopian host, and our Christianity ceases to be London-ward and New York-ward, but Heavenward, then will there be an end to Privy Councils, Governors, Colonels, Annexations, Displacements, Partitions, Cessions and Coercions. Telegraph wires will be put to better uses and even Downing Street be absent in the political vocabulary of the West African native.[40]

The psychological value of the Church to the elite at the time their ambitions were being thwarted in colonial administration was aptly put by one of them in 1902: 'In everything save religion, the black man is entirely in the hands and under the control of the white man as completely as the clay in the hands of the potter. In politics, business and in social intercourse, this statement has been verified and confirmed.'[41]

But it was not only within the Church that the elite visionaries were finding mental emancipation, and recording substantial success. Culturally, in a manner and to an extent never since repeated by the Nigerian press, the newspapers — especially the *Lagos Weekly Record* and *Lagos Standard*

The Reverend Ladejo Stone Church (Baptist) assumed self-support 1899
The Bethel African Church, Oct. 1901
The African Shalom Church, 1901
The Yorubaland Episcopal Church of Christ the Saviour.
[40]*Sierra Leone Weekly News*, 12 Nov. 1892.
[41]*Lagos Standard*, 5 March 1902.

— gave prominence to discussion of the values of Nigeria's cultural heritage, its importance and the denationalising effects of European civilisation upon Nigerian society. By 1902 the educated elite had discussed two major institutions thoroughly, and had come to the conclusion that Nigerians should prefer these institutions to alien ones. These were polygamy and indigenous secret societies, both of which they had become convinced were not incompatible with the practice of the Christianity of the Bible. Hints were also being made that other cultural values should be subjects for research. Apart from the attempts to chronicle local histories the educated elite drew attention to the advisability, and urgency, of the study of the healing properties in local herbs. In 1896 the Reverend E. M. Lijadu of the CMS mission was bold enough to write a pamphlet entitled *Yoruba Mythology (Ifa)*, drawing attention to the legitimacy and advantages of studies of African traditional religion. By 1900 a 'Professor' Abayomi Cole, who established the Psychical Research Institute of West Africa in Lagos, could go to the extent of rating Yoruba religion as superior to Christianity, a rating that would have scandalised the Holy See and Lambeth Palace. 'It appeals to the highest faculty of Man. Its standard of morality is the highest and purest, and it is the most suitable and natural for us as a Race, if we only understand it, and do not confuse it with the inventions of man!'[42]

Thus by 1900 European civilisation had ceased to be exclusively worshipped by thoughtful educated people, who correspondingly began to appreciate the values of indigenous culture. In this sense, in practical terms, the visionary nationalists were the earliest exponents of the doctrine of African personality.

[42]*Lagos Weekly Record*, 15 Dec. 1900.

7

PETER MARSHALL

The Imperial Factor in the Liberal Decline, 1880–1885

The period of Gladstone's second ministry represented eventful and significant years for British politics and politicians: historians, while interpreting developments in the light of their particular interests, are agreed that it contains changes of much importance. The largest claim is that of Professor H.J.Hanham, who considers that 'the chapter of political history that opened with the general election of 1885 was . . . a completely new one'[1], since the reconstruction of the machinery of politics by the Corrupt Practices Act of 1883 and the franchise and redistribution measures of the following year transformed the situation. The imperial historian has no cause to feel that the current of events relegates his concerns to a backwater. Gladstone's victory in 1880 had followed upon the disasters in Afghanistan and Zululand, while in the course of his ministry the affairs of South Africa, Ireland, Egypt and India ensured a continuing prominence to questions of Empire. Yet events such as Majuba, Phoenix Park, Tel-el-Kebir, and Khartoum, which were to leave a lasting mark on imperial attitudes, are difficult to relate to the fluctuations in the fortunes of the Liberal administration. Professor R.E. Robinson does not regard imperialism as a doctrine commanding popular support or mass emotion among the electorate during the 1880s, a process which he locates only during the following decade. Political attitudes on Empire became aligned with party loyalties in relation to Home Rule: 'It was the Irish question, not imperialism in general, which split the Liberal Party and brought most imperialists together in the Unionist alliance.'[2] This verdict had not gone unchallenged: Rosebery's comment in 1901 that the split had been 'far more on what I call foreign and imperial questions, so far as I know, than on the Irish question' still commands support.[3] Despite an abundance of material and a variety of excellent studies, the difficulty of reconciling changes in political structure, party organisation, personal relations, and popular attitudes, with a rapid succession of events which cannot clearly be considered as

[1] H. J. Hanham, *Elections and Party Management* . . . (London, 1959), p. xvii.
[2] R.E. Robinson, 'Imperial problems in British politics, 1880–1895', *The Cambridge History of the British Empire* (Cambridge, 1959), III, 179–80
[3] Bernard Porter, *Critics of Empire* (London, 1968), p. 70 and n.

either relating wholly to imperial or foreign affairs remains formidable and perhaps insoluble. It can, however, be demonstrated that the particular force and method intrinsic to Gladstone's leadership of Liberalism imposed severe strains on party unity and contributed substantially to the disruption of 1886.

The general election of 1880 underlined a distinction between the outlook of the politicians and of the electorate which would be apparent throughout the closing decades of the century. The Midlothian campaign had set the tone for Gladstone's unremitting denunciation of a Conservative administration whose foreign and imperial ventures could be characterised as both immoral and unsuccessful. Although a recent study of the contest concludes that the electorate was concerned in the mass with economic issues and does not venture beyond the judgment that 'perhaps imperialist feeling was a regional sentiment which had an effect in the smarter parts of London and the Home Counties',[4] it nevertheless acknowledges that the electorate was 'brought to vote by men who were concerned about foreign policy' and that Gladstone excelled in criticism couched in moral terms.[5] A contemporary account had stressed the implications which the Liberals discerned both in the particular excesses of Conservative foreign policy and in its general tendencies. Events in Afghanistan and South Africa 'were regarded as further manifestations of tendencies adverse to parliamentary institutions and favourable to the *rôle* of an aggressive military empire'.[6] Emphasis on this development created a situation in which 'the Liberal party for the time being became the party of resistance. Of resistance alike to hazardous enterprises, and to the introduction of dangerous innovations by which the practice of the Constitution was being deteriorated.'[7]

Gladstone's return to office brought to power a leader intent on the redress of immoral foreign and imperial policies, an aim to be pursued to the exclusion of other issues. Even a devoted son was later to admit that the first legislation proposed to the new parliament, concerned with the coursing of hares and rabbits, did not make for an impressive opening. But, as he explained, 'The circumstances were different in 1880. In 1868 Mr Gladstone had a great scheme of legislative work. He had no such scheme in 1880, thinking his call was limited to the responsibilities he had incurred in attacking and defeating the external policy of Lord Beaconsfield.'[8] Moral revulsion was not accompanied by practical suggestions for the righting of past wrongs: perhaps this was unlikely to emerge from a Cabinet dominated by Whigs. Joseph Chamberlain, whose inclusion

---

[4]Trevor Lloyd, *The General Election of 1880* (London, 1968), p. 138.
[5]*Ibid.*, pp. 41, 156–7.
[6]George Carslake Thompson, *Public Opinion and Lord Beaconsfield 1875–1880* (London, 1886), ii, 511.
[7]*Ibid.*, ii, 521–2.
[8]Herbert Gladstone, *After Thirty Years* (London, 1928), pp. 182–3.

represented a somewhat reluctant and limited acknowledgement of the existence of a radical element, was sharply disappointed at this failure to provide specific remedies. He recalled that:

> In the first discussion as to the general policy of the Government, I stood alone in urging a complete reversal of the general policy of Lord Beaconsfield which I maintained had been condemned by the nation. I wanted to recall at once Sir Bartle Frere, to reconsider the annexation of the Transvaal and to recall Sir Henry Elliott (Ambassador to Vienna). For none of these proposals could I meet with any support at the time.[9]

Although it could be argued on Gladstone's behalf that the press of events after 1880 — Majuba, Ireland, Egypt, the German bid for colonies, continuing to the very end of the ministry with the Penjdeh crisis — precluded any extended period of calm during which the prime minister might have examined the relationship of principles and policies, the record remains one of crises rather than of achievements. If the Liberals had become 'the party of resistance', their ability to conserve was far from evident; nor was their unity of doctrine either apparent or real. Their leader represented both an irreplaceable asset and a crippling handicap. His growing tendency to conduct business through individual ministers, rather than endure conflicts in Cabinet, in the long run was even more dangerous than his preference for concentrating his efforts upon a single issue. A short-term remedy paved the way for a later political disaster.[10]

Imperial historians have observed in attitudes towards the Transvaal and Ireland a feature distinguishing coercive Whigs and conciliatory Radicals; radical pressure for Transvaal independence offered the additional benefit of combating the Whig stand on Ireland.[11] Yet this relationship of political allegiances and imperial attitudes becomes less clear when subjected to individual scrutiny: figures such as Leonard Courtenay, a constant opponent of the annexation and retention of the Transvaal but equally adamant in his resistance to Home Rule, and after reluctantly acquiescing in the occupation of Egypt an outspoken critic of involvement in the Sudan, cannot be dismissed as interesting exceptions to a general rule. If Gladstone's unquestioning following within the Cabinet was limited to Granville, his influence succeeded in modifying the views of several others who might have supported a Whig position: his colonial secretaries, Kimberley and Derby, have been described — the former after Majuba — as Gladstonians except for their Whig views on the

---

[9]Joseph Chamberlain, *A Political Memoir 1880–1892*, ed. C.H.D.Howard (London, 1953), p. 4.

[10]D.M. Schreuder, *Gladstone and Kruger* (London, 1969), p. 214.

[11]Ronald Robinson and John Gallagher, with Alice Denny, *Africa and the Victorians: the official mind of imperialism* (London, 1961), pp. 68–9. Schreuder, *Gladstone and Kruger*, pp. 31, 82–3.

Irish question.[12] It was true that involvement in Irish affairs could undo all Gladstonian persuasiveness: both Forster and Harcourt, whether dealing with Parnell in Dublin or terrorists in London, became totally disillusioned, though Harcourt did not cease to share Courtenay's views on South Africa and was lukewarm on the Sudan intervention. John Bright, impeccable in his views on the Transvaal and Egypt, could not jettison a belief in union which he had cherished since his support of the North in the American Civil War. Ministers' stands were shaped as much, if not more, by past experience and the responsibilities of present office, as by attachment to 'Whig' or 'Radical' positions. Northbrook, a former Viceroy, supported a complete withdrawal from Afghanistan in 1880, approved the controversial Ilbert Bill, and followed a Gladstonian line on the Boers and Ireland. But, as First Lord of the Admiralty, and with the importance of communications of India in mind, he attached great importance to the maintenance of Egypt within the orbit of imperial interests, though he stopped short of advocating annexation and was reluctant to support the Sudan expedition.[13] Even Chamberlain and Dilke, though overt antagonists of their Whig colleagues, did not follow a consistent path of dissent from the majority position. Opposed to government by coercion in Ireland, they drew nevertheless a clear distinction between the provision of local government and the yielding of Home Rule; they supported the occupation of Alexandria in 1882, but withheld sympathy from Gordon, denouncing his disregard of instructions. Although in March 1884 Chamberlain led in Cabinet opposition to proposals for an extension of the Zululand protectorate, leading Kimberley to drop the scheme with the comment 'I see the Cabinet do not want more niggers', he was, by October, willing to go to war with the Boers over Bechuanaland.[14] He then came into line with W.E. Forster, whose coercion proposals he had vehemently opposed. Dilke most succinctly expressed the selective nature of his willingness to abandon overseas responsibilities when he wrote to Lord Edmond Fitzmaurice: 'I'm as great a jingo in Central Asia as I am a scuttler in South Africa.'[15] Rosebery, Gladstone's host during the Midlothian campaign, moved steadily during the ministry towards an imperialist position without seeking to link himself to the Whigs: firm on Irish questions, on the ground that concessions not shared by Scotland were unjustified, he returned in March 1884 from a world tour with an undisguised enthusiasm for Empire.[16] With such a variety of views, which would change and develop in response to events and experiences, it would

---

[12]Schreuder, *Gladstone and Kruger*, pp. 103, 308–9.
[13]Bernard Mallet, *Thomas George Earl of Northbrook* (London, 1908), pp. 154–98.
[14]Stephen Gwynn and Gertrude M. Tuckwell, *The Life of Sir Charles W. Dilke* (London, 1917), II, 86–7.
[15]Quoted *ibid.*, I, 532.
[16]Robert Rhodes James, *Rosebery* (London, 1963), pp. 127, 158.

seem fruitless to attempt a description of controversies within the Cabinet in terms of definable factions, each possessing a predictable and agreed form of response to imperial crises.

Confusion of attitudes at a ministerial level extended broadly and vehemently throughout the ranks of political opinion. In the first flush of electoral victory the triumph of morality appeared sufficient remedy: as the task of righting wrongs was commenced it became clear both that immediate revulsion had been mistaken for a fundamental change of heart and that the nation was far from extending its recently delivered vote of confidence in Gladstone to include all aspects of political and parliamentary life. The instability of views on imperial questions was not countered but accentuated by a series of episodes that possessed both tragic and farcical aspects: their effect was to strain and erode confidence in the efficacy of party politicians and in their chosen arena, parliament.

In 1880 T.H.S. Escott, a shrewd journalist, referred in a survey of national affairs to 'the vague popular desire for an indefinite extension of the dominions and the responsibilities of England'.[17] Gladstonian condemnations might submerge but could not destroy a sentiment stimulated, if not efficiently managed, by Disraeli. Popular willingness to respond to military glory in the same measure as to denunciations of immoral policy was demonstrated in the tumultuous welcome offered by the London crowds as the victorious force returned from Egypt in October 1882. An observer denied radical charges of careful preparations and affirmed the spontaneity of the reception. The moral that he drew for his American audience was that

> it proves more than the popularity of this Egyptian war. It proves how popular any war is, or any successful war. Mr Henry Richard may preach peace till Domesday; he cannot preach out of the soul of the Englishman his passion for war. The Manchester school has never educated and never will educate him into forgetting how he has won, and how he must keep, his Empire. To the average Briton this war in Egypt is an imperial war, a war for the safety of India, and as such he approves it with all his heart. He does not care much about the Khedive or the Control, and not even the continued efforts of Mr Wilfrid Blunt have made Arabi a hero to him, nor yet very hateful to him. He likes Mr Gladstone better because a war has been fought under his Ministry.[18]

Relief at escape from Afghan and Transvaal entanglements was the predominant feeling of the ministry, but one not universally shared. In Ladysmith, when news of the decision to withdraw was received in June 1881, a traveller observed that the landlord of his hotel had posted up this notice:

---

[17]T.H.S. Escott, *England* (New York, 1880), p. 5.
[18]George W. Smalley, *London Letters* . . . (London, 1890), ii, 264–5.

> Sacred to the memory of
> HONOR
> The beloved wife of John Bull
> She died in the Transvaal and
> Was buried at Candahar, March 1881.
> Her end was peace.

and it was curious to see the soldiers and civilians crowding round the placard and to listen to their very candid if not complimentary remarks on the Gladstonian ministry.[19]

'Remember Majuba' was to be employed as a popular patriotic slogan during the Second Boer War, a humiliation recalled long after the Gladstonians had thought it laid to rest.

The change of ministry had not therefore reflected a change of sentiment. Gladstone may have persuaded himself that this was the case, but the evidence does not bear this out. If opinions had altered, the cause was not the immorality but the ill-success of expansion. Even this was not certain to provide the sole consequence: time would indicate that disasters would prove as effective carriers of imperial sentiment as would triumphs. The mood of 1880 was one of disturbance as well as of repugnance, and from the very beginning of the new parliament threats to the established order were seen as endangering imperial security, even if the challenge seemed of the most remote kind. *The Rock,* a Low Church family newspaper, opposed to Romanism, Ritualism and Rationalism, proclaimed its opposition to Bradlaugh's entry into the House of Commons on the grounds that the taking of the oath 'is not a mere political test. It is a national, an imperial question involving the stability of the throne, and the very existence of the empire'.[20] The behaviour of the House and the bungling management of the problem posed by Bradlaugh's atheism did much to expose politicians to ridicule and contempt, an opinion reinforced by the systematic obstruction practised by the Irish Nationalists as they exploited, for two years, the absence of closure in order to defer coercive legislation.[21] To this general reduction of parliamentary prestige could be added the particular conflicts between order and protest, landlord and tenant rights, national integrity and Nationalist repudiation of unity, which fostered Liberal discord and began the process of ministerial resignations. Ominous though this was, the Irish question was to broaden its significance as it came to be seen as a domestic outbreak of a general epidemic which threatened the existence of the international order.

These fears were confirmed by the assassination on 6 May 1882 of Lord Frederick Cavendish, W.E. Forster's successor as chief secretary

---

[19]J.W. Mathews, *Incwadi Yami* . . . (London, 1887), p. 326.
[20]Quoted Walter L. Arnstein, *The Bradlaugh Case* (London, 1965), p. 169.
[21]Edward Hughes, 'The changes in parliamentary procedure 1880–1882' in Richard Pares and A. J.P. Taylor eds., *Essays presented to Sir Lewis Namier* (London, 1956), pp. 289–319.

for Ireland, and of the permanent under-secretary, T.H. Burke, as they strolled through Phoenix Park. The crime appeared to justify beyond question Forster's resignation in protest at willingness to reach an understanding with Parnell before lawlessness had been suppressed. That the murders were not the work of the Nationalists was irrelevant: horror at the news destroyed any sense of proportion. Gladstone's reputation, which had reached great heights in unaccustomed quarters when he had, during a speech at a Lord Mayor's banquet, announced the arrest of Parnell, suffered greatly from an event which followed so closely on the release of the Irish leader. To those with experience of imperial rule the situation appeared all too familiar and the remedy both obvious and essential. Disillusionment was acquiring further recruits.

From India, Sir Albert Lyall, lieutenant-governor of the North West Provinces, a staunch Liberal, declared to Morley that the news had destroyed his confidence in Gladstone's ability to govern. He considered it time for

> simply going back to the first duty of Governments — the protection of life — and stick to that resolutely, discarding all other issues, such as whether the revolt is political or social, on which Gladstone periodically lectures. If ever the word 'blood-guiltiness' should be used against a politician, it applies to the men who let women and their own officers be cruelly killed by assassins who could be put down in three months. Our country is being disgraced in the eyes of the civilised world; not is it the fault of our rulers at home that misrule and violence do nor spread abroad. India is just now wonderfully quiet; but what sort of a lesson are you teaching to the dangerous classes in this country, when you show that men can terrorise by assassination within a few miles of England? What has just happened in the Phoenix Park is exactly what might have occurred in the heart of Afghanistan to English officers; it is almost too bad, I think, for one Afghan to have done to another. But I suppose you are all deafened by the roar of London talk. I think it stupefies our public men, and is thus bringing parliamentary government to paralysis of all organs but the tongue.[22]

Lyall wrote in similarly gloomy tones to his sister. After the immediate excitement had died down, stringent measures would give way to 'Gladstone again explaining that the qualities of real statesmanship are patience, long-suffering, and consideration for the oppressed'. Only the police could suppress murder: the Thugs had been put down before the state of the peasantry had been improved, and this was the correct sequence of actions.

On the whole [he found],

[22]Quoted Sir Mortimer Durand, *Life of . . . Sir Alfred Comyn Lyall* (Edinburgh and London, 1913), pp. 258–9.

the survey of England from this distance impresses one with gloomy forebodings, not of immediate but of gradual decadence; owing to a great concentration of wealth and luxury among certain classes, producing a general indifference, relaxation of fibre, and carelessness of what goes on in the outlying parts of the empire. . . I doubt if 'society' would much care if India were lost, so long as their Indian dividends were secured.

I won't write more about Ireland or Egypt. The Lord deliver us, in any way that may seem fit, from W.E.G., who is evidently a helpless and futile man in rough times. He is the sort of person who brings us, eventually, the Saviours of Society, Cromwells and Napoleons, by whom he is contemptuously hurled aside and stigmatised as 'ideologue'.[23]

With some reason, Lyall considered himself as a Liberal until 1910. His mistrust of politicians and parliament; his perception that domestic decadence was breeding indifference to Empire; his emphasis on the challenge to authority, which led him to expect another 1857 in India, constituted views shared by many others who had served the Empire. As Lyall and his like observed the fashioning of policies apparently intended to conciliate Fenians and Boers, alarm and cynicism grew more widespread, the more so in the absence of an adequate alternative party allegiance. The Conservatives showed little sign of recovery from the electoral defeat of 1880 and the death of Beaconsfield in April 1881. The division of responsibility for leadership between Salisbury in the upper house and Sir Stafford Northcote in the Commons did not make for effective opposition. Salisbury's sense of the subordinate function of imperial in relation to foreign policy did not offer those whose first concern was the Empire a reliable spokesman for their interests; Sir Stafford Northcote was by general consent completely inadequate as an opponent of Gladstone. He had, indeed, forty years previously, been Gladstone's private secretary, an experience which had inculcated a veneration hopelessly superfluous in his present role. Yet the choice of Northcote as Leader was testimony to the merits of the Conservative front bench. What was the case for preferring to select Sir Michael Hicks Beach, R.A. Cross, or W.H. Smith? The outstanding speaker from the Tory benches was undoubtedly Lord Randolph Churchill, but it was very difficult to discover whom he was opposing: far too often he appeared allied with Joseph Chamberlain in hostility to Salisbury. Lacking an effective front bench, the Conservatives made no effort to revive the party platform from the cataleptic condition in which Beaconsfield had left it.[24] Disenchantment with Gladstonian Liberalism was not, therefore, open to correction by a transfer of loyalties. Conservatism offered a creed at even lower ebb.

[23]Lyall to Mrs Webb, 2 June 1882, *ibid.*, pp. 264–5.
[24]L.P. Curtis Jr, *Coercion and Conciliation in Ireland 1880–1892* (Princeton, 1963), pp. 23–6.

Against Liberal weakness and Tory disintegration, demonstrated for all to see at home by the incapacity of the House of Commons to conduct business with dispatch or decorum, the evidence of imperial failure offered additional proof of political inadequacy. After 1880 the hero of the age was not Gladstone but Sir Garnet Wolseley, defending the Empire against Irish, Egyptian, and Boer nationalism while despising the politicians whose orders deprived him of further glory. Loyal settlers buried the Union Jack in Pretoria as they suffered the abandonment of the Transvaal. Egyptian policy satisfied none and could only be tolerated by Gladstone himself on the supposition that the occupation was temporary. In India the Ilbert Bill roused the Europeans of Bengal and Assam to a pitch of hatred against Ripon and Liberalism which led some to dream of the day when an expeditionary force would recover Britain from the radicalism and republicanism to which Gladstonian rule had condemned it.[25] To many of less extreme views the Bill offered proof of the decay of imperial interests under Liberalism. Sir Bartle Frere, though he had favoured the entry of Indians into administration, was strongly opposed to the proposal; J.F. Stephen, whose objections to Liberalism had been steadily mounting over the years, denounced the Bill in *The Times* in natural consequence of his opposition to Irish Home Rule. The two questions were to him inseparable for, as he explained, 'the fear of imperial disaster, caused by a breach with Ireland, naturally led those who opposed it in the imperialist direction'.[26] With the Colonial Office interpreting unrest in South Africa in terms of Fenianism[27] it is clear that 'informed' official and unofficial opinion was explaining the turn of events against imperial interests as the work of a connected series of nationalist challenges surfacing in Ireland, South Africa, Egypt and India. The inability or unwillingness of Gladstonians to resolve these threats to imperial security was apparent not once but repeatedly; with each episode disillusionment grew.

The remedy, in a period of Conservative inertia, was not easily found. Whatever might prove their ultimate destination, a number of personalities of some political prominence departed the Liberal ranks in the early 'eighties through disagreement on imperial questions. W.E. Forster's resignation from the ministry was not accompanied by withdrawal from the party, though he did not subsequently refrain from passing damaging comments in the House on the management of both Irish and South African affairs. His viewpoint was sustained and broadcast by a sympathetic and articulate family. Matthew Arnold, his brother-in-law, had welcomed

[25]Christine Dobbin, 'The Ilbert Bill: a study of Anglo-Indian opinion in India, 1883', *Historical Studies Australia and New Zealand*, XII (1965–7), 87–102.
[26]John Martineau, *The Life and Correspondence of Sir Bartle Frere* (London, 1895), II, 440–1. John Roach, 'Liberalism and the Victorian intelligentsia', *Cambridge Historical Journal*, XIII (1957), 73.
[27]Schreuder, *Gladstone and Kruger*, pp. 82–3.

the Liberal victory in 1880. Within a few years he had adopted Forster's opinion that Gladstone was not a man to be trusted, had become deeply concerned that Ireland should be retained in the name of the Empire, and by 1886 was writing more extensively on politics than on literature.[28]

Forster's adopted son, Hugh Oakeley Arnold-Forster, associated himself even more closely with Liberal dissent. After publishing in 1882 a pamphlet conveying *The Truth About the Land League* he proceeded, through the instrumentality of W.T. Stead, to publish a series of articles in the *Pall Mall Gazette* which spread 'The truth about the Navy'. This declared that the Navy, the only shield of Empire, was completely unable to guarantee protection against German rivalry and a France now hostile to Britain following the unilateral decision to occupy Egypt. This interest, which had been stimulated by his prospective Liberal candidacy for Devonport, proved irreconcilable with Gladstone's leadership of the party. Arnold-Forster withdrew from the constituency in 1885 after rejecting Government policy in Egypt, which he held responsible for the death of Gordon.[29] Joining the Conservatives was not, however, a practicable alternative, for as he wrote: 'I wish the names Liberal and Tory were both at the bottom of the sea, and then we could start afresh, and begin to judge men and policies, not by virtue of the particular catalogue in which they are placed, but by the light of their conformity with honesty, reason, and common sense.'[30] His immediate solution was to become secretary of Cassells, the publishers, taking charge of the education department and producing patriotic readers for schoolchildren.

Herbert Vincent was another potential member lost to the Liberal party. He had resigned the post of director of criminal investigations at Scotland Yard in 1884, with the intention of entering parliament. His connections were Liberal: he admired Sir William Harcourt, the home secretary, and was married to the daughter of a Liberal member. Moderate Liberalism of the Goschen variety appeared appropriate to his outlook. Before securing a constituency Vincent undertook a world tour, from which he returned to find himself in process of being adopted as Liberal candidate for the City of Westminster. He informed the local association that his Liberalism had been completely undermined by his observations on the journey.

> I have come back to England absolutely aghast at the deliberate neglect of British interests in almost every quarter of the globe during the past five years, and with the firm conviction that a continuance of such

[28]Patrick J. McCarthy, *Matthew Arnold and the Three Classes* (New York, 1964), pp. 142–72.
[29]Arthur J. Marder, *The Anatomy of British Sea Power* (New York, 1940), pp. 121–2. Mary Arnold-Forster, *The Right Honourable Hugh Oakeley Arnold-Forster. A memoir* (London, 1911), pp. 49, 57–60.
[30]Arnold-Forster to Mary Story-Maskeleyne, n.d., Arnold-Forster, *A Memoir*, p. 52.

a policy can only lead to the early overthrow of the unity and commercial prosperity of the Empire, even though it is still the greatest the world has ever seen. Australia, India, Central Asia, South Africa, and, not least of all, Egypt afford more than ample evidence of this lamentable state of affairs.[31]

He could not represent such a party.

Disquiet at the purpose of parliament and the contribution of its members was widespread. In March 1884 Herbert Spencer declined nomination as Liberal candidate for Leicester on the ground that 'it is becoming a common remark that we are approaching a state in which laws are practically made out of doors and simply registered by Parliament'. He attributed the decay to undue publicity and discussions by journalists.[32] In May 1885 Alfred Austin, the journalist and poet, declined to stand as Conservative candidate for a Leeds division. He declared that entry into the House required a man to believe that, 'by so doing, he can serve his country and strengthen the Empire'. Austin was of opinion that 'the country is being demoralised and the Empire is being imperilled by that Assembly'. Gladstone indicated, rather than was directly the cause of, a situation developed by general constitutional malpractices. Austin concluded that his task must be to 'do what little I can, outside the House of Commons, to discredit its authority and to curtail its functions. To ask a man to enter it, in order to serve his country, is to ask him to waste his life, and break his heart, over an impossible undertaking.'[33]

In this mood of uncertainty and instability which entered discussions of parliamentary and political behaviour during these years, considerable attention was drawn to a yet further complicating factor: the role and power of the press. At the end of the century Reginald Brett wrote to remind Balfour 'that all the disasters of 1880–1885 came from the Government of the day allowing themselves to be swayed by the newspapers. Never once did they hold straight on to the end with the policy which (right or wrong in its inception) they had adopted'.[34] Unacceptable as an explanation, the comment does draw attention to a development of some importance. Politicians and publicists were becoming aware of a changing relationship in which previous functions could no longer be taken for granted. If Kennedy Jones is to be believed, Joseph Chamberlain was initiated at an early stage in his political career into the value of harnessing newspapers in his support. Schnadhorst should not have received credit for the development of the Birmingham caucus. It should have gone to William

---

[31]S.H. Jeyes and F.D. How, *The Life of Sir Howard Vincent* (London, 1912), pp. 147–58.
[32]Smalley, *London Letters*, II, 221–4.
[33]*The Autobiography of Alfred Austin* (London, 1911), II, 130–1.
[34]Reginald Brett to A. J. Balfour, 1 April 1898, in Maurice V. Brett (ed.) *Journals and Letters of Reginald Viscount Esher* (London, 1934), I, 211.

Harris, a leader writer on the Birmingham *Daily Post*, who provided the idea 'that it was possible by using the newspaper as the means of communication so to direct the voting power of the city that a popular party could make sure of carrying all its candidates at municipal elections'. Victory at a school board election immediately confirmed the efficacy of the technique. 'An important result was that Mr Joseph Chamberlain learnt and never forgot the value of newspaper publicity.'[35] Chamberlain was certainly aware of the importance of maintaining close links with the press by the time he entered the Cabinet. He recalled that the question arose during a meeting in the autumn of 1880:

> At one of these Cabinets there was a warm discussion on the subject of the communications between Cabinet ministers and the press and this question was revived from time to time afterwards. The fact was that several of the ministers were in intimate relations with the Editors of newspapers. Thus, Forster was continually communicating with Chenery of *The Times*, and I believe with Mudford of the *Standard*. Dilke was intimate with Hill of the *Daily News*, and I was in constant intercourse with Morley, Editor of the *Pall Mall Gazette*, and Escott who was a writer at that time on the *Standard*.
>
> In the course of the discussions it was pointed out that without special intercourse it was impossible to secure in the press an adequate defence of the decisions and policy of the Government.[36]

The Times, under the editorship of Chenery, had become, immediately prior to the 1880 election, more sympathetic to Liberalism. Gladstone entrusted the management of the press largely to Granville, who maintained a constant correspondence with Chenery, providing confidential information and dispatches thought suitable for publication. His materials, however, referred almost entirely to foreign affairs, and *The Times*, never happy with concessions to Parnell, hardened its stand appreciably after Phoenix Park.[37]

This form of press management, traditional and limited, became rapidly obsolete with the rise to prominence of W.T. Stead, who succeeded Morley as editor of the *Pall Mall Gazette* in 1883. Stead was to provide practical examples of the application of a belief in which he completely shared and which he was to proclaim more vehemently than any of his contemporaries. His predecessor, John Morley, held to the popular notion that the real power in the land was wielded by journalists and formers of opinion. Goldwin Smith had assured Morley that he should welcome his defeat in the 1880 election since he would have 'ten times more influence' as an editor because 'power is quitting Parliament and passing to the leaders of opinion'. Morley was fully in agreement, holding

[35]Kennedy Jones, *Fleet Street and Downing Street* (London, 1920), p. 94.
[36]Chamberlain, *Political Memoir*, p. 9.
[37]*The History of The Times* (London, 1939), II, 522–3.

that those who thought deeply on political and social questions and propagated their ideas were the real leaders, 'not the men who come in at the eleventh hour and merely frame the bills for Parliament'.[38]

Stead had grown aware of his powers and purposes while editor of the Darlington *Northern Echo* during the agitation against the Bulgarian massacres. A unique blend of religious hysteria, assertive nationalism, and social uplift led him one night, after securing consolation from reading a chapter out of one of the minor prophets, to formulate commandments of which the tenth and last read: 'More earnest desire to make the profession of the Press the worthy leader of a regimented people. At present it does not lead, it follows, reluctantly. The higher element in the nation is badly represented in the Press.'[39] In 1879 he summed up his political creed, taking as his first point a declaration that the 'English race, like Jews and Romans even more, has a world wide mission to civilise, colonise, Christianise, conquer, police the world and fill it with an English-speaking law-abiding Xian race. I am an Imperialist "within the limits of sanity and the ten Commandments", the phrase quoted by Forster.'[40] The manner of the *Pall Mall Gazette* could not be expected to remain unchanged when Stead succeeded Morley: it excoriated the living conditions of the London poor; initiated the defence scare of 1884 through the publication of Arnold-Forster's articles on the Navy, and reached even greater heights in its arraignment of the ministry for permitting the murder of Gordon at Khartoum. A popular newspaper of this kind required a readership whose interests and attitudes differed substantially from those of previous decades.

The death of Lord Frederick Cavendish had been felt as a parliamentary tragedy; that of Gordon provided the Empire with a martyr. The news of the failure to relieve Khartoum was greeted in the country with far deeper feeling than it was in parliament. The Conservatives were bound to denounce the ministry, but the debate on the Vote of Censure lacked real conviction. The Opposition offered no alternative policy: both parties saw the Nile valley less as the grave of Gordon than as a region where their own political reputations could all too easily be buried. No such considerations inhibited the expression of sentiment by the public at large. A literary outpouring of the most extensive, popular, and uncritical kind — even including a Little Golden Book of the Thoughts of General Gordon — could not aim at results other than the rousing of imperial at the expense of Liberal sentiment. Evangelical Anglicans felt that in another Church canonisation would have been the only appropriate reward as Sunday, 18 March 1885 was marked by Memorial services in every Cathedral:

[38]D.A. Hamer, *John Morley* (Oxford, 1968), pp. 77–8.
[39]J.W. Robertson Scott, *The Life and Death of a Newspaper* (London, 1952), p. 106.
[40]*Ibid.*, p. 109.

The circumstances of his death encouraged the belief that here was an uncalendared saint, a Christian hero and martyr, whose death had exposed the sins not only of the Liberal Government which had so signally failed to serve Khartoum but of all Britain which in its pride of Empire had forgotten God. A great nation knelt in self-abasement.[41]

And, unlike the great moral upsurges of the previous decade, it was directed against rather than by Gladstone.

The reaction against the ministry was severe and would continue in various forms until the disruption of 1886. Wolseley's campaign journal, as he made his fruitless advance to Khartoum, provides a model example of imperialist vituperation.[42] Entry after entry denounced Gladstone, party opportunism, the decay and degradation of English life, the superiority of rule by oligarchy or intelligent despotism, his regret that 'I have no sons to hang the spawn of men like Mr Bright, Chamberlain & Co.', the dwindling of manly virtues, now to be observed in a mere handful of military figures and, on one rare occasion of optimism, the belief that disaster might prove the prelude to a cleansing of the nation, though he warned that 'it is only a great war with all its ups & downs that can make men of us again'. News of the crisis with Russia over Penjdeh did not signal the moment of revival since the nation was totally unprepared for war. The best that could be hoped was that 'if war is forced upon us now the people in their anger may lynch the coward Harcourt, hang the plucky Gladstone and throw Dilke and Chamberlain into the River. As for men of the Northbrook calibre, merely tar, feather and kick them with the contempt they deserve.'

If Wolseley's outbursts represent an extreme of verbal violence, the themes he emphasised were widely debated and offered the basis for a moral fervour which had hitherto been considered a Gladstonian monopoly. This was the more significant at a time when Evangelicals and Nonconformists were less able to detect that sense of mission which was so essential to the retention of their fidelity. As Gladstone's purpose seemed increasingly confined to the conciliation of Irish nationalism their alarm grew at the prospect of submitting fellow Protestants to the domination of a Catholic majority. The coalition of interests which had accepted Gladstone's leadership and secured the victory of 1880 was beginning to disintegrate. Ireland was to supply the proximate cause, an issue on which radicals delighted to attack the Whigs in the course of a conflict which touched at times on all parts of the Empire. It would, however, simplify the problem of the causes of the Liberal disruption to the point of distortion if an explanation was restricted to consideration of the Irish

---

[41]Richard Hill, 'The Gordon literature', *The Durham University Journal*, XLVII (1955), 97–103.
[42]Adrian Preston, ed., *In Relief of Gordon . . . The Khartoum Relief Expedition 1884–1885* (London, 1967), *passim*.

Question. Gladstone's attitude towards subject nations was not universally accepted by radicals: his 'moral' attitudes were to many of them merely 'sentimental'. Although by no means in perfect agreement on detail, Chamberlain, Dilke and Morley rejected views of national equality within the international order and stressed the distinction between greater and lesser, advanced and backward, peoples. To them might be applied a description of the outlook of R.W. Dale of Birmingham:

> He did not regard government as a necessary evil, nor empire as a peril to the imperial race, necessarily involving injustice to subject races. He welcomed every enlargement of national enterprise that promised to achieve its purpose with efficiency, and any extension of imperial territory where our rule might establish order and justice in the place of strife and iniquity.[43]

The reinterpretation of Liberal doctrine, which revealed the inadequacy of its expression by Gladstone, drew its materials and examples from throughout the Empire and not merely from Ireland. It was this diversity of sources that accounted for the apparently irreconcilable interest of the Liberal seceders. What common factor linked Whig aristocrats, Chamberlain and Dilke, Bright and Rylands, Forster and Goschen, intellectuals such as A.V. Dicey, Warden Anson of All Souls, Matthew Arnold, Henry Sidgwick, H.M. Butler and Sir John Seeley, other than a rejection of Gladstonian leadership? In the first instance they believed themselves to have abandoned a party rather than a creed as they observed the old faith, to which they still adhered, displaced by a new Liberalism intent on abdicating the role which Britain should still exert in international and imperial affairs.[44] The Irish Question alone would not have brought them to this conviction.

The decline of Gladstone's appeal to the electorate should not be exaggerated. The forces set in motion by his policies during his second administration exerted a long-term rather than a short-term effect on the fortunes of the Liberal party. Comparisons between the outcome of the general elections of 1880 and of 1885 are virtually impossible: the Reform and Redistribution Acts of 1884, preceded by the Corrupt Practices Act of the previous year, markedly changed the political scene. Although the Liberals made gains in the counties due to support from the newly enfranchised, redistribution benefited the Conservatives through the creation of smaller constituencies. Parnell instructed his supporters to vote Conservative on account of the Irish Question; the Catholic Church opposed the Liberals on educational matters. In 1885 it was the Liberals' turn to suffer the effects of economic depression. It is the conclusion of

[43]A.W.W. Dale, *The Life of R.W. Dale of Birmingham* (London, 1899), p. 419. Peter Fraser, *Joseph Chamberlain* (London, 1966), pp. 26–9.
[44]Roach, 'Liberalism and the Victorian intelligentsia', pp. 79–81

one authority that of all the elections in the period 1885–1910 that of 1885 'is the most difficult of all to associate with one dominant issue'.[45]

The absence of recent imperial issues from a list of factors influencing the decision of the electorate is not as significant as it might appear. For their own reasons neither Gladstone nor Salisbury was anxious to give prominence to these questions. When Gladstone returned to Midlothian on a speaking tour during August and September 1884, an accompanying journalist complained that Egypt was almost totally ignored as a subject in favour of repetitive insistence upon the significance of electoral reform. He accused Gladstone of deliberately suppressing discussion of Egypt in order to stress details of a Franchise Bill which did not matter this year or next. 'But the decisions, the irrevocable decisions, to be taken at Cairo within the next twelvemonth, are decisions which must affect the destinies of this Empire for centuries to come.'[46] Gladstone's sense of moral imperatives did not, either in domestic politics or in imperial policy, obliterate his views of practical needs and possibilities. Advocacy of conciliation in Ireland did not rule out of the question resort to coercion if all else failed; abandonment of the Transvaal did not imply that war with Kruger was impossible.[47] It was not the end, but the means, of the preservation of the Empire which he queried, and in the last resort even the means were subject to adaptation to circumstances. In 1884 he privately welcomed German expansion into southern Africa and New Guinea as a valuable deterrent to demands for a greater measure of colonial self-government.[48] When, as in 1885, no external issue proved fit for illumination by Gladstonian moral exhortations the election was fought on other, less exotic issues.

To this decision Salisbury would also subscribe, though for very different reasons. His criticisms of Liberal policy in Egypt and the Sudan were founded on judgments of futility rather than of morality. As extrication grew more difficult, so his indignation mounted. To Salisbury the failure and waste of Liberal policy was epitomised by the irrelevant destruction of Arab forces by the expedition dispatched under General Graham to relieve the Red Sea forts. Their garrisons had already surrendered or been slaughtered and the reprisals were both brutal and pointless.[49] Salisbury's charge against the Liberals was not that Gordon had been murdered at

---

[45]Henry Pelling, *Social Geography of British Elections 1885–1910* (London, 1967), pp. 15–6. James Cornford, 'The Transformation of Conservatism in the Late Nineteenth Century', *Victorian Studies*, VII (1963–4), p. 58.

[46]Smalley, *London Letters*, I, 513–9.

[47]Schreuder, *Gladstone and Kruger*, pp. 177–8.

[48]Gladstone to Granville, 29 Jan. 1885, Agatha Ramm, ed., *The Political Correspondence of Mr Gladstone and Lord Granville 1876–1886* (Oxford, 1962), I, 329–30. Schreuder, *Gladstone and Kruger*, p. 475

[49]Lady Gwendolen Cecil, *Life of Robert, Marquis of Salisbury* (London, 1921, etc.), III, 97.

Khartoum but that he should never have been sent there in the first place. He was therefore unwilling to encourage imperialist emotions which might serve only to worsen the situation still further.

Salisbury's response to the attempts of Lord Randolph Churchill to gain control of the Conservative party has, coupled with his rejection of popular involvement in international affairs, obscured the skill with which he adapted his methods to changed political conditions. After 1880 Salisbury broke decisively with his own and his party's tradition of eschewing mass meetings. Accepting Gladstonian precedent he addressed more than seventy public gatherings in all parts of the country during the next six years.[50] Gladstone's rigid aversion to 'construction', the undue interference of the state in social and economic affairs, was contrasted with Conservative willingness to examine the living conditions and means of livelihood of the working class; the middle classes had, as early as 1874, indicated an unwillingness to continue their mandate to Gladstonian Liberalism. By 1886 the Irish Question could be presented as a flagrant interference with property rights rather than as a necessary act of moral redress.[51] The erosion of Liberal support was well advanced in two major areas. The process would be protracted but Salisbury was well aware that Cecils had dwelt at Hatfield House for centuries: time was not necessarily of the essence.

The significance of imperial episodes which provided such spectacular incidents during Gladstone's second ministry was not, therefore, immediately apparent in terms of electoral behaviour. The effect on relations between Liberal politicians was another matter: divisions arising out of questions of imperial policy were to weaken links which would snap the more easily under the culminating pressure of Home Rule. By the end of the century, however, it would appear that Gladstonian disasters had contributed more than Disraelian triumphs to the development of imperialist sentiment. In the course of adjustment to the problems posed by a greatly enlarged electorate the Conservatives sought to turn Liberal attacks back on their progenitors: in their arguments the Liberals constituted a class party, while Conservatism alone stood for national interests. A recent study of the literature produced for working class consumption in the last decades of the century stresses the Conservatives' continuous attack on the unfitness of the Liberals to manage matters of Empire. Prolific from 1880 it swells to the point that after 1886 'the Tory literature of this period addressed to the electorate abounds with examples of the most ruthless attempts to make party capital out of the imperial issue'.[52]

---

[50]*Ibid.*, III, 90.
[51]Robert Blake, *The Conservative Party from Peel to Churchill* (London, 1970), pp. 124, 159–60.
[52]Robert McKenzie and Allan Silver, *Angels in Marble* (Chicago, 1968), pp. 50–2, 72.

Political pamphlets of this kind combined with press innovations to reduce the impact of Gladstone's previously incomparable appeal. Organisations such as the Primrose League — a body that gave expression to Salisbury's belief that 'there is a great deal of Villa Toryism which requires organisation'[53] — ensured that Gordon's memory should remain fresh. The death of Colonel Burnaby, one of the earliest members of the League, as the relief expedition neared Khartoum, provided an additional hero of only slightly less stature. Lectures, lantern slides, charitable institutions named after the General, kept the sacrifice in public view and gave special significance to Kitchener's reconquest. As late as 1901 the camel harness used by Gordon was one of the most popular exhibits at Madame Tussaud's.[54] The mythology of imperialism would reach its fullest expression at the turn of the century: its themes were in large part born of events between 1880 and 1885. Such was the totally unexpected consequence of the entry into office of a prime minister whose first purpose was to destroy utterly the immoral aims of imperial aggrandisement.

[53]Salisbury to Northcote, 25 June 1882, quoted Cornford, 'Transformation of Conservatism', p. 52.
[54]Janet Henderson Robb, *The Primrose League 1883–1906* (New York, 1942), pp. 183–8.

8

JOHN S. GALBRAITH

Origins of The British South Africa Company

The British South Africa Company is usually identified with Cecil
Rhodes. Historians agree that he created it and gave it vitality. It was his
instrument for the advancement of his vaulting ambition. The Company
was an international power so long as he was in the ascendant. The disaster
of the Jameson Raid not only toppled Rhodes from his dominant position
but nearly wrecked his Company. So runs orthodoxy. The line is largely
true. Rhodes was the driving force of the Company. Without his energy
and his money the Company might well have collapsed in its early years
as did its contemporary, the Imperial British East Africa Company. But
Rhodes did not 'create' the South Africa Company; it was not merely an
extension of his personality or the agency for the realisation of his
dreams of Empire. The Company carried the ambitions and interests of
other men, and its antecedents and characteristics are not subsumed in the
biography of Rhodes. The amalgamation which produced the charter was
an alliance of avarice and megalomania. For several years the London
directors gave their loyalty to Rhodes because he enriched them. When
his complicity in the Jameson Raid threatened the Company's interests,
they accepted his resignation as Managing Director; but as soon as
possible thereafter restored him to favour, since public confidence in the
Company — and the price of its shares — depended on his involvement.[1]

The fortunes of the Company also had significance for the Imperial
government, which would not — dared not — ask parliament for money
for imperial purposes but desired to preserve for Britain as much as
possible of Africa. Whether the government was Liberal or Conservative,
the official policy in the 1880s was to use chartered companies to advance
imperial interests — 'imperialism on the cheap,' Harcourt aptly called it.
The operations of the chartered companies came under imperial scrutiny
only when they threatened international complications, particularly with
a great power, or required subsidies from the Exchequer. The government
consequently, like the London board of the British South Africa Company,

---

[1]For a discussion of the effect on the Company of the Jameson Raid, see my
article, 'The British South Africa Company and the Jameson Raid', *Journal of
British Studies*, x (1970), pp. 145–161.

provided little surveillance over the activities of Rhodes until he was embroiled in failure, the ultimate immorality. Rhodes enunciated as part of his creed 'never have anything to do with a failure,'[2] and his associates applied the same rule when they condemned him. But both government and board in pursuit of their interests had contributed to the fiasco of the Jameson Raid, which they condemned.

Gold was the attraction which directed European attention to the country of the Matabele and the Mashona. From the 1860s, when Carl Mauch, with more enthusiasm than accuracy, had described the vast mineral deposits of the area, more and more prospectors had made their way to Bulawayo to seek concessions which would make them wealthy. Diamonds in Griqualand West, gold deposits at Lydenburg, and finally the discoveries on the Witwatersrand further stimulated zeal to exploit the 'land of Ophir'. The great deterrent was fear of the Matabele, but by the 1880s it was evident to Lobengula that he and his people could not long remain isolated from Europeans and that he must seek the best possible accommodation either with Britain, which in 1885 established a protectorate over adjacent Bechuanaland, or with the Transvaal. By his treaty with John S. Moffat in February 1888, after similar negotiations with Piet Grobler of the Transvaal, he sought British protection against inundation. He would soon find that his hopes were vain. Humanitarians in Britain might protest against the subordination of African welfare to European interest, but their appeal could not override practical business considerations. At a meeting of the London Chamber of Commerce in May 1888, at which the missionary John Mackenzie was the principal speaker, Joseph Chamberlain expressed the dominant opinion of Britain accurately, albeit baldly:

> So far as the unoccupied territories between our present colonial possessions and the Zambesi are concerned, they are hardly practically to be said to be in the possession of any nation. The tribes and Chiefs that exercise dominion in them cannot possibly occupy the land or develop its capacity, and it is as certain as destiny that, sooner or later, these countries will afford an outlet for European enterprise and European colonisation.[3]

Chamberlain had no doubt that the Europeans who would develop the country must be British. Since in the conditions of the 1880s there could be no direct governmental involvement, the opportunity was presented for associations of private capitalists who would undertake the responsibility for development and accept the attendant risks. In 1888 two major contenders had appeared — a London group headed by Lord Gifford

---

[2]Rhodes to Rudd, 10 Sept. 1888. MS s. 134, Rhodes Papers, Rhodes House, Oxford.
[3]Pamphlet *Austral Africa*, London, 1888. Copy in Grey Papers 184/6, Durham.

and George Cawston, and Cecil Rhodes, backed by his own fortune and the revenues of Gold Fields of South Africa and De Beers.

Rhodes has often been credited with a dedication throughout his adult life to the acquisition of a solid band of British territory from Cape to Cairo. His youthful essay on the manifest destiny of Britons has been cited and recited to document either the nobility of his ideals or the crassness of his racialism. But he did not originate the idea of 'Cape to Cairo',[4] and his views on the survival of the fittest were hardly distinctive from the spirit of Social Darwinism which pervaded the British society of his day. Rhodes did not live for ideals. He lived for the exercise of power, the excitement of industrial diplomacy and the satisfaction of outwitting or 'squaring' his rivals in the contest. He was the 'great amalgamator'; he succeeded in deluding himself, as he convinced others, that his cause was Britain; in fact his cause was Rhodes.

There is some uncertainty as to when Rhodes first focused his attention on Matabeleland. His involvement in Bechuanaland in 1885 and his contretemps with Sir Charles Warren over the intrusion of the 'imperial factor' are well known. But as late as July 1885 he described the land between Khama's country and the Zambesi as 'fever-stricken' and unfit for settlement. Any colonisation plan was 'absurd' to anyone acquainted with the country. At that time he professed his object to be to tap the Great Lakes by a railroad from the south along the 'healthy ridge' of Central Africa.[5] The project of reaching the Lakes was at this time the favourite theme of geographical societies and explorers.

Even in 1885, however, Rhodes was preoccupied with assuring that Matabeleland would not fall under non-British control, primarily because of its importance as a link with the north. In 1885 the major threat seemed to be from Germany;[6] two years later, from the Transvaal; but action by the British government he considered imperative, and his pressure contributed to the Moffat Treaty of February 1888. His opinion of the prospective value of Matabeleland changed at the same time; he convinced himself that there were possibilities of mineral development rivalling or exceeding those of the Rand. In 1887 he employed John Fry, who had been a share-

---

[4]There are various claimants to the honour of coining "Cape to Cairo". Sir Harry Johnston attributed the origin to Sir Edwin Arnold in 1876, but a similar expression was used in 1875 by H.B.T. Strangway in connection with a telegraph, and Albert Grey, the future fourth earl, refers to a Cape to Cairo telegraph in a notebook of 1878 in the Durham Archives. Johnston took the credit for introducing the idea to Rhodes. See Lois A. C. Raphael, *The Cape-to-Cairo Dream* (New York, 1936). Sir Charles Metcalfe claimed credit for the idea of a Cape to Cairo railway. Notes by Basil Williams, s. 134, Rhodes Papers, Rhodes House.

[5]Ralph Williams, *How I Became a Governor* (London, 1913), p. 131; Williams refers to a letter from Rhodes to himself in May, 1885, on this subject, but he evidently refers to a letter dated 12 July 1885, contained in s. 134, Rhodes Papers, Rhodes House.

[6]Rhodes to Shippard, 3 Jan. 1885. RH 1/1/1, Rhodesian Archives.

holder in the Tati mines, to seek a concession from Lobengula. This was to be no mere right to hunt for gold as others had sought but a scheme for the monopoly for mining throughout the entire territory subject to the Matabele.[7] Fry was ineffective; ill with cancer which soon killed him, he left Matabeleland with the same lack of success as the numerous other would-be-concessionaires. In his stead Rhodes dispatched the famous 'Rudd mission', composed of his long-time friend and partner Charles D. Rudd; Rochfort Maguire, a fellow Oxonian; and Frank 'Matabele' Thompson, selected for his knowledge of native languages. The resources of the mission were provided by Gold Fields of South Africa, Limited, which Rhodes and Rudd had created and from which they were entitled to Founders' shares carrying three-fifteenths of the profits, in addition to another two-fifteenths of the profits while they retained their offices with the firm.[8]

At the same time that Rhodes was pressing for his great concession a formidable rival group was being organised in London, headed by Gifford and Cawston. Gifford in 1888 was thirty-nine years of age. As a young man he had served with Wolseley in the Ashanti campaign of 1874 and had been awarded the Victoria Cross. Subsequently he had participated in the Zulu War. Thereafter he held positions in the colonial service in Western Australia and Gibraltar, but his interest in the potentialities of southern Africa which had been stimulated by his stay in Natal continued. In particular his attention was directed to Matabeleland and Mashonaland where in 1880 he had unsuccessfully sought an exclusive mining concession in the basin of the Mazoe River.[9] Apparently he enlisted Cawston's interest, but Cawston soon dominated the partnership. Cawston, two years Gifford's junior, was of the type who exercise great influence without attracting attention, a man of grey in contrast to the charismatic Rhodes. But he was the architect of the formidable financial combination which was Rhodes's principal rival. He had joined the family firm on the London Stock Exchange, and in the 1880s was the head of the company which now bore his name. Among those with whom he became well acquainted was Francois I. Ricarde-Seaver, a member of a prominent Parisian financial house who was at that time representing his firm's interests in London.

From the conversations among these three there emerged by the spring of 1888 a scheme for the exploitation of lands from the Bechuanaland

---

[7]Fry's son stated that his father had a written contract by which he would receive £55,000 if the concession was granted through his work. 'Reminiscences of Ivon Fry' Sept.–Oct. 1938. FR 2/2/1, Rhodesian Archives. Rhodes's intentions soon leaked out. Heany to Dawson, 16 March 1888, DA 1/1/1, Rhodesian Archives.

[8]Consolidated Gold Fields of South Africa, Limited, *'The Gold Fields,' 1887–1937* (London, 1937), p. 10.

[9]Copy, draft agreement, —— , 1880, in HO 1/3/4/, Rhodesian Archives. Gifford offered £100 for the concession.

border with the Cape to the Zambesi River. The nucleus was provided by a mining concession in 1887 from Khama, chief of the Bamangwato, to Frank Johnson and Maurice Heany, on behalf of the Northern Gold Fields Exploration Syndicate of Cape Town, by which they received the right to prospect for a payment of five shillings a month, and to select up to 400 square miles for £1 per year per square mile and a royalty of two and a half percent.[10] The Syndicate's concession was bought by the Caisse des Mines of Paris, represented by Ricarde-Seaver, which in turn negotiated the transfer of rights to the Bechuanaland Exploration Company, registered in April 1888, with a capital of £150,000. The terms of the transaction were of the stock-jobbing sort which became increasingly characteristic in the world of the 'Kaffir circus'. The Caisse agreed to contribute £10,000 in cash in exchange for 19,000 shares in the Company and the right to offer 50,000 shares for subscription.[11] The other insiders received similar stock privileges. Among the first subscribers were Baron Henry de Rothschild and such City magnates as Henry Oppenheim and Messrs. Mosenthal and Sons. The Company was organised not only to exploit the concession from Khama but to promote a railway from the Cape border through the Bechuanaland protectorate.[12]

At the time the Bechuanaland Company was being organised, news reached London of the Moffat treaty with Lobengula, and Gifford and Cawston immediately saw the opportunity to capitalise on the chief's treaty of friendship by reviving Gifford's proposal for a mining concession. The original articles of association of the Bechuanaland Exploration Company being too restrictive, they formed the Exploring Company with the nominal capital of £12,000[13] and appointed Edward A. Maund to act as their agent to seek a mineral concession from Lobengula. Maund had first visited Lobengula in 1885 as one of three emissaries from Sir Charles Warren to notify the chief of the establishment of the protectorate in Bechuanaland and to assure him of the friendship of the British government.[14] Subsequently he had been involved in bizarre events in Tunis, but at the time he was approached by Gifford and Cawston in London he was seeking employment which would be both adventurous and lucrative. Many years later he recalled that he was about to leave for Australia to

[10]Agreement, 16 Dec. 1887, replacing an agreement of 16 April 1887. CO 879/32/392.

[11]Agreement, 16 May 1888 between La Caisse des Mines and Bechuanaland Exploration Company, File 26499, Registrar of Joint Stock Companies Office, London.

[12]Bechuanaland Exploration Company reports in *ibid*.

[13]The Exploring Company, Ltd, BT 31/4176/26995, Public Record Office.

[14]Marshall Hole, in *The Making of Rhodesia* (London, 1926), p. 68, states that Maund showed Cawston specimens of gold from the Matabele area in 1885 and made proposals for an expedition to secure a concession. This Maund branded as 'a fairy story'. He stated that the suggestion for the expedition was first made in the spring of 1888, and that he had not met Cawston before that time.

report on a coal mine and a railway.[15] He gave Cawston a somewhat different and much more alarming story. He stated that he had been offered
the leadership of an expedition sponsored by a German firm to take
wagons from German Southwest Africa to the German sphere of influence
in East Africa, thus laying a claim to a band across the continent which
could shut out Britain from the access to the northern interior beyond
Bechuanaland.[16] The two versions do not seem to be reconcilable, but
Maund's later recollections seem to have a ring of authenticity while his
tale to Cawston seems to have been calculated to enhance his value to his
new employers.

Maund's mission represented one prong of a campaign which collided
with Rhodes on two fronts. The Bechuanaland Company sought the right
to build the railway which Rhodes was attempting to block, and the
Company's offspring, the Exploring Company, competed with him for
the favour of Lobengula. Each of the contenders was vulnerable to the
other's strength. The London groups, backed by influential financiers
in London and Paris, had the initial advantage with the imperial government; and Rhodes, with the riches of De Beers behind him and his developing power in the Cape Assembly, was much more potent with local
imperial representatives and with the Cape government. The high
commissioner, Sir Hercules Robinson, had already shown himself susceptible to Rhodes's charm; Francis Newton, a friend from Oxford, was
Robinson's private secretary; Sir Sidney Shippard, deputy commissioner
of Bechuanaland, was a trustee of Rhodes's will.

These imperial officials were undoubtedly not 'bribed' in the sense
that they received money as an inducement to cooperation. Such a direct
bargain would have been both risky and unnecessary. But they clearly
supported Rhodes at least in part because he had power which could affect
their futures, and all subsequently benefited. Robinson became a director
of De Beers and a shareholder in the Central Search Company and its
successor, the United Concessions Company, which held the Rudd
Concession,[17] and Rhodes's support contributed to his return to South
Africa in 1895 as high commissioner. Shippard looked to Rhodes for help
in advancing his career in government[18] and in 1896 was appointed a
director of the British South Africa Company. Newton in 1902 was
appointed treasurer of the Company.

[15]Maund to Hole, 24 Sept. 1926. Maund Papers, University of Witwatersrand.
[16]Extract, Cawston's speech at Stafford, *Staffordshire Chronicle*, 29 Sept. 1900.
British South Africa Company Papers, V, Miscellaneous, Rhodes House.
[17]In October 1889, he held 250 shares in Central Search. In 1890, he was registered
as holding 2500 in United Concessions, and by January 1892, he owned 6250
shares. *Daily Chronicle* 1 Nov. 1895.
[18]In 1891 he was in communication with Rhodes about an appointment to a
judgeship in Cape Colony. Rhodes to Shippard, 11 Jan. 1891. RH 1/1/1,
Rhodesian Archives. He decided eventually to stay in the Imperial service,
where he remained until Nov. 1895.

Cawston and Gifford in May 1888 opened their campaign on both fronts. Cawston inquired of Knutsford whether the Colonial Office would give its blessing to an expedition to Matabeleland to secure a trading and mining concession.[19] The first response was cool — Cawston was directed to the high commissioner.[20] But when Cawston and Gifford made a personal appearance and presented their list of backers, the staff became receptive. The position remained that Robinson must be consulted, and concern was expressed about granting exclusive mining and trading privileges, but the Colonial Office made it clear there was no question about the desirability of encouraging British capitalists to get a footing in Matabeleland before foreigners were attracted to the area.[21] The petitioners received a similar unofficial response from the Foreign Office. The only tangible evidence they received of governmental favour was that there was no objection to Maund's being sent out[22] — he was recommended by, among others, the director of military intelligence[23] — but Gifford and Cawston felt encouraged enough by their interviews to proceed.

The proposal for support of railway construction had a similar cautious reception. Gifford asked whether the government would consider a project to extend the railway system from the border of Bechuanaland to Vryburg, and eventually to Shoshong in the Bamangwato territory, and received the reply that the government would indeed consider granting free land to a company with adequate backing but that for the present there was no prospect of any governmental financial assistance. Privately, however, the Colonial Office staff entertained doubts that the Cape government would in the immediate future undertake construction to the border because it had higher priorities.[24]

It was clear that the Colonial Office would do nothing without the advice of the high commissioner. It soon also became evident to Cawston and Gifford that immediate action was imperative. Cecil Rhodes, who was in London at the time, had heard of the negotiations with the Colonial Office, and had presented his case to Lord Knutsford.[25]

Rhodes and his rivals were now in a race to anticipate and to outwit. The Exploring Company in June sent Maund off to South Africa, and in July the Bechuanaland Company dispatched the noted engineer Sir Charles Metcalfe and R. W. Murray of Cape Town to negotiate with the Cape government and with Sir Hercules Robinson and to conduct preliminary

[19]Cawston to Knutsford, 4 May 1888. Maund Papers, Witwatersrand.
[20]Colonial Office to Cawston, 14 May 1888 in *ibid*.
[21]Note by R. G. W. Herbert, 1 June 1888, on Cawston to CO, 30 May 1888. CO 417/26.
[22]Herbert to Cawston, 4 June 1888. Maund Papers.
[23]Brackenbury to Fergusson 31 May 1888. FO 84/1922.
[24]Gifford to Herbert, 30 May 1888, and notes thereto. CO 417/26.
[25]Telegram, Exploring Company to Maund, 27 June 1888. Cawston Papers, Rhodes House, Oxford.

surveys of the proposed railway.[26] A few days before their departure, Rhodes had sailed for Cape Town.

The first of the contenders to arrive was Maund, who had an interview with Robinson at the end of June which he described as 'very satisfactory'.[27] Robinson assured him that he was favourable to the development of Matabeleland by a company with the impressive credentials of Maund's backers, but stopped short of giving his endorsement. There were others in the field, principally Rhodes, and Robinson stated he was not willing to assume the responsibility of blessing any project without a sign from Westminster clearer than the communications he had thus far received.[28] The interview, however, underscored the urgency of reaching Lobengula before some competitor could consummate an agreement with him. Maund hurried off for the north.

Metcalfe and his associates had a similar experience with Robinson. The high commissioner was friendly but evasive. Metcalfe developed the impression that beneath his pretence of impartiality, Robinson was already committed to Rhodes.[29] The judgment was correct. Before their interview Robinson had seen Rhodes and given his warm support to a scheme for a chartered company in Central Africa with powers similar to those of the British North Borneo, Royal Niger, and Imperial British East Africa companies. Rhodes's company would acquire control over those parts of Matabeleland and Mashonaland 'not in use'[30] by the African residents and provide protection for the natives in the lands reserved for them. Native welfare would be safeguarded and the interior would be developed at no expense to the British taxpayer. This proposal, said Robinson, merited acceptance by the imperial government. The extension of British interests into the interior by a chartered company based in South Africa would have a much more favourable reception from the Afrikaner community than the creation of another Crown colony.[31]

The conception of a chartered company as the instrument of Rhodes's ambitions was not foreshadowed by any previously recorded expressions of his intentions, and its sudden appearance in the record of an interview with Robinson is intriguing. Earlier in the year, Cawston had laid out similar plans which he was at this time developing into a formal proposal. One possibility is that Maund may have described Cawston's plan during discussion with Robinson, or Rhodes may have acquired the idea some time during his visit to London. Whatever the antecedents, Rhodes

[26]Gifford to Herbert, 12 July 1888. CO 417/26.
[27]Telegram, Maund to Exploring Company, 29 June 1888. Cawston Papers.
[28]Maund to Cawston, 2 July 1888, in *ibid*.
[29]Notes of interview Metcalfe with Basil Williams. s. 134, Rhodes Papers, Rhodes House.
[30]The expression is Robinson's, but it may well have been used by Rhodes.
[31]Robinson to Knutsford, 21 July 1888, quoted in [Cave] 'Minutes of Proceedings of the Commission,' in continuation of Cmd 1129, May 1921.

anticipated his London rivals, who produced their draft charter for the 'Imperial British Central South Africa Company' in September 1888.[32]

In the race to reach Lobengula, however, Maund initially was ahead of Rhodes's agents. He reached Kimberley at the beginning of July and continued with no delay toward Khama's country.[33] Rudd and his associates were not yet on the way. Maund left Kimberley several weeks ahead of his rivals. But his advantage disappeared in the Bamangwato territory. His explanation to Cawston for the delay was that the administrator, Sir Sidney Shippard, had requested him to arrange for the defence of Khama's capital in the wake of the death of Grobler and the threat of a Boer invasion.[34] His service to Khama, he reported exuberantly, could give him sufficient favour to obtain a concession to the 'disputed territory' lying between the Shashi and Macloutsie rivers to which both the Bamangwato and Matabele laid claim. He would then seek the same concession from Lobengula, thus eliminating the problem of rival claims.[35] Cawston was incensed at Maund's deviation from his instructions. In pursuit of a peripheral object he had sacrificed precious time. He ordered Maund to end his stay in Bechuanaland immediately and to proceed with utmost speed to Bulawayo,[36] but a month had been lost, during which Rhodes's agents had arrived at Lobengula's kraal.

Maund belatedly resumed his journey. He boasted to his employers that he had entered Matabeleland by a ruse when other parties had been turned back. The king had allowed him to enter because Maund portrayed himself as the representative of great men in England.[37] Shippard gave a somewhat less complimentary version. From Baines' Drift, on the borders of Lobengula's country, he reported that Maund had arrived from Shoshong in a famished state, representing himself to be a correspondent for *The Times*. Shippard knew him to be a concession hunter but allowed him to proceed on the assurance that he had permission from Lobengula to enter Matabeleland. In fact, Shippard said, he had had to order his self-invited guest to leave after Maund had imposed himself for ten days. Again the facts are in doubt. The Bechuana had christened Shippard 'Marana-maka' — the Father of Lies.[38] Bulawayo in the latter part of

---

[32]Draft Charter, Sept. 1888, Maund Papers. The charter, like the title of the Company, seems to be modelled on Mackinnon's Imperial British East Africa Company. Maund noted on the margin: 'this proves the BSAC was not Rhodes' scheme but was formed under auspices of Exploring Co.'

[33]Maund to Cawston, 8 July 1888. Cawston Papers, Rhodes House.

[34]Maund to Cawston, 27 Aug. 1888, in *ibid.*

[35]Extract, Maund to Cawston, 29 July 1888, in *ibid.*

[36]Telegrams, Cawston to Maund, 19, 28 Sept., in *ibid.* The telegraph reached only to Mafeking, and the message had to be delivered by messenger on horseback.

[37]Maund to Cawston. 250 cf. 1888, Cawston Papers, Rhodes House.

[38]On all this see Shippard to Robinson, 1 Sept. 1888. CO 879/30/369; and William Plomer, *Cecil Rhodes* (Edinburgh, 1933), p. 58.

1888 was enveloped in a miasma of lies and deceit. Each of the contenders assumed that the others were men of no principle, and their collective judgment was essentially correct. Marshall Hole was certainly justified in his description of the environment as 'an atmosphere of intrigue, plot, counter-plot and chicanery'.[39]

When Maund arrived there were several parties in Bulawayo jealously watching each other and doing their best to expose the others while concealing their own intentions. In addition to the Rudd party and Maund, there were agents for interests in Port Elizabeth, Kimberley, and Johannesburg, as well as a number of freelance traders who sought concessions which they could turn into gold. Maund, acting on the assumption that Lobengula distrusted the whites of South Africa, whether from the Transvaal or from the Cape, posed as the representative of imperial interests and did his best to muddy the distinction between 'the great men of England' whom he represented and the government itself. His previous visit as an imperial representative made it easy to convince Lobengula that he indeed had some relationship with the imperial government. John Smith Moffat, now resident commissioner in Bulawayo, warned Maund not to imply that he was an official, but Maund was not deterred from communicating widely that those he represented were in favour with the Colonial Office. As allies who hoped to gain a share of the proceeds if he were successful Maund enlisted his companion of the 1885 visit to Lobengula, Sam Edwards, 'Far Interior Sam'; George A. 'Elephant' Phillips;[40] and C. D. Tainton, another prominent trader, who served as interpreter. With such influential residents who enjoyed the confidence of Lobengula, Maund hoped for success.[41]

Maund's principal rivals, however, had great assets. Rhodes had given them a free hand to use whatever arguments and resources were necessary to achieve their object. Lobengula, Rhodes assumed, would be ignorant of the meaning of corporate enterprise; if necessary, they could offer to act as the chief's agents in exchange for a large share of the profits; with that undertaking as a base, they could then proceed to make themselves the *de facto* monopolists of Matabeleland and Mashonaland. He advised them to 'square' Tainton and any other white men who might be useful.[42] But the trump card on which Rhodes relied was the support of local imperial officials. With their backing he could neutralise Maund's claims to favour and influence Lobengula to grant the concession to Rudd, Thompson, and Maguire. Robinson could be relied upon, as could Shippard and Newton, Shippard's assistant. Both Shippard and Newton made

[39]Hole to Maund, 25 Nov. 1927. HO 1/3/4, Rhodesian Archives.
[40]Phillips was known to the Matabele as 'Elephant' because of his enormous size and great strength.
[41]Maund to Gifford, 10 Oct. 1888. Cawston Papers, Rhodes House.
[42]Rhodes to Rudd, 10 Sept. 1888. s. 134, Rhodes Papers, Rhodes House.

it clear to Moffat that they favoured Rhodes's interests,[43] and Shippard's journey to Lobengula's kraal at a critical stage of the negotiations was certainly not that of a disinterested imperial official, giving impartial advice.[44] Though Shippard for obvious reasons made no mention in his reports of any representations to Lobengula on behalf of Rhodes, he almost certainly indicated a preference that Lobengula put his trust in Rudd rather than the 'unscrupulous adventurers' who were his competitors. After Shippard's departure, Maguire wrote to Newton that 'Sir Sydney's visit did a great deal of good removing much misunderstanding which was steadily growing worse', and that 'Shippard and Moffat did all they could for us'.[45] Rudd noted in his diary: 'The King talked to Moffat about so many white people coming into the country and as to how it could be avoided, and Moffat took the chance of putting in a good word for us.'[46] Moffat's motivations may have been somewhat different than that of the other local imperial officials. Like them, he was helpful to Rudd and his companions. But Moffat also gave encouragement to Maund's party, and Sam Edwards whom Maund considered a supporter was consulted by Rudd about his group's proposals and 'thought well of them'.[47] Moffat clearly believed that the imperial interest would be served if a 'respectable' syndicate acquired a monopoly of mining rights and he may well have thought that Rhodes and his agents best fitted his specifications, but his indictment for complicity is unproved.

A similar accusation has been levelled against Charles D. Helm, the missionary who interpreted the Rudd party's proposals to Lobengula. A biography of Rhodes goes so far as to suggest that Helm had 'become one of Rhodes's men' and misled the chief as to the nature of the concession.[48] A recent writer cites the biography as documentation that Helm was 'a mere mercenary, a paid hack of Rhodes'.[49]

The corrupt missionary is an appropriate companion to the bought government official as supporting actors in the amorality play of the Rudd concession. But there is no evidence that Rhodes 'bought' Helm, only that he tried. There can be no doubt that Helm hoped that the Rudd party would be successful, but his support came from other considerations than personal enrichment. Like his associates in Matabeleland, Helm had been a missionary without converts, a pastor without a flock. Nor had he been able to modify the Matabele way of life toward Victorian standards

[43]There are several communications in this vein in the Moffat papers, MO 1/1/4, Rhodesian Archives.
[44]Richard Brown, 'Aspects of the scramble for Matabeleland,' in Eric Stokes and Richard Brown, eds, *The Zambesian Past* (Manchester, 1969). pp. 76–9.
[45]Maguire to Newton, 27 Oct. 1888. NE 1/1/10, Rhodesian Archives.
[46]Diary, 29 Sept. 1888, in V. H. Hiller, ed., *Gold and the Gospel in Mashonaland* (London, 1949), p. 187.
[47]*Ibid.*, p. 185.
[48]J. G. Lockhart and C. M. Woodhouse, *Cecil Rhodes* (New York, 1963), p. 137.
[49]Stanlake Samkange, *Origins of Rhodesia* (London, 1968), p. 67.

of behaviour. The white men who came into the country in search of wealth he considered little better than the Matabele and he was convinced there would be chaos if the rush of concessionaires were not checked. If a strong company were given a monopoly and had the power to keep out adventurers, he foresaw a new era in which the Matabele would gradually be converted to civilised ways and the missionaries might have the opportunity for useful work both in conversions and in assistance to the new regime.[50] These views were like those of his fellow missionaries. David Carnegie was delighted to hear of the Rudd concession and disconsolate when he heard that Lobengula had repudiated it. The way was now open, he feared, for the invasion of hundreds of filibusterers who would overrun the country.[51] Helm stated that he had received no personal inducement, and there seems no reason to disbelieve him, for his motivations to be of assistance were already compelling.

Allegations of bribery and corruption derive in large part from the assumption that Lobengula could not have agreed to concede a mining monopoly over his entire domain for the paltry price of £100 a month and one thousand rifles, and that he must have been deluded. Lobengula was well aware that the Matabele were in danger of being overrun by white men who coveted the resources of his land, and it seems unlikely that he would have put his faith in a great monopoly headed by Rhodes as a means of protecting himself against petty prospectors.[52] But if Rudd's account of the final negotiations is to be believed, the proposals were not only understood but considered in great detail by the indunas as well as by Lobengula. Lobengula finally agreed to sign after a brief conference with Thompson and Lotje, a trusted induna who had favoured the concession, at which no one else was present.[53]

The most likely explanation for Lobengula's insistence that he had been duped is not that the provisions of the concession document were mistranslated but that oral assurances were given him which misrepresented its meaning. Helm later stated to his directors that the grantees had assured Lobengula that all that they wished was the right to dig for gold and to

[50]Helm's reactions to the prospect of the Rudd concession are contained in a letter, Helm to Thompson (LMS), 11 Oct. 1888, LO 6/1/5, Rhodesian Archives. After the concession, 'Matabele' Thompson offered Helm £200 a year to act on behalf of the concessionaires but Helm referred the proposal to the headquarters of the LMS with the notation that he assumed the Society would not approve. He was correct. Helm to Thompson (LMS), 22 Dec. 1888, and enclosure. 'Matabele' Thompson to Helm, 9 Nov. 1888, in Hiller, *Gold and the Gospel*. The only Matabele missionary recorded as acquiring shares in the British South Africa Company was W. A. Elliott who in 1893 had 100 shares. London to South Africa, BSAC, 7 April 1893, LO 3/1/13, Rhodesian Archives.
[51]Carnegie to Thompson, 15 Jan. 1889. LO 6/1/5, Rhodesian Archives.
[52]Brown, 'Aspects of the scramble,' 80.
[53]Hiller, *Gold and the Gospel*, p. 202. Lotje was killed by order of Lobengula in Sept. 1889, allegedly for his support of the concession. Maund thought he had been killed because of his wealth.

bring in the necessary machinery, that they would not bring in more than ten white men, and that they would abide by the laws of his country and 'be his people'. These promises were not put in the concession.[54] In November 1888 Lobengula did not yet know that the verbal promise of a maximum of ten white men would not be kept, but he had received disturbing reports that he had been tricked into 'selling his country'. One of the concession hunters, Edward R. Renny-Tailyour, who had allied himself with Maund, admitted that on instructions from Maund he had told Lobengula that the chief had given away his country,[55] but Renny-Tailyour was not alone in the attempt to upset the concession, and reports in South African papers which were communicated to Lobengula also indicated that he had in fact conferred rights far more extensive than he had been led to believe. His young regiments were already restive over his protection of the whites whom they were eager to kill and many of his indunas were disquieted by the terms of the Rudd concession. Confronted with a grave crisis for his leadership, Lobengula twisted and turned. On the one hand he continued to assure Maguire and Thompson who had remained to protect their interests that he had not repudiated the concession itself, merely the suggestion that he had given away his country. Maguire maintained that Lobengula, in mid-January 1889, told him not to worry, that when the guns arrived all would be well and the concession would be honoured. But at the end of November 1888 Lobengula had asked Maund to accompany two of his indunas to England with the official mission of presenting a letter to the queen protesting at the encroachments of the Portuguese but also to seek advice on the crisis confronting him from the increasing pressure of Europeans on his country. The first object of the mission was public — his letter was witnessed by Helm, among other Europeans — the second was secret, though no one was deluded that he would at his own expense send a mission to England merely to deliver a letter regarding the Portuguese.[56]

Maund was jubilant. The chief's protest against the Portuguese involved encroachments in the Mazoe valley where Maund sought a concession for the Exploring Company, and his verbal message repudiating the Rudd Concession Maund hoped would eliminate the threat of Rhodes's monopoly. He had not seen the Rudd concession — Rudd in his haste to depart had not left a copy — but was assured by Lobengula and his indunas

[54]Helm to LMS, 29 March 1889, in *ibid.*, p. 227. Lobengula later referred to this promise when he protested to Rhodes against the entry of the pioneer column.

[55]Memo of conversation with Maund, 24 Jan. 1889, by Graham Bower. CO 879/30/369.

[56]Helm after hearing of the chief's intentions wrote to Moffat that he hoped Lobengula would also inform Robinson. Helm to Moffat, 22 Nov. 1888. MO 1/1/4, Rhodesian Archives. Rhodes and his associates were never under any illusion about the mission's being directed against them.

that the chief had conceded nothing. Maund concluded that even if there was a concession, the pressure of the Matabele would compel Lobengula to repudiate it.[57] Maund maintained that he knew nothing of the concession to Rudd until after he left Matabeleland, which led Maguire to observe that it was difficult to understand how Maund could have advised Lobengula to disavow an arrangement of which he was unaware.[58] Also difficult to believe was Maund's later insistence that the initiative for the mission came from Lobengula and that Maund had reluctantly agreed to serve for fear of offending the chief. Maund also averred that the oral message which the chief entrusted to the indunas was entirely Lobengula's own.[59] This assertion was undoubtedly correct. Lobengula had great reasons of state for his initiative, and he must have been led to hope by Maund, still posing as the representative of 'the great men in London', that the imperial government across the seas could be a source of succour against its South African representative. For his services to Lobengula, Maund extracted the promise that there would be no more concessions or negotiations until the return of the indunas from England. The response to Maund's request for a concession in the Mazoe valley was less explicit. Lobengula replied : 'Take my men to England for me; and when you return, then I will talk about that.'[60] Lobengula's caution was understandable.

Whatever its antecedents, the mission to London provided a magnificent opportunity for the Exploring Company, as both its directors and Cecil Rhodes were keenly aware. The issue was not merely the Rudd concession. The document was of doubtful validity, and its value would be even more doubtful if Lobengula were expressly to repudiate it. If the indunas were to convey the message that Lobengula had been defrauded they would have support from British humanitarians as well as from the financiers who backed the Exploring Company. Rhodes's plan to use the concession as the basis for a charter might well be frustrated.

The news of the mission came as a shock to Rhodes. He had congratulated himself on the removal of what he thought to be the last obstacle to the concession — the right to ship rifles. The compliant Robinson had accepted Shippard's argument that arming the Matabele with firearms was in fact humanitarian because they would not know how to fire them and would become less formidable than if they used assegais. Bishop George W. H. Knight-Bruce, who sought to establish a mission in Mashonaland and who had denounced the 'deviltry and brutality' of providing the Matabele with rifles to massacre the Mashona had been converted by Rhodes with unspecified arguments into a 'cordial supporter'.

[57]Maund to Gifford, 5 Dec. 1888. BSAC Misc. I, Rhodes House.
[58]Maguire to Moffat, 4 Jan. 1889. MO 1/1/4, Rhodesian Archives.
[59]Maund to Hole, 7 Oct. 1926. Maund Papers, Witwatersrand.
[60]Memo by Maund of meeting held at King's Kraal, 24 Nov. 1888, witnessed by Helm, Tainton, and J. W. Colenbrander. Maund Papers, Witwatersrand.

Rhodes had assured Rudd that 'Matabeleland is all right for the future',[61] but now he was confronted with a threat far greater than that from a mere bishop. His first response was to attempt to discredit the indunas as people of no standing and to prevent their departure from South Africa.

Maund suspected that Rhodes would make such an effort. Before any orders for his detention could be received he travelled to Khama's capital where he arrived on 22 December and left the same afternoon. He told Moffat, who was now back in residency with Khama, that Lobengula had 'all but forced on him' the mission. Moffat was contemptuous; Maund was 'phenomenally untruthful'; he lamented to Shippard that he had no authority to put down 'this kind of thing',[62] but before any such authority could arrive Maund had departed, proceeding through the Transvaal to avoid any complications from Shippard or his agents, reappearing in British territory at Kimberley in the freedom of Cape Colony where Shippard's writ did not run. Rhodes, hearing of his arrival, sent Dr Jameson to invite Maund to his cottage and Maund, though 'scenting trouble', accepted.[63] The interview was in the Rhodes style. Rhodes was first casually friendly and then turned to business — if Maund would 'chuck' his people in London and join him, he would 'make' him. When Maund refused to betray his employers, Rhodes stormed that he would see to it that the high commissioner stopped him and the indunas.[64] Robinson did his best. He had previously tried unsuccessfully to discourage Maund from proceeding by warning him that the imperial government would not receive the deputation without the recommendation of the local authorities,[65] and when they arrived in Cape Town he reiterated that they should not proceed on a hopeless mission. Robinson sought to ensure the futility of the mission by discrediting it in communications to the Colonial Office. Maund, he quoted Shippard as saying, was 'a mendacious adventurer', 'a dangerous man'; the interpreter Colenbrander was 'hopelessly unreliable', and the 'natives' were not indunas or even head men.[66] Robinson's opposition might well have checked the departure of the deputation. Cawston after a fruitless plea to the Foreign Office wired Maund that it was useless to proceed until the High Commissioner's opposition had been removed.[67]

At this critical moment, Rhodes arrived in Cape Town. His mood was far different from that he had displayed in Kimberley. There was no

---

[61]Rhodes to Rudd, 6 Dec. 1888. RU 2/1/1/, Rhodesian Archives.
[62]Moffat to Shippard, 24 Dec. 1888. CO 879/30/369.
[63]Maund apparently came to Kimberley not with the intention of meeting Rhodes but because it was on the railway to Cape Town.
[64]Samkange, *Origins of Rhodesia*, pp. 94–95.
[65]Robinson to Administrator, Vryburg, 15 Jan. 1889. CO 879/30/369.
[66]Robinson to Knutsford, 23 Jan. 1889, confidential, enclosing extract, Shippard to Robinson, 17 Jan. 1889. CO 537/124B.
[67]Telegram, Cawston to Maund, 28 Jan. 1889. BSAC Papers, Misc. I, Rhodes House.

bluster or attempts at bribery. Instead he asked to see the letter which Lobengula had addressed to the queen, and professed to see in the appeal and the mission an opportunity to strengthen the Rudd concession and his plans for northern expansion if the London group and he were to join hands in an amalgamated company, and he authorised Maund to cable the Exploring Company to this effect.[68] Maund assumed that the threat posed by the mission and his own persuasiveness had been responsible for Rhodes's change of front. But the initiative for amalgamation had come from the Colonial Office. In December 1888 Knutsford advised Cawston and Gifford that their prospects of receiving a charter would be greatly enhanced if they worked together with Rhodes. Accordingly they cabled Rhodes, who was in fact responding to the London overture when he agreed to unite with the Exploring Company.[69]

With Rhodes's opposition removed, Robinson modified his position. He could not without loss of credibility shift to outright endorsement, but he informed the Colonial Office that on further examination of the Matabele whom Lobengula described as head men he had concluded that they should be allowed to proceed. Their sole object was to see the queen to prove that she existed, and 'in good hands the visit may be advantageous to British interests'.[70]

Rhodes's decision to seek an amalgamation came as a great relief to Gifford and Cawston, for they and Rhodes were in stalemate. They believed that they had sufficient weight to frustrate his hopes for a charter. They had enlisted the support of prominent men in British commerce and politics who were concerned about the extension of the Cape Colony's interest into Bechuanaland and the north. The South African trade section of the London Chamber of Commerce had notified the government of its opposition to Bechuanaland Colony being transferred to the Cape, and had sought support for the Bechuanaland Exploration Company's railway scheme.[71] Another influential group, the South African Committee, sought to promote the same objects. Included in its membership were Earl Grey and his nephew Albert, Joseph Chamberlain, Sir Thomas Fowell Buxton, and other men of prominence.[72]

These were powerful allies, but the London interests could not hope to succeed without the cooperation of the Cape government and the High Commissioner. In the last months of 1888 the railway project had been stalled by an impasse between Downing Street and Cape Town. The Colonial Office would not negotiate an agreement for Bechuanaland with-

[68]Maund, 'Reminiscences', 22 June 1923, in Maund Papers, Afr. 5229(4), Rhodes House, Oxford.
[69]Cawston to Colonial Office, 1 July 1889. CO 879/30/372.
[70]Telegram, Robinson to Knutsford, 4 Feb. 1889. CO 879/30/369.
[71]*South Africa*, 11 Jan. 1889.
[72]See circular, South African Committee, n.d. (early 1889). CO 879/30/372.

out assurances from the government of Sir Gordon Sprigg that it would build a railway to the Bechuanaland border, but the Sprigg government would take no action without knowing the terms of the Exploration Company's agreement with the Imperial government, and the obduracy of the Cape was strengthened by opposition in Britain to the transfer of the Crown Colony of Bechuanaland to the Cape.[73] Rhodes was a powerful member of the Cape Assembly, made more formidable by his alliance with the Afrikaner Bond, whose opposition to railway extension into Bechuanaland had been a factor in the delay. Rhodes could be the means to removing the block in Cape Town. Most important, Rhodes would bring into the amalgamation the substantial resources he derived from De Beers and Gold Fields, and the Rudd concession which would become far more valuable if the London group's opposition to it were to be withdrawn. Amalgamation with Rhodes had become essential to the Exploring Company, as cooperation with the Exploring Company had become essential to Rhodes.[74]

The union of interests took place as the Colonial Office was considering an inquiry by Gifford as to whether the government would be willing to grant a charter to a merger of the Bechuanaland Exploration and Exploring Companies. The subordinate staff was cautious to hostile. Edward Fairfield was opposed in principle to chartered companies,[75] and predictably condemned the proposal:

This is a mere piece of financing. Something is to be got which will look well enough to invite fools to subscribe to. Such a Chartered Company could never really pay. It would simply sow the seeds of a heap of political trouble, and then the promoters would shuffle out of it, and leave us to take up the work of preserving the peace, and settling the difficulties. The existing system of chartering has not been such a success as to make us augur well for its extension to a poor inland country, the seat of political troubles.[76]

Fairfield's colleague John Bramston agreed that there was danger in chartering a company in an area dominated by grave political questions. Their superiors agreed that there was a risk, as there was in any extension of the British presence in Africa. But the issue was not whether Britain

---

[73]Gifford to Herbert, 3 Dec. 1888, and enclosures and minutes. CO 417/26.
[74]Metcalfe, who was a close friend of Rhodes though employed by his rivals, later wrote: 'There is no doubt that without the aid of the Exploring Company, the Charter would not have been granted or even thought of. The amalgamation made it possible.' 'My Story of the Scheme,' in Leo Weinthal, *The Story of the Cape to Cairo Railway & River Route, 1887–1922* (3 vols, London, [1923?]), I, 99.
[75]It is ironic that several years later Fairfield should be saddled with the indictment of having been an accessory to the Jameson Raid.
[76]Note by Fairfield, 4 Jan. 1889, on Gifford to Knutsford, 3 Jan. 1889. CO 417/38.

should refuse to be involved; the government had already involved itself by the Moffat Treaty. The questions for decision were whether the recognition of a chartered company would lighten or remove the burden on the British Exchequer in Bechuanaland and the interior, and whether such a company could be regulated in such a way that it would not contribute to international complications or native disturbances. Lord Knutsford and his permanent under-secretary Sir R. G. W. Herbert, already impressed with the financial backing of Gifford and Cawston, were convinced that, with the reported accession of Rhodes, there was no problem of resources — there was now 'a plethora' of funds available to the promoters.[77] The Colonial Office, therefore, replied that it would defer a decision until it had considered the effects of a charter on the financial and political condition of Bechuanaland and had received a recommendation from the high commissioner.[78] The campaign for a charter was on the verge of success. Gifford wrote to Cawston in mid-March: 'I am convinced we are going to win, it is a grand game. I was dreaming of it last night, but my damned gun would not go off as the natives rushed to turn us out.'[79]

At this juncture Maund arrived in London with Lobengula's indunas. The Colonial Office, which had previously been adamant that the mission could have no official recognition and that Queen Victoria could not receive them, had changed from frigidity to ardent welcome. The reception at Windsor was arranged, and when the indunas refused to go without Maund, Knutsford hastened to assure them that an exception would be made to the rule that British subjects could not attend such an audience since it would be 'a matter of great regret to him both on account of the indunas themselves and of the relations between Lobengula and the British government if their proposed visit to the queen were in any way to fall through'.[80] The envoys delivered the letter protesting about Portuguese encroachments, which was useful to the new combination, and Lobengula's oral message, which was not. The response of Knutsford, speaking for the queen, was all that the Exploring Company could have desired in the circumstances of late 1888 but was directly contrary to its interests in 1889: 'A King gives a stranger an ox, not his whole herd of cattle, other-

---

[77]Notes by Herbert and Knutsford, on *ibid.* At the time Knutsford referred to Rhodes's joining forces with Cawston and Gifford, they were still in opposition. The origin of the premature report that they had combined is obscure and interesting.
[78]Colonial Office to Gifford, 10 Jan. 1889. FO 84/1995.
[79]Gifford to Cawston, 13 March 1889. BSAC Misc., Rhodes House.
[80]Baillie Hamilton to Maund, 1 March 1889. Maund Papers, Witwatersrand. Maund gave the credit for the change of front to the influence of Lord Lothian, Secretary of State for Scotland, and Lady Frederick Cavendish, who were his shipboard acquaintances. 'The Matabele Mission to Queen Victoria,' n.d., Maund Papers, Witwatersrand. It is likely that Robinson's changed position and the agreement with Rhodes had made the Colonial Office more receptive.

wise what would other strangers arriving have to eat?'[81] This counsel, written in what Knutsford conceived to be the Matabele style,[82] evoked dismay among the promoters. Rhodes, who had arrived in London to formalise the amalgamation, concluded that Maund was the culprit and denounced him as a traitor to his employers. A letter from the Aborigines Protection Society to Lobengula reinforced the Colonial Office message in more explicit terms, that white men would make war for gold, just as Africans fought for cattle.[83]

Maund left London with instructions to do all that he could to undo the damage of the letters. He was to pose as the king's adviser with no thought of personal gain but to use every opportunity to strengthen the hands of the Rudd concession-holders. This feat of gymnastics Maund performed with great finesse. He advised Lobengula that the concession was undoubtedly legal and that the chief had no alternative but to accept it.[84]

While their agents in Matabeleland devoted themselves to salvaging the Rudd concession, Rhodes, Cawston, and Gifford proceeded with the organisation of their monopoly and their campaign for a charter. At the end of May, Rhodes and Rudd on behalf of Gold Fields of South Africa, which had provided the funds for the Rudd mission, and the Exploring Company negotiated an agreement with a new entity named the Central Search Association, Limited, by which they sold to the new body all their claims to mineral rights in 'the domains of Lobengula and adjacent territories'. The directors of the Central Search Association included Rhodes, Gifford, Cawston, Beit, John O. Maund, and C. D. Rudd and his brother Thomas. In essence, therefore, the creators were selling to themselves. The Central Search Association, the creation of the vendors with a nominal capital of £120,000, paid its creators £92,400 in shares, distributed as follows:[85]

Gold Fields of South Africa, Ltd	£25,500
Exploring Company, Ltd	22,500
Cecil J. Rhodes	9,750
Charles D. Rudd	9,000
Alfred Beit	8,250
Nathan Rothschild	3,000
Rochfort Maguire	3,000
Rhodes, Rudd, and Beit	9,000
Austral Africa Exploration Company	2,400

[81]Message to Lobengula, 26 March 1889, in Knutsford to Robinson, 27 March 1889.
[82]Maund maintained that the parable of the ox was Knutsford's own idea, that Maund tried to get the sentence changed or eliminated but the message had already been approved by the queen. Maund to Hole, 7 Oct. 1926. HO 1/2/1, Rhodesian Archives.
[83]Buxton and Fox Bourne to Lobengula, 19 March 1889. MA 23/1/1, Rhodesian Archives.
[84]Maund to Exploring Company, 11 June 1890. MA 23/1/1, Rhodesian Archives.
[85]Memorandum of Agreement, 30 May 1889. BT 31/4451/28988.

The Austral Africa Company was among those claiming a prior concession from Lobengula which gave up its rights in exchange for shares, and other rivals were transformed into supporters by the same process. The Rudd concession costing £1200 a year now supported a capital of £120,000, and in July 1890 Central Search was transformed into the United Concessions Company, with a capital of £4 million most of which was paid to Rhodes and his fellow insiders for their rights.[86] In May 1889, also, the old Exploring Company was liquidated and from its dead body emerged a new company of the same name which included Rhodes as a director and Beit as one of its prominent shareholders.[87] This pyramiding of largely paper capital which eventually would be converted into fortunes for the favoured few took place unknown to the investing public and to the government, which when it granted the charter in October assumed as did investors that the British South Africa Company was the possessor of the Rudd concession. In fact it remained the property of the Central Search Association and its successor the United Concessions Company which retained the right of 50 per cent of the profits.

The participants also agreed to provide a total of £700,000 as initial capital for the chartered company, of which £500,000 would be for railway construction and £200,000 for development of the country assigned by the charter. In addition Rhodes provided from his own funds £30,000 for a telegraph and £4,000 for the salary and expenses of a British resident in Matabeleland. The capital came from the following sources:[88]

	Railway	*Development*
Gold Fields of South Africa	£170,834	£68,334
Rhodes, Rudd, Beit and various minor interests in South Africa	£204,166	£81,666
Exploring Company, Bechuanaland Exploration Company, Southern Land Company, and other smaller interests	£125,000	£50,000

The predominant financial support for the chartered company therefore came from Rhodes and his associates, and with money went power. Rhodes, in addition to being with Beit a member of the London board, was made chairman of the local board in South Africa and Managing Director with plenary powers.

Rhodes and the Exploring Company also agreed to seek extension of the scope of the Charter beyond the Zambesi to the Great Lakes. It is usually assumed that this enlarged vista reflected Rhodes's grandiose dreams and this may well have been the case, though Cawston had also

---

[86]Agreement, 23 July 1890. BT 31/4815/3926.
[87]Agreement, 7 June 1889. BT 31/4468/2152.
[88]Cawston to Colonial Office, 1 July 1889. CO 879/30/372.

talked in similarly expansive terms.[89] Whatever the source of the idea, it was accepted by the promoters and negotiations had been begun by the beginning of May 1889 for the absorption of the African Lakes Company into the chartered company.[90] By mid-May the Colonial Office had formally endorsed the grant of a charter to the Exploring Company–Rhodes combination, on the argument that a charter would bring the Company more directly under governmental control and would relieve the government of diplomatic difficulties and heavy expenditures.[91] Salisbury had no objections to the grant of the charter but left in abeyance the issue of the extension of its purview north of the Zambesi.[92] Unofficially, also, Salisbury suggested that the character of the proposed company would be enhanced with the addition to its Board of Directors of some men of standing in Britain.

Rhodes approached Sir William Mackinnon of the Imperial British East Africa Company and the steamship magnate, Sir Donald Currie, both of whom declined. Lord Balfour of Burleigh, the first choice to be president of the Board, accepted but then withdrew because of a possible conflict of interest with his position in the ministry as secretary of state for Scotland.[93] Thereupon the promoters invited the Duke of Abercorn and the Duke of Fife to become chairman and vice-chairman respectively, and they accepted.[94] Abercorn, the owner of large estates in Ireland and Scotland, was then fifty years of age. He was *persona grata* at court, a prominent member of the Conservative party, and a close friend of Salisbury's. Fife, about the same age, was the husband of the Prince of Wales's eldest daughter, a wealthy man who had augmented his fortunes through his partnership in the London banking firm of Sir Samuel Scott and Company. Fife belonged to the Liberal party.[95] The third of the 'public' members of the board was Albert Grey, nephew of the third earl and heir to the title. At the instance of Fife, the board appointed to its membership his banking partner, Horace B. Farquhar, 'an aristocrat

---

[89]Harry Johnston probably was the means of communicating the plans of the Company to Salisbury. Johnston recalled that Salisbury had had only a vague idea of who Rhodes was: 'Rather a Pro-Boer M.P. in South Africa, I fancy.' H. H. Johnston, *The Story of My Life* (New York, 1923), p. 221. Johnston may indeed have suggested the idea to Cawston and Rhodes of extending the company to the lakes. Ricarde Seaver to Cawston, 21 April 1889. BSAC Misc. I, Rhodes House.

[90]Ewing to Salisbury, 3 May 1889. FO 84/1994.

[91]Colonial Office to Foreign Office, 16 May 1889. FO 84/1995.

[92]Foreign Office to Colonial Office, 27 May 1889. FO 84/1996.

[93]Euan Smith to Salisbury, 15 June 1889. File A/79, Salisbury Papers, Christ Church, Oxford. Sir Charles Euan Smith, the consul-general of Zanzibar on leave in Britain, acted as an intermediary in these negotiations.

[94]Again Euan Smith was centrally involved. He suggested the names of Abercorn .and Fife, and represented the company in inducing Fife to accept. Cawston to Colonial Office, 1 July 1889. CO 879/30/372.

[95]*South Africa*, 14 March 1891.

whom strong commercial abilities and a capacity to make money turned into a business man.'[96] With such glittering adornments of British society, the Company had the respectability to match its financial power which assured it a charter. Rhodes attempted to provide an additional guarantee of success by offering to make Salisbury's son Robert a barrister for the new company, but Robert prudently declined.[97] After some delay caused by the opposition of Sir John Swinburne, MP, who objected to the monopoly because it ignored the claims of his company, Swinburne was bought out and the charter of the British South Africa Company was approved on October 29, 1889.[98]

This imposing combination of prestigious names and working capitalists, the imperial government hoped, would bring about economic development in the African interior and serve the public interest under the constraints imposed by its charter. The three public members were expected to ensure that the Company acted responsibly. But Abercorn and Fife showed little interest in the drudgery of corporate administration. Their interests were directed to the fluctuations of Company shares and as prices rose, they sold their holdings at handsome profits.[99] Rhodes's energy and money buoyed that rise and they gave him their unquestioning confidence. Grey was an active member of the Board but he also fell under the spell of Rhodes. Cawston and Gifford also accepted Rhodes's leadership. His position of dominance was formalised when the Board in May, 1890 assigned him 'absolute discretion' to act for the Company.[100]

The combination of indolent or deferential directors with the driving ambition of Rhodes was institutionalised irresponsibility. The government assumed that the Company's directors would supervise Rhodes, and the directors assumed that Rhodes would control his subordinates. Neither assumption was correct. Rhodes had undertaken too many responsibilities to devote his unremitting attention to the affairs of all and in July 1890 he added to his power, prestige, and burdens when he became prime minister of Cape Colony. Rhodes thus advanced his ambition to become master of southern Africa, but his personal aims were not necessarily congruent with the interests of the Company. Abercorn complained to Cawston that he was 'not happy' about Rhodes having accepted the prime ministership, and that this position and a directorship in the Company

[96]Paul H. Emden, *Money Powers of Europe in the Nineteenth and Twentieth Centuries* (London, 1937), p. 338.
[97]McDonnell to Salisbury, 10 July 1889; Euan Smith to McDonnell, 17 July 1889, both in File E, Salisbury Papers. Salisbury noted, 'Rhodes magnificence rather alarms me'. The ubiquitous Euan Smith was also the intermediary in this offer.
[98]Council Office to Foreign Office, 1 Nov. 1889. FO 84/2005.
[99]Galbraith, 'The British South Africa Company and the Jameson Raid', pp. 147–8.
[100]Power of Attorney, 14 May 1890, enclosure in Hawksley to Fairley, 12 July 1896. CO 879/47/507.

seemed incompatible.[101] But neither Abercorn nor any other member of the board had the temerity to ask Rhodes to make a choice.

Rhodes devoted his principal attention to diamonds, politics, and development south of the Zambesi. His interest in Gold Fields of South Africa was minimal except in terms of the profits he received, and his involvement in the operations of the chartered Company north of the Zambesi was spasmodic. Even in Mashonaland he did not supervise the management of his administrator Jameson. Rhodes reposed complete confidence in Jameson, who 'never makes a mistake'.[102] Rhodes discussed plans with Jameson during occasional visits and through telegraphic communication, but Jameson had great discretionary authority. As Rhodes said to him in one of their telegraphic interchanges: 'Your business is to administer the country as to which I have nothing to do but merely say "yes" if you take the trouble to ask me.'[103] Jameson's administration was highly permissive to favoured insiders who received lavish land and mining grants in terms of promises to provide capital, but were not held to the terms of their contracts.[104] William Milton who was sent to Mashonaland in 1896 to establish an efficient administration looked at the shambles of Jameson's land policy and concluded that he 'must have been off his head for some time before the Raid'.[105] When Rhodes did intervene, however, it was frequently to make the shambles worse, for he on several occasions ordered Jameson to make huge land grants without any guarantees for effective development.[106] The London board protested, but took no action.

The British South Africa Company between 1889 and 1896 bore little resemblance to the responsible agency for economic development and the protection of native welfare which the imperial government had visualised in the grant of a charter. Most of the directors were preoccupied with enriching themselves without undue sensitivity as to the manipulations which caused gullible investors to bid for shares at higher and higher rates. The Company, it is true, was not unique in its pyramiding of a mining concession into a large amount of paper capital — dozens of syndicates in South Africa made fortunes for insiders in a similar way. But the British South Africa Company was the only chartered company with such characteristics. When the Duke of Fife with watery eye and quivering lip resigned after the Raid with a denunciation of Rhodes, he was indicting himself and his co-directors who had abdicated their

---

[101]Abercorn to Cawston, 19 July 1890. BSAC II, Misc., Rhodes House.

[102]Thomas Fuller, *Cecil John Rhodes* (London, 1910), p. 75.

[103]Memo of conversation held Sunday, 15 May 1892. A 1/3/10, Rhodesian Archives.

[104]Memorandum, 'Beneficial Occupation of Land,' n.d. [1898] A 1/5/1, Rhodesian Archives.

[105]Milton to his wife, 18 Sept. 1896. MI, 1/1/1, Rhodesian Archives.

[106]Jameson protested to Rhodes on at least two occasions against giving away land without requiring development. Telegrams, Jameson to Rhodes, 10 March 1892, 12 March 1892, both in LO 5/2/17, Rhodesian Archives.

responsibility. The imperial government likewise had used the Company to achieve imperial purposes' on the cheap' but had not devoted sufficient attention to the manner in which it carried out these responsibilities. The Company was like an engine without a governor; like such an engine, it was likely to be involved in a disaster. The events of December 1895 were long foreshadowed.

9

D.M. SCHURMAN

Historians and Britain's Imperial Strategic Stance in 1914

When the war clouds gathered over Europe, as the summer began in 1914, neither responsible Britons nor interested continental observers were certain how, or even if, the United Kingdom would react if a general conflict ensued. This ambivalence is sometimes obscured for more recent observers by the disadvantage of hindsight. For it is well enough known that in the First World War, some nine and a quarter million of men were mobilised from the British Isles and the attendant Empire, of which a high proportion served, suffered and eventually triumphed in France and Flanders. It is also well known that, on the water, by stretching itself across the North Sea approaches, the mighty fleet of Great Britain took a stranglehold on Germany's overseas trade and contributed heavily to the ultimate result of November 1918 — although it may well be doubted if the lipservice eventually paid to the value of 'blockade' represents deep appreciation of its true potency. Because the war in France had become static, due to the superiority of the means of defence over the power of attack, suggestions were soon made about ways to break that frustrating immobility. These suggestions were translated into the Gallipoli, Salonika, and Palestine offshoots of the war, and the advocates of these operations were later dubbed as the 'easterners' as opposed to 'westerners' who backed the ideal of eventual victory in France. Since victory could be *seen* to have occurred in the western theatre, no matter what had been the causes contributing to it, the epithet 'sideshow' so tellingly applied to efforts in the Eastern Mediterranean during the war, acquired additional pungency in retrospect.

It was inevitable that historians, writing after 1914, should have argued the merits of one approach over the other even as it seems to have been inevitable that some writers should identify with one 'strategy' and some with the supposed alternative.[1] Furthermore, it was, if not inevitable, at least natural, that these pen-wielding artists of the post-mortem should support their viewpoints with references to the 'traditional' currents of

[1]The best one-sided example of this literature is Trumbull Higgins, *Winston Churchill and the Dardanelles* (London, 1963), and the controversy is well enough known to make exhaustive documentation superfluous.

British strategy stretching back in historical time at least as far as Queen Anne's war. Undoubtedly the most widely known of the protagonists for the 'easterners' was the late Sir Basil Liddell Hart. Liddell Hart, a journalist whose naturally penetrating mind acquired strength and perspective from constant refreshment from the storehouse of history, had recoiled from the high casualty rates and apparently unimaginative leadership attendant upon the slow push to victory on the western front. Not only did he deprecate the generalship revealed under those conditions, but he suggested that heavy commitment to such stultifying warfare methods was not in tune with what he dubbed 'the British way in warfare', which 'traditionally' involved the use of a superior fleet to give the British army the mobility that would allow its small numbers to achieve maximum effect — operating in an alliance.[2] However, this thrust of Liddell Hart's mind, while it may be supported with historical examples, was not developed as the result of any deep study of sea power, and seems to have rested on disillusionment with what happened in 1914–18 much more than it did on historical considerations. That is to say, it was an unimpeachable proposition that Britain had always relied on sea power to gain her greatest military effects in the past; it was quite another to relate this true but complacent consideration to the genesis and progress of the First World War. For it seems clear that Liddell Hart's mainspring of judgment owed more to his contempt for British generalship in France than it did to serious detailed historical contemplation of the background to Army–Navy cooperation or lack of it before the war.

In this connection, it is instructive to note that the paramount defender of Haig, John Terraine, many of whose judgments Liddell Hart so plainly rejected,[3] does not deny that the naval mobility pattern was the traditional British way.[4] Their argument has been really about whether Haig was a military dunce or top of the class. But Terraine, like Liddell Hart, has not been a dedicated student of sea power. It is true that he has understood something of the forces dividing the two services before 1914, despite the fact that the Navy is treated as a less strategically perceptive force when compared with his military heroes. No one would deny that there were faults in the naval thinking apparatus, but a viewpoint claiming that Great Britain has produced no naval Clausewitz or thinker equal to Mahan seems to want some refining.[5]

This whole subject of 'easterner' versus 'westerner' has been discussed by the present writer in an earlier article, where some of the disadvantages

---

[2]B.H. Liddell Hart, *The Real War* (Boston, 1930), p. 42.
[3]For instance, on 24 April 1963, Liddell Hart wrote to *The Times* to state that Mr Terraine had not looked at the Liddell Hart evidence on the First World War, and Haig's part in it 'in a genuine spirit of enquiry'.
[4]John Terraine, *The Western Front, 1914–18* (London, 1964), p. 251 especially.
[5]*Ibid*, p. 26.

of hindsight have been pointed out.[6] The Chichele Professor of War at the University of Oxford, Norman Gibbs, has grappled with the problem in a broader context, and has noted the way in which 'easterner' views have tended to be linked with Britain's 'traditional' sea strategy, and 'westerner' views linked to 'continental' strategic priorities in the past. Quite properly, he has pointed out that a 'continental' strategy has every claim to be regarded as 'traditional' and, a far more important argument, he refers to the fact that the iron law of international politics is that tradition must bow to the overwhelming circumstances of the moment when there is a conflict, or seems to be a conflict between them.[7] The proposition that the eighteenth century and the Napoleonic era saw the two traditions poised for use as circumstances appeared to dictate, is a true enough observation if one eschews the difficult matter of weighing the importance of one tradition against the other. Consequently, Professor Gibbs's sane observations help to clear away the emotional overtones of post-World War I argumentation masquerading as history. Again, Admiral Sir Herbert Richmond has indicated that the dichotomy between the two approaches was discussed as early as 1909, and that Admiral Lord Fisher understood clearly that important national strategic conclusions were being reached that would have a strong bearing on service conduct in the war when it came.[8]

It seems possible, indeed, that consideration of what postwar apologists and historians thought was 'traditional' doctrine is not, in itself, sufficient to allow the problem to be seen most advantageously. It may well be illuminating to link the postwar arguments of justification with a short consideration of what happened when the war began, and those happenings, in turn, with the events preceding the war. This method seems to be valuable in dealing with past political argument that has since hardened into historical controversy. It seems to be widely accepted that theories of war have a great bearing on the conduct of war. No doubt it is true that in some mysterious way theory does affect war, but it appears to the present writer that this effect seldom occurs in ways that either protagonists of theory or postwar explainers like to think. This essay, among other things, will attempt to demonstrate how a theory of great strength based on historical study carried out by powerful minds fell before a combination of ignorance and circumstance when warfare actually occurred.

When the events of 1914–15 are examined with such a linking purpose in mind, it is possible to observe, as Professor Gibbs does, that circumstance

---

[6]D.M. Schurman. 'Easterners v Westerners', *Purnell's History of the First World War*, no. 26, pp. 712–15.

[7]Norman Gibbs. 'British strategic doctrine', in Michael Howard, ed., *The Theory and Practice of War* (London, 1965), pp. 187–212 – see esp. pp. 193–4.

[8]Fisher to Esher, 15 March 1909. See M.V. Brett, *Journals and Letters of Reginald, Viscount Esher*, (London, 1934), II, 375–6; quoted by H.W. Richmond in *British Strategy : Military and Economic* (Cambridge, 1941), pp. 134–35.

governed the turn of events.[9] However, this controlling factor held true for *both* the British Army and the Royal Navy. A good part of this argument is set out with compelling force in the Lees Knowles Lectures for 1936.[10] There, C.R.M.F. Cruttwell looked at military dispositions in 1914. He has shown that the British Army, no matter what its final arrangement, was not a force at once committed to operations of an almost unlimited nature on the Franco-Belgian flank of the French armies, any more than it was committed to large-scale operations on its own in support of the Belgian neutrality that the force purported to defend. After all, military staff conversations had predisposed the British to action, if it came to that, in some conjunction with the French army. It is not at all clear that this predisposition was in any way a blank cheque submitted for General Joffre, the French Commander-in-Chief, to draw upon. This becomes evident when it is considered that the Expeditionary Force itself (although well trained, carefully armed and powerful) was not of a strength that would make heavy operations extending over any length of time viable. After all, manpower was limited. It was thought that the war would be a short one, and it is clearly impossible to give Lord Kitchener credit for the vision that proclaimed a long costly war — after it had been well begun — and, at the same time, to allow that vision to such luminaries as Sir Henry Wilson, who proposed continental action with a *limited* force as early as 1911.[11]

Surely the war produced its own logic. Consider the instructions, quoted by Cruttwell, given to Sir John French as he took up his new command in 1914:

> It must be recognised from the outset that the numerical strength of the British Force, and its contingent reinforcements, is strictly limited, and with this consideration kept steadily in view it will be obvious that the greatest care must be exercised towards a minimum of losses and wastage. Therefore, while every effort must be made to coincide with the plans and wishes of our Ally, the gravest consideration will devolve upon you as to participation in forward movements, when large bodies of French troops are not engaged and where your force may be unduly exposed to attack.[12]

It would be difficult to find a more non-committed Cabinet instruction to a military commander.[13] It does not indicate that anyone in the Cabinet

[9] As he put it, 'Traditions in themselves are neither right nor wrong. What makes them so is their relevance to changing circumstances.' See Gibbs, 'British Strategic Doctrine', p. 194.
[10] C R.M.F. Cruttwell, *The Role of British Strategy in the Great War* (Cambridge, 1936).
[11] At the Committee of Imperial Defence meetings of August, 1911. See Samuel R. Williamson, *The Politics of Grand Strategy* (Harvard, 1969), pp. 191–3.
[12] Cruttwell, *Role of British Strategy*, pp. 22–3.
[13] But admittedly it was in the tradition of the lack of instruction given to Sir Redvers Buller when he left for South Africa in 1899, and, later, to Sir Ian Hamilton when he left for Gallipoli in 1915.

considered that the British Expeditionary Force was required to produce any effect other than a defensive one. This was not the language of the saviour of Belgium against the field grey 'masses' of the Germans. In fact, the force was not expected to be decisive. The Germans did not expect the British to provide a strong check to its movements, any more than the French were of the opinion that scales would be turned or even balanced by the khaki representatives of King George V.[14] It is true that the firepower of French's force, due to good rifle shooting ability, was a surprise to the foe: it is true that this firepower served important requirements of delay; it would be impossible to say much more of it. Indeed, what seems clear in retrospect, is that the British Army had been earmarked for participation in a short war, the destiny of which it could only peripherally hope to affect. This uncommitted attitude is further revealed by the partial withdrawal of British soldiers, after the Marne, to the all but left flank of the Entente line, from whence, had it proved impossible to hold on, the ultimate withdrawal behind the sea wall of south England would clearly have been attempted. It was at the end of the First Battle of Ypres that the policy of 'no firm commitment' gave way to 'we must hold'. At that point, the pill box and machine gun allied with trench and barbed wire dictated a new policy — guns and more men with which to *attack*, and for long years new armies were drawn into an old vortex. Undoubtedly, in this concentrated killing ground, continentalising assumed a new shape. Not for General French and his successor Haig was the Peninsular style of Wellington available. Wellington's policy had been one of conserving men under the protection of natural defences until the foe had become worn with the failure of attack. The new stance was different. Its implementers constructed a pipeline for the extermination of British manhood. They maintained it in the face of failure. They were saved by the French, the Americans and the Royal Navy.

The idea that any tendency to gloat over the place of the British Army in 1914–15 gives pleasure to naval historians should, at this point, be resisted. If the function of the British Army was at the mercy of circumstance, so was that of the Royal Navy. Prescient strategic genius was not demonstrated by the directors of the Royal Navy, a force that assumed decisive strategic importance despite its inclinations and training. When the Royal Navy dispersed from Spithead for its stations in June-July 1914, it went into the North Sea skulking and apprehensive of an anticipated attack from a foe who would make every effort to disturb its majestic symmetry by submarine, torpedo and mine attack rather than manfully facing the British for a Trafalgar-type scrap, ship to ship, fleet to fleet in a devoutly to be wished armageddon.[15] This attack did not materialise

[14]Cruttwell, *Role of British Strategy*, pp. 17–20 and Richmond, *British Strategy*, p. 132.
[15]Julian S. Corbett, *Naval Operations* (London, 1920) I, 29.

and the Navy was able to prepare itself, gathered in might, and sound in tactical plan, for that Great Day. Almost at once it was perceived that the role of guard for the army commuter passage to France was within the Navy's capability, and did not seriously detract from what was assumed to be its main task – the attack and destruction of the German Fleet. On the broad reaches of distant oceans it was possible to destroy Germany's overseas ships almost piecemeal, not without such unpleasant events as the Battle of Coronel and the success of the *Emden*, but relentless and successful none the less.

All this is well known. But two points are worthy of notice. The first is that overseas defence of communication was almost unbearably complicated by an unlooked-for imperial manpower convoy role. The second is that the stationing of the Fleet based on Scapa, for the purpose of inciting and prosecuting decisive naval action, placed it almost inadvertently in a position to throttle German trade with the outside world. As Cruttwell so significantly observed, the real power of the Navy as expressed in the blockade, which was a highly decisive weapon for winning the war, came about as a result of a doctrine and disposition for a 'grand-slam' fleet action which was not a way of winning the war,[16] but only a possible way of losing it.[17] With regard to convoy, Sir Julian Corbett, the official historian, observed that the need to convoy men anxious to participate in the war on land was the one thing that surprised British planners both naval and military.[18] Plans were made to defend the Empire, but plans to allow the Empire to participate in the war in Europe were almost non-existent. The British are often a people to whom sentiment makes little appeal politically except when that sentiment embraces 'loyal' peoples doing what they are told to do. In this case, Empire populations directed by highly motivated governments defined their own concepts of 'imperial defence' in bewilderingly short order and demanded transportation to armageddon. A reluctant but real sense of gratitude forced on an already overstretched Navy the task of shepherding the lambs to the slaughter. In the face of confinements imposed on general British ship movements by over-preoccupation with the probability of battle in the North Sea, it was a miracle that the fleet could rise to the occasion. Luck played a more important part in the successful movement than did advance planning, and luck plus German dilatoriness in responding to the opportunity made the movement largely dry-shod for the overseas soldiers.

In short, as Professor Gibbs has divined, the British naval and military response to the war was dependent on circumstance. Or, as Richmond judged, the 'hard unescapable facts of war soon disclosed the fallacies

[16]Cruttwell, *Role of British Strategy*, p. 24.
[17]Author's judgment.
[18]Corbett, *Naval Operations*, pp. 130–1.

on which the restraints imposed upon power rested'.[19] Both services moved to fulfil a role that presupposed little in the way of cooperation. Both took up a stance that led, through circumstances at best dimly envisaged at the time, to eventual victory. For the ultimate success of the almost inadvertent naval economic stranglehold was a product of First World War developments often commented on in retrospect but not so clearly understood at the time.[20] The final success of the Army owed much to the gallantry that attrition in modern war demanded, but much more to factors in France, Russia, America and on the sea, whose conjunction was only dimly felt by the soldiers in France. Furthermore, it should be stated boldly that the ultimate successes of blockade and attrition war were at the expense of any successes that might have shortened time and perhaps saved lives, such as heavy antisubmarine convoy warfare or 'sideshow' attacks on Gallipoli might have provided. This was because the commander-in-chief of the Grand Fleet resolutely set his face against any disbursements of his collection of ships that would place the possibility of decisive victory in a big battle beyond his means. At Jutland, Jellicoe had the numerical means, and the victory eluded him — and in fairness to him it should be said that, in this writer's opinion, the result was not the fault of his tactical errors. Nevertheless, it may be conjectured that fewer ships would not have produced a lesser result. In brief, the ultimate disposition of Britain's naval and military forces owed most to the reactions of British military, political and naval leaders to circumstances as they unfolded in 1914. It owed little to prewar planning or strategic doctrine.

It is now necessary to penetrate behind the days of decision in 1914, and view the predispositions which made this tyranny of circumstance ultimately operative. On the practical military level, the main lines of development that contributed to this result are complex, but some main lines may be suggested. The Navy, the very mention of whose name fertilised the flower of security in British breasts, was heavily and almost continually engaged in experiment and internal argument over ship design and type. While Admiral Fisher forced new technical apparatus on a service with no unanimous appetite for a single fare served up by him, thought that might have been applied to strategic matters was lavished on the acquisition and improvement of technical expertise. Although Fisher and a few others (even the dimly perceiving Lord Charles Beresford) saw the need for sound strategic thinking, the development of such thinking was not a congenial ancillary to the disagreements over ship type. If Fisher had some sound strategic appreciations they took second place to his preoccupation with numerical and technical superiority to Germany, the admitted rival. As a result, by 1914 the Fleet was ready for the great

[19]Richmond, *British Strategy*, pp. 136–7.
[20]Richmond has argued that lack of British support for more traditional international rules regarding blockade in war limited the fleet's effectiveness. *Ibid*, pp. 123–9.

sea battle that everyone dwelt on to the exclusion or demotion of so much else.

The British Army, for its part, began the first decade of the twentieth century with one of the most inefficient central organisations for war of any army in Europe. But some of its personnel held strategic ideas based on Germanic studies. Further, soldiers were able to attract attention to themselves through the efforts of anti-invasion scaremongers whose objective was conscription, but whose main effect was to alarm the populace, detract from confidence in the Navy, and finally to give them the best conceit of themselves of any British soldiery since Marlborough's time. These tendencies were aided by an organising personality of genius in the person of Richard Burdon Haldane, who took an amorphous scattered collection of regimental soldiers and gave them the staff of a coherent and cohesive army force. The irony of the whole thing was that an army with continental preoccupations had by 1908 settled upon a small, highly trained force excellently suited for such service as cooperation with ships and sailors involved, but which held virtually no serious war planning converse with them. It was a paradox that this centralised, horsedrawn and foot-marching little army of formidable efficiency, possessed of alien doctrine, was able, by 1914, to maintain successfully that the main role of the modern mechanised steel and engined Navy was to convoy an archaically equipped soldier force to France. The politicians supported these men, with Napoleonic tendencies and ancient accoutrements, against any ideas of the sons of the blast furnace, steam engine and fifteen inch gun. Seldom has the idea that modern equipment determines the largest say in strategic priorities been so conclusively refuted.

It would not be correct, however, to say that the Army displaced the Navy in British affections — even measured in terms of monetary support. The Navy got its ships even as the small Army received the right to play its (apparently) minor role in concert with the French. What happened was that while these strange developments took place, the Navy lost any position of primacy it might have had in the determination of *overall* British strategy in war. It can be argued that the Navy never in history (except for isolated cases) possessed such primacy. If that be accepted, and it is an unpalatable but arguable proposition in the mind of the present writer, then the result of this division between the services was division, lack of concert, and disenchantment with what used to be called conjunct operations. The Army was not only not what Fisher wickedly used to call 'a projectile to be fired by the Navy', it was not even a coequal supporting or conjunct force. Each service, in short, had its own training, rationale, objectives. Seventy years before, Lord Durham had described French and English in Canada as 'two nations warring within the bosom of a single state'. This hackneyed but arresting phrase might easily have been applied to the British Army and Navy in the years 1905–14. When they went to war, much of the strife ceased, but when they fought they fought separate wars — one hesitates to add 'for separate reasons'.

That statesmen and military thinkers were undecided about ultimate British strategic roles in future wars was mainly the result of two factors. One was the overbearing prestige that accrued to land warfare as a result of Prussian military successes between 1861 and 1871. Military prowess that dictated a sharp change in the chief power relationships of Europe was bound to arrest the eye of the general observer as well as that of the military specialist. The second factor was that, as this profound power change was taking place, naval power was being seriously called into question as ship design was caught up in a protracted process of material change. Until ship design experiment ceased, to the extent that a settled design could be accepted as not only the prototype but the actual combat vessel of a future war, strategic speculation about the effect of ships on war remained merely that — speculation. Consequently, the crushing effects of the Prussian system captured the public eye, even as sea experimentation puzzled it.

It is important to note that if Prussian victories made mistrust of the Navy an apparently practical occupation, the more potent cause of that distrust in the Navy predated those successes. The Duke of Wellington's famous letter to General Sir John Burgoyne in the late 1840s, in the face of ship design change, raised the question of the Navy's ability to protect the heartland of Great Britain against invasion. This thought was aimed at fear of French military power under Napoleon III and resulted in both the Volunteer movement of the 1860s and a mania for fortification that lingered in subdued fashion until the beginning of the twentieth century. This is not to say that prominent sailors tended to agree with such a panic-prone mentality, but it is undeniable that in a time of flux the customarily silent service found no stimulus to uncharacteristic articulation. Furthermore, the general cast of anti-Empire thinking that looked to domestic rather than worldwide responsibilities fostered the idea of fixed coastal defences at home rather than of proud activity on the high seas. This naval hiatus stretched roughly from 1859 to 1889. From the point of view of naval history, it was helped by the fact that books dealing with that Great (Napoleonic) War were mainly of the type that dealt with sea warfare as a question of profit and loss in capital ships, and not basically with the important question of the influence of sea power on the purposes for which the war appeared to have been fought. Furthermore, most of the printed Napoleonic war writing was army literature: a point made by Richmond.[21] Put more bluntly, this attitude to sea warfare induced people to look for tradition in battle lore and not in broad sea effects. This meant that sea traditions tended to become bastardised in slogans,

[21]*Ibid*, pp. 114–15.

most of which were grouped around the name of Horatio Nelson in a way that would have horrified that professional sailor.

In the 1880s, there was an attempt to produce a hardheaded doctrine of sea power. A Royal Commision under the leadership of Lord Carnarvon sat and reported on the connection between imperial responsibility and the military (Army and Navy) stance. Its conclusions, focus strategic strength in the English Channel and free ships for trade protection and blockade, were both sane and extensive. But a Liberal government that did not wish to marry might and responsibility in a way that called for financial outlay buried its main conclusions and only produced a hackneyed version for public consumption. Furthermore, the Reports were largely dealt with at the War Office. That is to say, they were Army dominated and, secrecy aside, the conclusion urging cooperation could not be made operative simply because machinery did not exist which could knock the heads of the two services together. Indeed, it was inadmissible to the Gladstonian cast of mind then so prevalent.[22]

The defensive thought behind the Carnarvon Commission was not primarily historical. On the other hand, the chief propagandist who prompted its formation was Sir John C. R. Colomb and he and his brother, Admiral Philip Colomb, were not unaware of historical precedents. Long after the Commission concluded its work, the Committee of Imperial Defence was set up in 1904, ostensibly to secure high level support for joint service planning. The support did not materialise.[23] It is significant that on that occasion the prime minister, Arthur James Balfour, saw fit to reward Sir John Colomb with the Grand Cross of the Order of St Michael and St George.[24]

The strongest historical thrusts in favour of naval strategy came from the pens of an American Admiral Alfred Thayer Mahan, and the British naval historian Julian S. Corbett. Admiral Mahan published his book, *The Influence of Sea Power Upon History*, in 1890. It was followed, in quick succession, by others written in the same vein. Whatever his books may have been meant to engender in the way of the regeneration or growth of American sea power, they became available in Great Britain just at the moment when ship design had acquired enough stability to allow for the formulation of doctrine. Consequently, the work of Mahan was warmly welcomed by British sea enthusiasts as tracts for the times carrying with them the sanction of history. Mahan was not the first to conscript history

[22]D.M. Schurman. 'Imperial defence, 1868–1887'. Unpublished Ph.D. thesis in the University of Cambridge, 1955.
[23]Long before Professor John Mackintosh wrote his article pointing out the in-effectiveness of the CID as an effective planning body ('The role of the Committee of Imperial Defence before 1914', *English Historical Review*, LXXVII, 1962), the point was made by Admiral Richmond, who wrote, 'those discussions got no further than the Committee room'. Richmond, *British Strategy*, p. 135.
[24]D.M. Schurman, *The Education of a Navy* (London, 1965), p. 32.

on the side of naval strategic doctrine, but his own brilliant formulations and the circumstances of the moment combined to make his work congenial, popular and important in the United Kingdom. He has retained this position amongst naval propagandists, the great bulk of the population, and many serious thinkers about naval matters.

Mahan's doctrine was congenial because it brought into conjunction two favourite thoughts of pro-navy men: first, that sea power by itself was sufficient to change or maintain the course of power politics; second, that this maintenance presupposed great decisive battles between the fleets of great powers at sea. Mahan is too complicated a thinker to invite the comment that he intended this to be a rule admitting of no exceptions. There were such, but the exceptions were not what sea-addicted contemporaries drew from perusing his works. The lessons drawn from Mahan were naturally reinforced by the patriotic retrospective endeavours of sea-power enthusiasts in England. The grand conclusion in England among such people was that 'grand slam' sea power would determine, even as it has determined, the successful course of British history. With the formation of the Navy League, and its opposite number, the National Service League, positions that accepted or rejected the paramount naval role were taken up. By 1897 these roles were fixed and different in the popular mind, as indeed in the minds of important statesmen, sailors and soldiers. The greatest effect of Mahan in Great Britain was to stimulate the tendency to polarisation of the two services.

The year 1897 has been singled out because in that year a naval journalist, James Thursfield, and an army engineer, Sir George S. Clarke, were worried about this hardening of attitudes to separate service functions and published a volume of essays expressly aimed at exploding the simplifications attendant upon the uncritical acceptance of Mahan's thought. It was called *The Navy and the Nation* and its main purpose was to show how it had been, and would be, the conjunction of the two services, united in doctrine and practical training, that made for British success in war. Mahan had related a broad concept to the effects that could be deduced from the study of history from secondary sources. It was brilliant and convincing. Clarke and Thursfield attempted to set out a more complicated doctrine that emphasised service cooperation, also based on secondary accounts. They were no less intelligent but much less successful. A Navy just emerging from forty years of naval change was understandably impatient with roles when it could find a role.

Clarke's influence was, for a time, immense. He had, eight years earlier, written a book entitled *Fortifications* that made an impact both in the Army and the Navy. By 1903 he was considered important enough to be brought back from a governorship in Australia to help set up the Committee of Imperial Defence, of which he became secretary, and to advise on the 'reconstruction' of the War Office. As he attempted to achieve practical results in the way of service cooperation, his historical torch passed to a different kind of writer, but one with similar service-healing objectives, Julian S. Corbett.

This is not the place to delineate Corbett's career, and his books have been discussed by the present writer elsewhere.[25] However, it is important to note that from the first his historical productions were based on careful research into British primary military materials. Secondly, and again from the beginning, his historical work repeatedly emphasised his steadily reinforced conclusion that the Army and the Navy could exert the most valuable force as extensions of British policy when they acted in concert. He did not deny that the separate activities of the services had been valuable, but stressed that their total value increased in proportion as their *rapport* was real. Finally, it must be claimed that Corbett was a military thinker of a stature equal if not greatly superior to Mahan, or any other naval writer that the world has yet produced. As will be seen, his influence did not match his cognitive genius.

There was, of course, a real link between Corbett and Clarke, for by Corbett's own admission it was Clarke's great concern for interservice harmony that moved him to write *England in the Mediterranean*, where, to use one example, the strategic links between Marlborough's European movements were strikingly linked to naval activities in the Mediterranean. In this work, as in all of his others, the powerful effects of combined strategic policy in pursuit of the clear, but eternally shifting British aims in warfare were demonstrated with clarity. An antiquarian with almost unrivalled knowledge of military minutiae, Corbett never allowed this specialised occupation to interfere with his delineation of broad effects. It is even more important to grasp that battle description and tactical speculation never dominated the narrative of any of his broad historical works. Battle was for him only a means to the securing of strategic ends. Sea fights were never an end in themselves: nor, in his opinion, would they ever be anything else than means.

Between 1898 and 1914, Corbett wrote six books in which the themes of state and joint service cooperation were omnipresent and central.[26] In addition, between 1900 and 1914, he lectured every year, sometimes three times a year, to the Naval War Course. Corbett's work and ideas engaged the attention, even as he personally held the friendship, of Admiral John Fisher, possessor of the most powerful and influential naval mind within the service during the prewar period. At the same time, he made contact with important men within the naval service, and of soldier

---

[25]*Ibid*, pp. 147–84.
[26]*Ibid*. In addition to the books discussed in *The Education of a Navy*, Corbett wrote an important staff history of the Russian-Japanese War for the Naval Intelligence Department at the Admiralty. The book has not yet been made public.

writers whose predilection was for service cooperation. Indefatigably he used his pen and his contacts to press for Army-Navy *rapport*. By 1914 he was of the opinion that his teaching was known, appreciated, and assimilated. His conviction that his views were accepted received striking corroboration from Maurice Hankey, the secretary of the CID, who told him that the amphibious doctrine and joint planning had won the day, that their separatist opponents were routed.[27] This is certainly an arresting observation in view of the 1914 tyranny of circumstances discussed above, and gives added point to the cautious instructions issued to Sir John French. Indeed, it seems clear that by 1914 lipservice was paid to the idea of joint action based on combined plans. But never in the field of human statements has such a judgment as that of Hankey been proved so illusory in the face of the relentless events of the next few months.

The power of the accepted practice of the moment over the dominance of theory can be seen at work in 1916. In the autumn of that year, Sir George Clarke, now raised to the higher eminence but less influential position as Lord Sydenham of Coombe, spoke out in the House of Lords against the doctrine that gave naval primacy in big battle second place to the accomplishment of the strategic aim. Sharing the general sense of frustration over the less than complete victory achieved at Jutland, he attacked the strategic guide that had been used to instruct prewar Naval War Course students. Corbett had written much of that guide, entitled *Notes on Strategy*, and he wrote to Sydenham to protest stating that the latter had been shown the original draft years before and had not only endorsed but praised it. Not surprisingly, Sydenham refused to acknowledge *publicly* this earlier belief, and the correspondence languished.[28]

By 1916, also, it was Sir Maurice Hankey's view that the soldiers held such control of the mainsprings of strategic activity that it was no longer possible, in the Cabinet, to question their strategic or tactical dispositions.[29] Thus in two short years had the tail come to wag the dog, and this judgment is worthy of notice in view of the fact that 1916 was also the year in which the German politicians hardly dared question the decisions of Ludendorff and Hindenburg. Lloyd George never lost his distaste for the situation of khaki dominance, but neither did he break its stranglehold. If the reasons for this dominance can be traced to the terrible circumstantial tyranny of war, its genesis can be seen in the fact that the strategic props of the Navy as set out by historians never acquired sufficient strength to buttress policy successfully. That shrewd observer, Lord Esher, had grasped the nub of the problem when he wrote, on 15 March 1915:

[27]Corbett *Diary*. 2 April 1914. Papers in the possession of Richard Corbett, Esq. Hereafter RCP.
[28]Sydenham to Corbett. 1 Dec. 1916. Papers in the possession of Mrs W.C.B. Tunstall. Hereafter CP.
[29]Corbett *Diary*. 19 May 1916. RCP.

Why . . . do we worry about history? Julian Corbett writes one of the best books in our language upon political and military strategy. All sorts of lessons, some of inestimable value, may be gleaned from it. No one, except perhaps Winston, who matters just now, has ever read it. Yet you and I are fussing about a strategical history of the war. Obviously history is written for schoolmasters and arm-chair strategists. Statesmen and warriors pick their way through the dust.[30]

It also needs to be pointed out that Corbett, if he was the most erudite of the advocates of amphibianism, was not the only advocate of service cooperation. In the Navy, Admirals Sir Charles Ottley and Sir Edmund Slade, successive holders of the office of Director of Naval Intelligence between 1904 and 1909, were 'amphibians'. So, for the Army, were Major General Sir Charles Callwell and Major General Sir George Aston.[31] All four were able men, but the sailors did not carry the Admiralty defences any more than the soldiers were successful in storming the Horse Guards. They found their common viewpoint with each other. Even at that, it would be wrong to think that there were not sympathisers with their viewpoints in each service — Sir John French himself, for instance, was far from being in opposition to them.[32] The hard fact was that they did not succeed in converting those at the top, a point that was noted by such an astute and sympathetic observer as Haldane.[33] The First Sea Lord and the Chief of the Imperial General Staff pursued their own courses unmoved by such writing.

It is important to emphasise, at this stage, that this essay does not put forward the argument that a joint strategy involving the close cooperation between the Army and the Navy would have been preferable to the one or ones adopted in the event. It may indeed be that opinions of interest would arise from such an exercise. That, however, would be to deal heavily in conjecture, and there is enough conjecture involved in attempts to assess the extent to which actual military theory determined actual practice without complicating the matter further. Also, any attempt to measure an intelligence such as Lord Haig's by comparison with that of Lord Fisher might invoke a smile or even impassioned reaction, but it would not help in the understanding of the juxtaposition of events and theory here described unless to show how even the greatest or least of minds were trapped by the contingency of circumstance in a war fought by a constitutional monarchy. As G. K. Chesterton has written with perception 'it is not familiarity but comparison that breeds contempt'.[34]

---

[30]Brett, *Journals of Viscount Esher*, III, 221
[31]See, for instance, C.E. Callwell, *Military Operation and Maritime Preponderance* (London, 1905), and G.G. Aston, *Letters on Amphibious Wars* (London, 1911).
[32]Slade to Corbett. 12 Dec. 1907. CP.
[33]Corbett *Diary*. 19 July 1908. RCP.
[34]G.K. Chesterton, *Autobiography* (London, 1937), p. 332.

Why was it that such strong teaching based on history did not carry the field (or the oceans) before 1914? First of all, it is clear that the entrenched nature of the departments in the British Civil Service did not lending themselves by nature to cooperation. That this was so probably owed as much to the dead hand of procedural custom as it did to the Empire-building to which civil servants are disposed. Promotion does not come easily to the generous minded advocate who thinks outside the general patterns of his civil service area.

Next, it is clear that the intense nature of the political pressures on the military, as well as the intense pressures on the politicians pointed to the line of least complicated resistance. Had the power of the prime minister in his capacity of chairman of the Committee of Imperial Defence been directed heavily and consistently at the first lord of the Admiralty and the Secretary of State for War, then cooperation might have been forced from ambitious men. Such singleminded power direction was no part of either the nature of Sir Henry Campbell-Bannerman or Herbert Henry Asquith, who both wished to preserve a decent modicum of British prestige without adding to the natural tendency of Cabinets to wrangle while engaged in the struggle for power or recognition.[35] Whether these observations hold true it is undeniable that joint service planning bowed before the power struggles then extant, as indeed did the whole concept of the Committee of Imperial Defence as a joint planning body.[36]

For the Army it is sufficient to say that soldiers basked in, and were not prepared to relinquish, a political affection to which they were hitherto not accustomed. From a decidedly secondary rank in 1901–02 they advanced to such a position of high favour that their private policy since 1905 was advanced to declared state policy by 1911. At that time, the politicians acknowledged and supported a continental purpose, and they instructed the Navy to support it as well.

The Navy presents a more complicated picture. Nevertheless, it is safe to say that Fisher was so busy defending himself against attacks in his own service that he could not afford a further distractive element in negotiations with an Army whose *bona fides* in cooperative gestures he had good reason to distrust. However, it is true that the Navy, aside from regarding itself as a rival rather than a partner with the Army, was not prone to give any strategic concept serious attention if that approach did not focus on battle-worthiness almost to the exclusion of everything else. It is doubtful if Fisher, even if relieved of his chief opponents within the naval service, Charles Beresford and Reginald Custance, would have

[35]Mackintosh, 'The Committee of Imperial Defence'.
[36]Nicholas J. d'Ombrain. 'War Planning and High Policy', unpublished MS; d'Ombrain's whole book is an explanation of this thesis, the purpose of which he sets forth on MS, p. iii.

dared risk giving unequivocal support to ideas that his captains and admirals were mentally unfit to receive.

Two other factors suggest themselves. The first is that unless doctrine is in line with the latest thinking of either service or with the needs of the political hour of action, there is not much evidence to suggest that it has ever carried the barricades of decision. The laws of self-interest seldom succumb to the blandishments of historical argument no matter how powerfully or attractively displayed. Corbett was not the first, nor was he the last lecturer to face the military and mistake his own enthusiasm, or the politeness or dullness of a captive senior audience, for the conversion of the gold braided multitude. Audiences pulverised into quiescence are not the same thing as audiences converted.

Finally there is the place of naval history in British thought itself to consider. The British people are a people greatly uninterested in understanding the important rudiments of sea power. This may seem unfair to those who have pored over the charts of Trafalgar and Jutland, and it is true that the statement is not capable of refined proof. Nevertheless, speculative asides are within the realm of historical endeavour, and it may well be asked why naval history in its sublime strategic aspects is so little quoted and understood in British historical circles. Take two examples. Until very recently, it was standard for writers to mention the defeat of the Spanish Armada without appreciation of the fact that English gunfire did not sink *any* of the Spanish fleet. The function of the fleet, in fact, was strategically to prevent the landing of a Spanish force in England. This it did and therein lay the 'victory'. Another. In 1805 Napoleon moved his army from Boulogne almost two full months before Trafalgar was fought and we are still told that this strategically unimportant battle saved Britain from invasion. Let the reader reflect that these examples are taken from the two most famous events in British naval history, and consider what a judgment on say the Battle of Toulon, or the Kentish Knock may be worth. It is difficult to think that it would excite any breasts outside those stalwarts within the Navy Records Society. Naval history was acceptable, and still is, when it dwelt upon 'death and glory'; not when it dealt with real connections between the sea and the expanding British state. Mahan was popular because his British readers, professional and lay, could take what they wanted from him. Corbett and the 'conjunct' men were presenting thoughts as complicated as they were important, and they were incomprehensible to readers who wanted vicarious glory and not what Brian Tunstall once called *The Realities of Naval History*.[37]

For the rest the two services fought their wars. This paper is not constrained to point out that Britons and the attached sheep of the Empire would have been better to fight the First World War along conjunct

[37]Title of a book published in London, 1936.

lines. It is, however, to say that they did not fight it so because they rejected the conjunct advocates — if they really ever seriously considered them. Indeed, those weighty strategic voices hardly ruffled the grass over the White Cliffs, the poppies at Poperinghe, or the crests of the ripples in the Solent.

10

GEORGE P. GRANT

Ideology in Modern Empires

The classical way of asking 'what is politics?' was the unhistorical question 'what is the political?' What is that common quality which belongs to any event that we call political, the absence of which makes an event apolitical? Clearly if the word political means anything more than what happens, then some human events are not such. Modern common sense starts from the judgment that the political has to do with the activities of the state. But immediately a theoretical difficulty arises. If we are not totalitarians, we imply in so naming the political that there are some activities which transcend state control. For example, many modern men do not want education or religion to be totally controlled by the state, because they recognise that knowing and reverencing are not acts which are properly realised under political control. Within modern common sense we express this by saying that 'society' is a more comprehensive term than 'state'. But here the theoretical difficulty arises. The Greeks from whom we receive the words 'politics' and 'the political', and whose philosophers first thought consistently about these things, did not make any such distinction between 'state' and 'society'. Politics was that which had to do with the 'polis'. The polis was the community which included all communities, while itself being included by none. For this reason it is a mistake to translate the Greek 'polis' as 'city-state', because this implies the modern distinction between 'state' and 'society'. We can see the difference between what the political means for us and what it meant for the originators of our vocabulary when we remember that Plato says a central political fact is the way that music is taught to the young. Some liberals, like R. H. S. Crossman, have made out from such remarks that Plato was a totalitarian. Such a shallow misinterpretation is only made by those who are unable to think outside the distinction between 'state' and 'society'. But the refusal to make the distinction does not imply totalitarianism. The possibility of this distinction is the central issue politically between the deepest ancient and modern thinkers. This theoretical point is only made here to illustrate that when we think about the political from within modern common sense, we start from large assumptions which may or may not be true.

189

In terms of the modern common sense definition of the political as that which has to do with the activities of the state, it is clear that the modern practice of politics is increasingly occupied with the simply administrative. There is political conflict in the world because there are certain situations which some human beings want to change or preserve, while others want to prevent such changing or preserving or want to carry them out through different means. The decision that cars will stop at red lights and go at green is strictly administrative, in the sense that once the convention has been decided on, there can be no sane conflict about the rationality of the convention. On the other hand, there are some Québecois who want to preserve French culture in North America and believe certain political steps are necessary to counteract its menacing by the English-speaking institutions of the continent. At the same time, most English-speaking North Americans, when they are aware of the issue, want to integrate Quebec into the imperial continental heartland. This is not an administrative problem because in no fair definition of sanity can we say that those on either side of the conflict are necessarily irrational in taking one side. Admittedly there are many English-speaking North Americans who talk as if it were a question of insanity. What is all the fuss about? Why don't the French just settle with the continental system of private and public corporations and become like the rest of us? Many Québecois will not settle for these benefits because they believe to do so would be to throw away their particular humanness — or to use a misused word in its richest sense, to throw away their virility. One side wants to preserve Quebecness because it appears to them their particular good; the other side are willing to sacrifice that quality in the name of goods they consider higher. In short, the political which is not administrative has to do with matters of potential conflict, and the ultimate basis of conflict is a division as to what is good. Unlike the question of traffic lights, this division is irreconcilable by any negotiable standard of rationality.

It is clear that within the western world since 1945 there are fewer and fewer serious examples of the non-administrative political, and more and more of the purely administrative. In the English-speaking world elections have often been thought of as events where the political presents itself in its non-administrative form. Journalistic rhetoric is widely used to preserve this belief. But elections are more and more plebiscites in which the masses are asked to choose between alternative groups of the elite within the determined administrative system. No wonder the multitude largely grasp such politics as a spectator sport, sometimes amusing but more often boringly shallow. Indeed the ways to victory in these plebiscites can be increasingly 'routinised'.

It is clear why the political is becoming increasingly the administrative. There is almost no conflict in the western world as to what is the political good. The highest political good is thought by the vast majority to be the building of the technical society by the overcoming of chance, through the application of the natural and social sciences. The political only arises in disagreement about means. For example, should the realised technical system be brought in largely under the control of the English-speaking empire, or should state capitalist power be more divided between competing blocks within the northern hemisphere? (The Vietnam war seems to have helped solve that one.) In the relations between the western world and other societies the questions become less administrative. There is some real conflict between state capitalism and state communism. There are even societies in the southern hemisphere who would like to have some power over their own place in technical civilisation. Not only in the west, but in a worldwide context, questions move towards the purely administrative because there are few public doubts about man's highest political pursuit. Most of us must earn our living within one of the private corporations or within the coordinating public ones, and in such an environment there is no serious conflict about political good.

Indeed the modern project has from its origins in the dreams of thinkers believed that in the end politics would disappear except as administration. The end towards which the modern project was directed was the universal and homogeneous state — the worldwide society of free and equal men in which all but a few idiots would be open to the knowledge of science and philosophy and therefore increasingly ruled by it. As all men would be open to the dictates of reason, and these dictates would lead them to agreement about what was good, there would be no conflict, and thus communal life could be ordered by administration. Lenin, who took up with enthusiasm certain partialities of the modern dream a century after it had come to bloom in western Europe, said that in an advanced technical state, ruling would be so simplified that it would be open 'to every non-illiterate'. 'Under socialism', he wrote, 'all will rule in turn and quickly get used to the fact that no one rules.' To transcribe the rhetoric of Utopian Marxism into my language, ruling will be a matter of administration. Lenin did not live long enough after he came to power to face how quickly is quickly, but he was willing in the interval to 'teach' those who had not yet reached the modern conception of good. Certainly in the west we have not 'got used to the fact' that nobody rules or that administration is open to every non-illiterate. What remains of the liberal hope is that at least within the confines of particular blocs, living well together will be achieved by administration. As the secularised eschatological framework disappears because men can no longer hope for it what remains in the practice of modern politics is the purified conception of technical rationality. Whatever general or particular criticisms should properly be levelled against the thought of Max Weber, he laid before us what 'rationality' means in the souls of those who are most often influential in the realm of modern politics.

It may appear perverse to state that in this age the practice of politics has been procrusteanly reduced. Has there ever been a time so taken up with public events of conflict, when men have expected so much from the practice of politics or been willing to do so much in the pursuit of that practice? Is it not also perverse to say that men have come to understand the political as calculating rationality in an era when there have been sudden outbreaks of uncalculated irrationality from the very centres where such reason seemed incarnate? Indeed in their allegiance to the great ideologies — communism, English-speaking liberalism, national socialism — men have seemed to commit themselves to the belief that salvation is attained in the political. Two such consummately modern thinkers as Hegel and Nietzsche both emphasised: the reading of the morning newspaper has taken the place of the morning prayer. At the beginning of the day when we need to pay attention to what is necessary to our good, we turn that attention to reading about public events, not to the eternal. Nevertheless men may concentrate on something without being aware of its nature. For example, there are more books written about the practice of sexuality in modern North America than ever before. But who would say that modern North Americans are aware of the essence of sex — that they know what it is suited for? In our concentration on politics there is a clear reduction of its scope from what was included under that royal techne by traditional theorists. Moreover, the outbreaks of obvious 'irrationality' from the very centres of modern 'rationality' may be seen under the old tag *naturam expellas furca etc.*

The study of politics has been as technicised as the practice of it. The same modern account of 'rationality' operates in its study as in its practice. One supposes that departments of political science are the places where politics is most consistently studied; there the dominant method since 1945 may best be characterised (albeit generally and loosely) as behaviourist. Even in an essay dedicated in admiration to a noble historian, it is not my purpose to search out the origins of behaviourist social science. I will not even indulge in the comic description of why this conception of social science, first formulated and pursued by Germans, was taken up so enthusiastically in the English-speaking society, just after that society had expended itself in two wars against the Germans.

On the surface (and it is always best to start thinking about anything from its surface) the dominant characteristic of contemporary behavioural political science is the insistence of its practitioners on a clear cut distinction between what they name the 'normative' and the 'empirical'. At the surface, the most evident methodological assumption of this science is the distinction made between judgments about 'fact' and judgments about 'value', and the assertion that the scientist *qua* scientist is concerned only with facts, or with the values as psychological facts. Its practitioners are concerned with what happens in politics, not with making judgments as to what are good or bad purposes in politics. Judgments concerning what is valuable are considered beyond the purview of reason, and therefore have no place in the science *qua* science.

In formulating this methodological principle, Max Weber did not simply desire to get on the antiteleological bandwagon of modern physics and biology, but had also a pure political motive. Among the intensities of pre-1914 Germany, Weber was concerned that the study of political matters in the universities be free of the ideological pressures of the public world. The assertion of 'objectivity' in the human sciences, against Dilthey's formulations, was understood by Weber as a means to the transcendence of ideology. He was fearful of how easily the human sciences could be used by the passions of the world, whether by the ideology of democracy or of communism or of Bismarckian statism. It was not only in the name of an antiteleological science, but in the name of independent universities that he enucleated the method of a value-free social science.[1]

As is the case in so many German influences on North American life, the idea of a 'value-free' social science has been turned around to be used for a different purpose. Above all it has been used as an instrument of justification in the rhetoric of liberal pluralism. The chief domestic justification of our imperial state capitalism is that we live in a pluralist society in which the individual is free to pursue his life according to his inclinations. Therefore the classical view that the clearest minds could know what were the best purposes for human life seemed a particular enemy of our liberalism. It seemed to imply that certain 'dogmatic' and *a priori* conceptions of human excellence should be given official sanction at the expense of the individual's freedom to follow his individuality. By turning the language of good and bad ends into the language of values, and by removing any discourse about the goodness of such values from within the clear light of science, the Weberian methodology seemed to eliminate at one and the same time not only the traditional enemies of modern science, but also the enemies of the free life of the individual. Value-free social science was enthusiastically greeted in North America not chiefly for the protection of the free university, but rather for the protection of democratic pluralism.

It is no wonder that a political science dominated by a conception of objectivity taken from modern natural science, and seeing itself as serving the public rhetoric of democracy, should have become so much a servant of the ruling class of its society — a technique to be used in administration.

---

[1] It is interesting how close this motive is to a continuing one found in the life of G. S. Graham. In the Canadian context (so different from that of Germany) Graham and such close colleagues as H. A. Innis were concerned that their historical studies remain independent by not being handed over to the service of the ideological pressures, official or otherwise, which are always rampant and rapacious in North America.

An 'object' is a thing that has been thrown in front of us. Thrown in front of us, it lies there as at our disposal. Objectivity is a relation between things and our disposal.[2]

The relation of all modern science to technical use is not therefore something accidental, but is at the very heart of our apprehension of things (human or non-human) as objects. When the social scientists united this concept of objectivity with the rhetoric of pluralism, it followed that their work in the universities should become the servant of the administrative needs of the public and private corporations. 'Value-free' social science seemed to Weber an instrument for maintaining the independence of the universities; in North American hands it was a means to the universities becoming servants of the public realm. The word 'servant' is appropriate even when particular social scientists, such as Galbraith or Huntington, moved from their role of scientist into the role of influential advisor. The independence of the university is put just as much in question by being a recruiting ground of personnel as when its science is directed to immediate public usefulness. The 'objective facts' were used along with the men who discovered them. W. W. Rostow's 'facts' about the breakthrough necessary to the development of underdeveloped areas, were used, along with his person, in deciding American actions in Vietnam. Bacon's account of science was realised.

The use of the universities by the powers of this world is not surprising. It is surprising how little protection these liberal social scientists had against such use. What is essential about North American society is not its pluralism but its monism. We are the inheritors of the European beliefs of the last centuries that the best society would be built by the overcoming of chance through the knowledge reached by the 'objective' sciences. Power in that society is incarnate in the public and private corporations which organise the pursuit of that overcoming of chance. The rhetoric of pluralist liberalism was an extra tacked onto the monolithic certainty about the public good. What this extra in fact meant is that individuality is allowed, but only in the 'private' realm of sexuality and religion and art. As the objective facts of social science belong to the public realm, it is inevitable that they be used not in the interests of pluralism, but by the public and private corporations which control what happens in the public domain. It is surprising how little the good-willed social scientists expected their 'value-free' science to be so used — that is, saw the political consequences of their own methodological assumptions. As discussion of the goodness of ends (or, as they are called, 'values') has no place in political science, there is no reason within the science why its discoveries about the objective political behaviour of human beings

---

[2]One clear cause why ancient thinkers so concentrated on questions of good was just because these questions were not objective and therefore not easily negotiable.

should not be at the disposal of wicked men. The scientist *qua* scientist does not think about whether the practical rulers of his society are decent or wicked. By conceiving their science as 'value-free' the social scientists may have thought that they were clearing the ground of religious and metaphysical superstitions, and establishing their independence. But what in fact they have been doing is clearing out of the universities any coherent discussion of the political good, and so eliminating small barriers which stood in the way of the general public identification of that good with the totally technicised and administratable society. Whatever else may need to be said about the student rebellions of the 1960s, it is clear that among some of its members there was a recognition that the leading social scientists, in eliminating the question of ends, had in fact given themselves over to serving the ends of state capitalism at great profit, and at the expense of the independence of the university and the education of the young.

It is impossible to predict in any detail what these changes in the practice and study of politics will entail. It would be a foolish person, indeed, who thought he saw clearly into our future. So new is the society built on the principle of the conquest of human and non-human nature that who would dare predict the consequences of its working out. The future stretches before us as trackless, and the chief compasses of the western past (revelation and philosophy) have ceased to be readable by most of us.

However, I am going to speculate about the future influence of one political fact. Ideology is a particular characteristic of the modern world and it is likely that our future will be characterised by outbreaks of it. Ideology was not part of preprogressive empires. It has arisen in modern societies because of certain presuppositions of the progressive age. Before the modern era, the wisest westerners believed that the practice of both religion and philosophy were necessary if tolerably decent communities were to exist. But they distinguished these two activities. The proper relation between them was considered an extremely complex question and was at the root of many controversies of the preprogressive era. One mark of modern thought has been to believe that philosophy should not only play its old role, but that it also should take over the role once assigned to religion. But the need for reverence continued to be pressing for men and women, even at a time when the traditional reverences were under sustained public criticism, and when people were being told by the clever that philosophy was open to them as a substitute for religion. In that situation ideologies rose like demons out of the depths to fill the void created by progressive assumptions. Put one way: ideologies are surrogate religions pretending they are philosophies. Put the other way: they are surrogate philosophies trying to fulfil the role of displaced reverence. To repeat, the three leading examples of the recent past are Marxist communism, national socialism and American liberalism. They do harm to the political fabric because they consolidate the confusion about the proper place of religion and philosophy in communal life. Ideologies make public the modern denial that reverence is the matrix of human nobility; but as surrogate religions they slip reverence in. It is, however, reverence for something not truly worthy of reverence, suchas the state, the race, the multitude, the nation. Those of us who are Jews or Christians would say they are idolatrous in the worst sense of the word. On the other side, they claim to be rational, scientific and philosophic, and therefore to be giving knowledge of what is happening, when in fact they do not. In this sense they are destructive of common sense and moderation — the two great protectors of the health of the political realm.

The fact that 'value-free' multiversities can do little to restrain these demons is evident. English-speaking people are well advised to remember the German experience. The Germans were the first to build universities in which 'objective' science and scholarship was exalted above all questions about good. The scientists and scholars pursued their 'objective' work and scorned thought about ends as extra-scientific. Many of the most brilliant and ardent young therefore had to seek answers to such questions outside the discipline of coherent study, among the raucous voices of public ideology. The fact that our ruling classes have become technicised and that our universities have largely excluded from the curriculum the serious study of the most important questions, makes us open to the same occurrence.

This process is already far advanced in our society. At the beginning of the 1960s an influential American social scientist, Daniel Bell, wrote a book called *The End of Ideology*. In that book he described how North Americans had transcended that stage in the past in which men argued and indeed fought about ultimate good. All sensible men could now agree about the proper direction of American society. The 'value-free' sciences in the multiversities would play their role in thinking about the means to the further realization of the state-capitalist society. By 'ideology' and its end he clearly meant the dying away of debate, even when philosophic, about propositions that transcended the 'objective'. Soon after the book was published, Mr Bell's own multiversity was rent apart by a student uprising, the leaders of which claimed that that multiversity was not 'value-free,' but rather a servant to the ideology of the American empire. Peace at the 'value-free' university was reestablished by the occupation of the campus by the New York police. The lack of sympathy one may feel for some of the rebels' actions, is surely equalled by a lack of sympathy for Columbia which had progressively excluded from its midst over several generations anything but 'objective' science and scholarship and technology, while many of its faculty made their fortune by selling these to government and business. Be that as it may, 'the end of ideology' had not ended in an end of ideology. The behaviourist doctrine helped to open the university to the full force of ideology, whether that of the establishment or of the radicals.

196

While our species has existed, there seem to have been outbreaks of public madness of one kind and another. In this technical era, it appears that corporate madness will increasingly manifest itself in ideological forms. The question of how it is good to live cannot be eliminated from the world while human beings remain human beings. The attempt is made to eliminate that question from the public realm by thinking that political conflict can be solved by the techniques of administration; the multiversities try to eliminate it by conceiving the pursuit of reason as technique. Nevertheless, the question of how it is good to live continues to present itself to those of noble minds and open hearts. However those who seek an answer to it are driven by this official exclusion to seek that answer in terms of ideology — that is outside the theoretical discipline of philosophy and outside the ecstasy-sustaining discipline of received reverences. As the public realm is given over more and more to the iron maiden of realised administrative technique, the question of good will present itself in increasingly illicit and urgent forms to those who find no comfort in that iron embrace. As spontaneity has been excluded from the public realm, the desire for it, as part of human good, has asserted itself, and has been expressed in ideologies which are hostile to the public ideology of 'ideology-free' liberalism. The time of conflict between the public ideology and the illicit ideologies, cannot be happy for those who, in the name of philosophy or religion or prudence, fear both sides. It will be increasingly difficult to know how properly to respond in particular manifestations of that conflict. On the one hand, sensible people must have respect for the necessities of public order, yet they will find that that public order is expressed in the form of unspontaneous administration, backed by all the growing powers of physiological and psychological technique. On the other hand, sensible people may sympathise with the manifold, if impotent, revolts against this order, as expressing a fumbling towards human good, and yet be fearful as they are expressed in the form of illicit and even mad ideologies.

The Historical Writings of
GERALD SANDFORD GRAHAM

Compiled by George Metcalf

1930

British Policy and Canada, 1774–1791: A study in eighteenth-century trade policy (London and New York, Longmans, Imperial Studies Series, IV).

1931

'Cobden's influence on Bismarck', *Queen's Quarterly*, XXXVIII, 433–43.

1935

'The migrations of the Nantucket whale fishery: an episode in British colonial policy', *New England Quarterly*, VIII, 179–202.

1938

'Naval rivalry: the problem of the battleship', *Canadian Defence Quarterly*, XV, 178–82.

'Admiral von Tirpitz and the origin of Anglo-German naval rivalry', *ibid.*, 305–12.

'Sam Birnie's letter-book', *Queen's Quarterly*, XLV, 204–11.

'Grey's foreign policy: a retrospect', *ibid.*, 453–9.

'The gypsum trade of the Maritime Provinces', *Agricultural History*, XII.

1939

'Lord Castlereagh and the defence of British North America', *Canadian Defence Quarterly*, XVI.

'Napoleon's Baltic blockade and the birth of the Canadian timber trade', *Baltic and Scandinavian Countries* (Baltic Institute, Gdynia), V.

1940

'The aims of Gustav Stresemann', *Queen's Quarterly*, XLVII, 389–93.

1941

Sea Power and British North America, 1783–1820: A study in British Colonial Policy (Cambridge, Mass., Harvard University Press; London, Oxford University Press).

'The origin of free ports in British North America', *Canadian Historical Review*, XXII, 25–34.

'Fisheries and seapower', *Report of the Canadian Historical Association for 1941*, pp. 24–31.

1942

'Britain's defence of Newfoundland', *Canadian Historical Review*, XXIII, 260–79.
'The changing strategical problems of the British Empire', *Annual Report of the American Historical Association for 1942*, III, 163–72.

1943

Britain and Canada (Longmans Pamphlets on the British Commonwealth, no. 6, London and New York, Longmans).

1946

'Newfoundland: British strategy from Cabot to Napoleon', in R.A. MacKay, ed., *Newfoundland. Economic, Diplomatic and Strategic Studies* (Toronto: Oxford University Press), pp. 245–64.

1947

'The fourth British Empire', *New Empire* (Journal of the Empire Day Movement), I.

1948

'The naval defence of British North America, 1739–1763', *Transactions of the Royal Historical Society*, 4th series, XXX, 95–110.

1949

'Considerations on the War of American Independence', *Bulletin of the Institute of Historical Research*, XXIII, 22–34.

1950

Empire of the North Atlantic: the Maritime Struggle for North America (Toronto University Press; 2nd edn, 1958).
Canada, a Short History (London, Hutchinson's University Library).
'The maritime foundations of imperial history', *Canadian Historical Review*, XXXI, 113–25.
'The British Empire and Commonwealth', in *Chambers's Encyclopaedia* (London; rev. edn, 1959).

1952

'Canada — an experiment in compromise', in Drummond Shiels, ed., *The British Commonwealth: A family of peoples* (London, Odhams Press), pp. 61–77.
'Mission to Quebec, 1710', *Queen's Quarterly*, LIX, 273–90.

1953

[Edited, with Introduction] *The Walker Expedition to Quebec, 1711* (London, Navy Records Society; Toronto, Champlain Society).
'Views of General Murray on the defence of Upper Canada, 1815', *Canadian Historical Review*, XXXIV, 158–65.

1956

'The ascendancy of the sailing ship, 1850–1885', *Economic History Review*, IX, 74–88.
'The defences of Canada, 1710', *Canadian Historical Review*, XXXVII, 167–9.

1957
'The evolving Commonwealth', *University of Ceylon Review*, xv, 115–25.
'Monarchy and republic in the New World', *Pakistan Horizon*, x, 71–83.
1958
'The transition from paddle-wheel to screw propeller', *The Mariner's Mirror*, XLIV, 35–48.
1959
'Imperial finance, trade and communications, 1895–1914', in *The Cambridge History of the British Empire*, III (Cambridge University Press), pp. 438–89.
'Peculiar interlude: the expansion of England in a period of peace, 1815–1850', the fourth George Arnold Wood Memorial Lecture (University of Sydney).
1962
[Edited, with Introduction, by G. S. Graham and R. A. Humphreys] *The Navy and South America, 1807–1823: Correspondence of the Commanders-in-Chief on the South American Station* (London, Navy Records Society).
1964
'By steam to India', *History Today*, XIV, 301–12.
1965
The Politics of Naval Supremacy: Studies in British maritime ascendancy (Cambridge University Press).
1967
Great Britain in the Indian Ocean: A study of maritime enterprise, 1810–1850 (Oxford, The Clarendon Press).
'Canada, 1867–1967', *Commonwealth Journal* (the Journal of the Royal Commonwealth Society), x, 111–17.
'Paul Knaplund, historian of the British Empire', in *Paul Knaplund* (Madison, The State Historical Society of Wisconsin).
1968
A Concise History of Canada (London, Thames and Hudson).
1969
'Canada and Canadian history as viewed from the United Kingdom', in Mason Wade, ed., *Regionalism in the Canadian Community, 1867–1967* (Papers presented at the Canadian Historical Association Centennial Seminars, University of Toronto Press).
New Worlds to Conquer, vol. XII of the *Hamlyn History of the World*, with an Introduction by G. S. Graham, advisory editor (London, Paul Hamlyn).
1970
A Concise History of the British Empire (London, Thames and Hudson).
1972
Tides of Empire: Discursions on the Expansion of Britain Overseas (McGill-Queen's University Press).